MW01234902

Anticipation

Anticipation

✦

The Real Life Story of *Star Wars: Episode I—The Phantom Menace*

Jonathan L. Bowen

iUniverse, Inc.
New York Lincoln Shanghai

Anticipation
The Real Life Story of *Star Wars: Episode I—The Phantom Menace*

Copyright © 2005 by Jonathan L. Bowen

All rights reserved. No part of this book may be used or reproduced by any means, graphic, electronic, or mechanical, including photocopying, recording, taping or by any information storage retrieval system without the written permission of the publisher except in the case of brief quotations embodied in critical articles and reviews.

iUniverse books may be ordered through booksellers or by contacting:

iUniverse
2021 Pine Lake Road, Suite 100
Lincoln, NE 68512
www.iuniverse.com
1-800-Authors (1-800-288-4677)

ISBN-13: 978-0-595-34732-2 (pbk)
ISBN-13: 978-0-595-67148-9 (cloth)
ISBN-13: 978-0-595-79475-1 (ebk)
ISBN-10: 0-595-34732-0 (pbk)
ISBN-10: 0-595-67148-9 (cloth)
ISBN-10: 0-595-79475-0 (ebk)

Printed in the United States of America

This book is dedicated to the memory of Stu Schechter, a true *Star Wars* fan who waited for days outside of Mann's Chinese Theatre to see *The Phantom Menace*, but sadly will not have the opportunity to watch the completed *Star Wars Saga*. Stu passed away in 2000.

Special Thanks To:

Richard Curtis for his support and representation on the project in its early stages.

Craig Faris for suggesting the book to Richard and for his support of my career.

Vicky Stevens for her editing and publishing advice.

Jim Corbin, Steve Cote, Peter Genovese, Linda Gomez, Kolby Kirk, Clare Whipps, and Helen Winterbottom for their insight into the lineup for the film.

Michael Wendt for his help and encouragement throughout the process.

Scott Hettrick for his help on the video sales information for the film.

Joshua Griffin for providing commentary about TheForce.net, and for his interest in the book throughout its writing.

Maggi White for writing the first media article about the book and its author.

Homer Williams for his help connecting me with influential people.

George Lucas for inspiring millions of people worldwide.

My mother for editing the book and providing encouragement.

My father for making every effort to help me become a published author.

Contents

Introduction

By the late 1980s, interest in *Star Wars* had waned. With no new movies scheduled for release, most licensees allowed their contracts to expire. Merchandising came to a halt. By 1985, *Star Wars* fever had largely subsided. Only the most faithful fans remained subscribed to the *Star Wars* Fan Club newsletter, known as *Bantha Tracks*. While many people believed *Star Wars* dead, it was only a cultural phenomenon in hibernation, awaiting its triumphant return.

The *Star Wars* revival began with a novel titled Heir to the Empire, which was based on the popular characters from the classic *Star Wars Trilogy*. Well-known science fiction author Timothy Zahn wrote the novel, which Bantam Books released in June 1991. Heir to the Empire skyrocketed to the top spot on the all-important *New York Times* Bestseller List, where it remained for months and sold more than one million copies. The events in the book occur five years after the fall of the empire in the final *Star Wars* movie, *Return of the Jedi*. Heir to the Empire and its two sequels, Dark Force Rising (June 1992) and The Last Command (May 1993), have more than five million copies in print.

The success of the novels surprised many observers, and even Lucasfilm. The passion for *Star Wars*, which many had dismissed as sentiments of a past age, was still remarkable and quickly increased with Zahn's successful trilogy. Skeptics questioned the power of the saga to create enthusiasm even after years of inactivity, but fans realized that a *Star Wars* renaissance had just begun. Zahn deserves credit for returning glory to the *Star Wars* name. Without his impressive writing and captivating stories, the franchise might have remained dormant for many more years. Lucasfilm tested the market with Heir to the Empire, attempting to gauge public interest in the saga so that the company could decide how to proceed with future *Star Wars* projects. George Lucas had to confirm that interest in *Star Wars* still existed, so the phenomenal success of the first novel convinced him that the saga had not lost its timeless appeal. The first several novels began a much more aggressive effort to place *Star Wars* in the public spotlight once again.

In 1991, the same year as Bantam Books published Heir to the Empire, Hasbro, one of the nation's leading toy companies, purchased Kenner Toys. Kenner had manufactured *Star Wars* action figures and other related products since the beginning of the phenomenon in 1977, but released the first *Star Wars* action figures in early 1978. Few people anticipated the success of the first *Star Wars* movie, which left companies unprepared to produce merchandise based on it. Even more surprisingly, studios rarely considered merchandising deals for movies in the 1970s. Aside from T-shirts and hats, studios did not often authorize movie memorabilia before *Star Wars: Episode IV—A New Hope* changed the movie merchandising industry forever.

Although interest in *Star Wars* had seemingly disappeared after the final film in the original trilogy, the series only grew more popular over the late 1980s. An entire generation of fans who could not see the *Star Wars* movies in theaters could watch them on home video and play with previously released *Star Wars* action figures. Many people even believe that the action figures played a major role in keeping interest alive throughout the years following the release of *Return of the Jedi*. Videos played the most significant role in creating new fans, however. A poll conducted on the Official *Star Wars* Website revealed that 21% of the fans who voted became interested in the saga between 1984 and 1990.

In a *Variety* article published on October 4, 1993, the trade publication explained Lucasfilm's plans to produce three new *Star Wars* films, although the article noted that Lucas would most likely not direct any of them. Shortly after the early speculation, Lucas announced plans to direct all three films. Gordon Radley, president of Lucasfilm at the time, said the company was not worried about diminished interest in the saga. He said, "We're looking at these films as brand new franchises, separate from the originals." Before the prequels began production, though, another major *Star Wars* project was underway.

In the early 1990s, Lucasfilm began negotiating with Twentieth Century Fox about the possibility of adding scenes to the *Star Wars Trilogy* and making digital improvements to many of the shots. After the studio's enthusiasm about the plan, which involved re-releasing the films as *Special Editions* in honor of the twentieth anniversary of *Star Wars*, Lucasfilm began working on the new versions. The total budget for creating *Special Editions* of all of the three films was not much more than $20 million. Still, *Star Wars: A New Hope* occupied nearly half of the budget, which was almost as much as the entire original movie cost to produce in the 1970s.

Proving that few people knew *Star Wars* was still a powerful force in popular culture, *Entertainment Weekly* placed a picture of Luke Skywalker on the cover of their January 10, 1997 issue, calling the re-release one of the biggest gambles of the year. In the article, a passage read, "Of course, with the prequel on track, there's no turning the ship around if the reissues vanish into the black hole of low grosses." Fortunately for Lucasfilm, Twentieth Century Fox, and the *Star Wars Saga,* Hollywood had never seen an event that compared to the first re-release.

On January 31, 1997, *Star Wars* fans and excited moviegoers lined up at theaters nationwide to watch the most popular movie of all-time. Playing in 2,104 theaters, the movie grossed $35.9 million during its first weekend of re-release, which was by far the highest grossing weekend ever recorded in January, or February. Its average gross per theater of $17,066 indicated sold-out showings across the nation. The massive weekend gross was not only the best ever for a re-release, but one of the top ten highest weekend totals for any movie in history at the time, yet the film had already been released five times before in theaters and had sold tens of millions of videos. The magnitude of the success shocked analysts.

The *Star Wars Special Edition* reigned for three weeks as the top grossing film in America, before losing out to its own sequel, *The Empire Strikes Back*, which premiered on February 21, 1997. In exactly three weeks, the first *Star Wars* movie reclaimed its crown as the highest grossing movie in box office history. In the same span, it also became the first movie to gross $400 million at the North American box office.

The Empire Strikes Back re-opened with almost $22 million and held onto first place at the box office for two weeks. The final part in the trilogy, *Return of the Jedi*, grossed $16.3 million on the weekend beginning March 14, 1997; it reigned as the highest grossing movie of the weekend. *Star Wars: A New Hope* collected $138.3 million on its re-release, *The Empire Strikes Back* grossed $67.6 million, and *Return of the Jedi* ended with $45.4 million. The re-releases also catapulted all of the movies into the top ten highest grossing films of all-time. While the trilogy grossed $251.3 million in North America on re-release, it also added another $214.2 million in foreign ticket sales for a total of $465.5 million. The impressive success of the *Special Edition Trilogy* proved that interest in *Star Wars* was still strong. The value of all contracts surrounding the first prequel skyrocketed.

Even before the *Special Editions* arrived in theaters, PepsiCo never doubted the popularity of the *Star Wars Saga*. On May 16, 1996, PepsiCo signed a deal with Lucasfilm guaranteeing them the rights to link their products with *Star Wars* through the release of the first prequel. The agreement included PepsiCo's beverage, snack food, and restaurant brands worldwide, allowing the company the opportunity to stage a massive cross-promotional campaign for the *Special Editions* and *Episode I*. PepsiCo's deal was not the first major one struck with Lucasfilm for the prequels, but it was the largest. At $2 billion, the agreement was the most extensive promotional alliance in entertainment history. "Lucasfilm has and will continue to change the way movies are made, and this partnership will forever change the way movies are marketed," said Roger A. Enrico, the CEO of PepsiCo, Inc.

The success of the *Special Editions* also made the rights to distribute all three prequels extremely valuable because every studio wanted a percentage of the worldwide box office gross of the prequels. The toy rights for the movies were also highly valued, especially because the products released in 1997 in conjunction with the *Special Editions* sold very well. During the same year, the prequel toy rights sold for a record sum of money and *Star Wars* once again rewrote merchandising history.

Work on the first prequel began years before the *Special Editions* arrived in theaters, though, as Lucas began writing *Episode I* on November 1, 1994. "It's great to be able to sit by myself and just be able to do this. It's a real luxury, actually," he said on the first day of writing. He remarked that he could say, "Wouldn't it be great if..." but "then pounding that into reality takes a huge amount of effort." The immense effort began early and required years of work from thousands of talented people to bring *Episode I* to theaters and fans.

On January 18, 1995, Lucasfilm formed the *Star Wars: Episode I* Art Department. Doug Chiang, the head conceptual artist for *Episode I*, led the department, which produced thousands of drawings, paintings, and models to conceptualize the first film. The department worked with Lucas for more than three years and gave him the opportunity to visualize each element of the movie before he began filming.

Doug Chiang replaced Ralph McQuarrie, who was the production illustrator for the first *Star Wars Trilogy*. Chiang is a talented, award-winning artist who is well suited to the *Star Wars* universe because of his vivid use of colors and sharp drawing style. He began his career with the television show *Pee-Wee's Playhouse*, but soon began working on feature films such as *Back to the Future Part II* (1989), *Ghost* (1990), *Terminator 2: Judgment Day* (1991), *The Mask* (1994), and *Jumanji* (1995). He won an Academy Award for his work on *Death Becomes Her* (1992), a British Academy Award for *Forrest Gump* (1994), and advertising's highest honor: A Clio Award for Best Art Direction. His design work on *Episode I* helped give the film a unique style, but one that also fits with the past *Star Wars* movies.

The sixteen-year wait between *Return of the Jedi* and *Episode I* helped create an unprecedented frenzy surrounding information relating to the movie. The media began its hype machine years in advance of the film's release while fans had speculated about the fourth installment of the *Star Wars Saga* since the day they saw *Return of the Jedi*. The longer wait, more developed special effects techniques, and higher budget created even greater expectations for *Episode I* than for the past films.

No movie had ever suffered from the same degree of expectation, but no movie had the advantage of such a massive built-in audience either. Lucas had to rely not only on his own considerable fortune and hired talent, but also on his writing and directing skills, which ultimately decide the quality of a film. Though he is young as a director, most people recognize his considerable talent. Nevertheless, Lucas had not directed a film since the first *Star Wars* installment more than two decades earlier, so many people wondered whether he could handle the task.

After Lucas began writing his script and the *Episode I* Art Department convened for its first meeting, the casting process soon began, eventually followed by the start of filming on the most anticipated movie in history. The process was long and arduous, but ultimately rewarding and fulfilling for nearly everyone involved.

Would tens of millions of dollars and years of work from thousands of talented professionals create one of the most impressive movies of all-time, and a worthy addition to the *Star Wars Saga*, or would the weight of expectation crush the first prequel? Fans everywhere speculated about the movie and its plot, anxiously anticipating the first prequel to the greatest trilogy in movie history. The story of *Episode I* is full of glorious triumphs, technological advancements, incredible difficulties, fan backlash, and inaccurate media reporting, but few failures. With millions of fans awaiting its release, major companies striking unprecedented deals with Lucasfilm, and every studio in Hollywood wanting a piece of the film's box office gross, analysts knew that its theatrical premiere would be a major event. Some people doubted that *Episode I's* quality could match its hype, though nobody could deny the power of the Force to attract fans.

Casting Announced

The casting announcement is one of the most important for any anticipated film, but especially with *Star Wars*, where fans wanted to know who would play their favorite characters. With *Episode I*, the first *Star Wars* movie in sixteen years, the anticipation reached even higher levels than with past major blockbusters. In June 1995, Lucasfilm hired casting director Robin Gurland for *Episode I*. For most movies, casting directors are not hired years in advance of filming, but *Episode I* required special attention and a prolonged process of finding the most talented and capable actors.

The casting decisions for a few of the roles, such as Obi-Wan Kenobi and Queen Amidala, impacted all three prequels because of the characters' central roles in the entire trilogy. The actors and actresses who George Lucas and Gurland chose needed to be willing to sign a contract for all three *Star Wars* prequels. In an online chat at Talkcity.com in June 1999, Gurland said of the casting process, "It's a cooperative effort between the director and myself, as to which actors would work best for which roles."

Besides the expected complexities involved in the process because of the weight of expectation and the duration of the roles, Gurland enjoyed many advantages as the casting director for *Episode I*. In the classic *Star Wars Trilogy*, Lucas chose mostly unknown actors, with the notable exception of Sir Alec Guinness as Jedi Knight Obi-Wan Kenobi. For *Episode I*, Gurland said she "was given the freedom to choose actors that were right for the roles, known or unknown."

With three planned prequels to the *Star Wars Trilogy*, the casting announcements for the roles of Kenobi and the young queen were more important than those of any other characters. The young queen eventually becomes Luke and Leia's mother, as avid fans know. The unusual number of rumors traveling the Internet made determining who the actual cast members were in advance of the official announcements nearly impossible.

Immediately prior to Lucasfilm's public statements, however, the names mentioned in respectable media sources such as *Mr. Show Biz*, *E! Online*, and *Variety* proved accurate. On April 3, 1997, *Variety* announced that Liam Neeson had talked with Lucas and auditioned for the role of a respectable Jedi Master who is

1

the primary character in *Episode I*. *Variety* also announced that Lucasfilm had cast Ewan McGregor as the young Kenobi. The coveted role of Kenobi outweighed the role of the more important prequel character, Anakin Skywalker, because Lucasfilm required two separate actors for Anakin. One actor plays him for *Episode I* as a younger boy while another serves as a more mature Anakin in *Episodes II* and *III*, which take place more than a decade after the first film. Despite the announcement from *Variety*, a Lucasfilm spokeswoman insisted, "Absolutely no one has been cast in this film." Nevertheless, the *Variety* announcement quickly proved correct.

On April 9, 1997, *Variety* announced that Portman would play the young queen in all three prequels. The trade paper conceded that Lucasfilm had not issued an official announcement, although once again the report was accurate. Portman joined the talented prequel cast, which continued to grow throughout April and May.

Just days later, on April 15, *Variety* stated that Lucasfilm had cast Samuel L. Jackson in a small role in the upcoming prequel. His schedule already seemed busy with *The Negotiator* (1998) and *Jackie Brown* (1997) in development, but insiders claimed Jackson had landed a part. Once again, *Variety* was correct and Samuel L. Jackson joined the prequel cast.

At the end of May 1997, insiders speculated that young Jake Lloyd had won the part of Anakin Skywalker. Their unofficial reports were accurate. At the age of eight, Jake Lloyd played nine-year old Anakin Skywalker, who becomes one of the most evil villains in film history.

In an interview posted on the Official *Star Wars* Website on June 2, 1997, McCallum announced that Lucasfilm had nearly completed casting. He named Ewan McGregor, Jake Lloyd, Liam Neeson, Natalie Portman, and Samuel L. Jackson as the tentative lead actors, confirming reports published much earlier. He also announced Ian McDiarmid as Emperor Palpatine, Pernilla August as Anakin's mother, and Frank Oz as Yoda. With filming weeks away, and with casting having taken almost two years, Gurland and Lucas had finally shaped the cast for *Episode I*.

Among the talented main actors cast for *Episode I*, Irish actor Liam Neeson had the most experience. While Lucas had originally envisioned Neeson's character as a Jedi Master in his sixties, the role required the actor be able to participate in physically demanding scenes, so he chose a younger person for the role. Gurland considered nearly 30 actors for the part of Jedi Master Qui-Gon Jinn, but Neeson seemed the perfect choice with his dignified manner and wise appearance. Having received a Best Actor Oscar nomination at the 1994 Academy

Awards for his brilliant performance as Oskar Schindler in Steven Spielberg's powerful epic *Schindler's List* (1993), Neeson had the experience required to play a Jedi Master.

Natalie Portman claimed the role of the young queen, later revealed as Queen Amidala. At age sixteen, Portman already had significant acting experience. Her role in Luc Besson's *The Professional* (1994) earned her acclaim at a young age. Although Portman played a queen who is younger than she, the ten-year time difference between *Episodes I* and *II* required an older actress. In addition to being an excellent performer, Portman is extremely intelligent, holding nearly a perfect grade point average in high school and attending Harvard after completing her secondary school education. Gurland met with more than 200 actresses for the part of Amidala.

Lucasfilm chose Jake Lloyd for the role of Anakin Skywalker from more than 3,000 potential child actors. When Gurland first met with Lloyd, his young age seemed to exclude him from the role, but two years later, Lloyd, then eight, seemed a great choice to play young Anakin. He made his acting debut in *Unhook the Stars* (1996) and also appeared in *Jingle All the Way* (1996) with Arnold Schwarzenegger during the same year. In addition, he has made numerous appearances in television commercials and on NBC's popular show *ER*.

The role of Obi-Wan Kenobi, perhaps the most important of the trilogy, went to actor Ewan McGregor, who typically detests big budget blockbusters, but could not resist being in the newest *Star Wars* movie. McGregor gained fame for his role in the popular independent film *Trainspotting* (1996). Although he became well-known for his lack of modesty on movie sets, his notorious indiscretions had no place in his role in *Episode I*. Lucas and Gurland realized that McGregor had the charm and acting talent to play young Kenobi throughout all three prequels, so although Lucasfilm considered more than 100 other actors, McGregor was their first choice. He even perfected his accent so it meshed with the way Alec Guinness spoke in the first *Star Wars* film.

Samuel L. Jackson's casting has the most interesting story associated with it. While Gurland chose the rest of the cast from a pool of competent actors, Jackson actually requested to be part of the cast. While on numerous talk shows, and each time a reporter interviewed him, the actor hinted that he wanted to work with Lucas. Gurland heard that Jackson had expressed interest in being part of the cast and invited him to Skywalker Ranch, located just outside of San Francisco, California. Lucas had a small part for Jackson to play in the first prequel, but the director later revealed that the character would play a more significant role in the next episode. In an unusually minor role for an actor of his stature, Jackson played Jedi Master Mace Windu.

Ian McDiarmid reprised his role as Emperor Palpatine, although in *Episode I* he is only a senator who becomes the Supreme Chancellor by the end of the film. He found the experience of playing the same character again especially interesting because fifteen years had passed since he last played Palpatine, although the film takes place more than 35 years before the *Star Wars* film he worked on previously. Because of the extensive makeup used in *Return of the Jedi*, McDiarmid, just over fifty years of age when filming on *Episode I* began, could play a much younger senator in the prequel. McDiarmid earned a masters degree in social science before changing his emphasis and attending the Royal Scottish Academy of Dramatic Arts. He began a successful stage career in London and earned small roles in films such as *Dragonslayer* (1981) and *Gorky Park* (1983). Since playing the Emperor in the final chapter of the *Star Wars Saga*, McDiarmid had appeared in 1995's Oscar-winning *Restoration* and *Dirty Rotten Scoundrels*, a film starring Steve Martin and Michael Caine.

Another important person also returned to lend his services for *Episode I*. Frank Oz, who voiced Yoda in the previous films, also voiced the Jedi Master in the first prequel. He won four Emmy awards and worked with Jim Henson on the Muppets for many years bringing his classic characters to life. Many critics and film fans call Oz one of the greatest puppeteers of the twentieth century, but he is much more than just a puppet master. After his career with Henson, he turned to directing and has created an impressive portfolio of work including *Little Shop of Horrors* (1986), *Dirty Rotten Scoundrels* (1988), *What About Bob?* (1991), *Indian in the Cupboard* (1995), and *Bowfinger* (1999). Despite his busy schedule, he still found time to bring Yoda to life in the first prequel.

Perhaps equal in importance to the return of Oz as Yoda was Anthony Daniels again providing the voice for C-3PO. Daniels not only voiced the character throughout the entire first trilogy of films produced, but he also wore the golden costume and performed all of the physical acting, including in the scorching deserts of Tunisia. Since the release of *Return of the Jedi* in 1983, Daniels had remained an active contributor to the *Star Wars* phenomenon. He wrote a column that appeared in each issue of the *Star Wars Insider* magazine, called the *Wonder Column*. Daniels became Lucasfilm's golden boy and also a fan favorite. Although he was not active on the set of *Episode I*, he provided his voice for the popular character, who appears in all six films in the saga.

Ahmed Best played Jar Jar Binks, who provides comic relief in *Episode I*, but is also an important character in the film's plot. Gurland offered Best the part after she saw him perform on stage in the hit show *Stomp*. The show is unique because it features performers using common objects to create special song and dance routines. Best is primarily a musician, so *Episode I* was the first major motion picture in which he played a prominent role. Gurland chose Best because of his ability to use his body in a humorous way, which was useful for his character, who is actually entirely digital in the film. Despite the virtual nature of the Binks character, Best acted during every scene and Industrial Light & Magic used his body movements to guide the digital animation process. Best also voiced the character during post-production.

In *Episode I*, Hugh Quarshie played Captain Panaka, the chief of security for Queen Amidala. Quarshie, an actor in his forties at the time, appeared in *The Dogs of War* (1980), *Baby: Secret of the Lost Legend* (1985), *Highlander* (1986), *Nightbreed* (1990), and many other films. He was born in Ghana, but has lived in England since he was three. In addition to his success in the film industry, Quarshie has appeared on numerous British television shows and was also part of the Royal Shakespeare Company (RSC), where he performed such famous plays as *Faust*, *Macbeth*, and *The Great White Hope*. He also performed both *Romeo and Juliet* and *Guys and Dolls* on the German stage. Not only is he a talented actor, but he also co-directed a production of *Othello*, wrote the play called *The Prisoner of Hendon*, and produced a television show about the arts called *Signals* for Channel 4 in Britain.

Brian Blessed, an accomplished Shakespearean actor, provided his voice for Boss Nass, who is the leader of the Gungan race on the planet of Naboo in *Episode I*. A big *Star Wars* fan himself, Blessed was eager to be part of the ongoing phenomenon. He played Prince Vultan in 1980's *Flash Gordon* and Antonio in *Much Ado About Nothing* (1993). In addition to an acting career that has spanned more than 35 years, Blessed is an explorer and has undertaken three climbs up Mount Everest. Although he originally auditioned for the smaller role of Sio Bibble, both Lucas and Blessed realized he was not suited for the part. Nevertheless, his opportunity to become part of the phenomenon came when Lucas contacted him about the part of Nass, which Blessed eagerly accepted.

In perhaps the most enviable cameo appearance of the entire film, Ray Park played Darth Maul, the evil Sith Lord who confronts the two Jedi Knights, Jinn and Kenobi. A native of Scotland, Park has lived in London since he was just a toddler; he was in his mid-twenties. Park is an experienced martial artist and also has a background in gymnastics, which explains his incredible moves in *Episode I*. He is trained primarily in the Wu Shu style and philosophy of martial arts, but also in kick-boxing, Tae Kwon Do, and even fire-breathing. Landing the coveted role as Maul was somewhat of a coincidence for Park, who was rehearsing a fight scene with *Episode I's* stunt coordinator, Nick Gillard, but later received a call from the movie's producer asking if he would be interested in playing the villain.

Park worked as a stunt double before appearing in the first prequel, which has massively boosted his career within a short period of time. Although he had a solid role as a stunt double in *Mortal Kombat: Annihilation* in 1996, he has gained more notable respect in the film industry recently. Since appearing in the prequel, he played the Headless Horseman in Tim Burton's *Sleepy Hollow*, released in late 1999, and he also played the villain Toad in *X-Men*, which became a box office hit during the summer of 2000. *X-Men* also allowed audiences to see his true face and hear his real voice, instead of just marveling at his impressive physical skills.

Acclaimed actor Terence Stamp also appeared in *Episode I*, although his brief role as Supreme Chancellor Valorum did not grant him more than a few minutes of screen time. Stamp played General Zod in the first two *Superman* films and has acted in many other movies including *Far from the Madding Crowd* (1967), *The Hit* (1984), *Wall Street* (1987), *The Sicilian* (1987), *Young Guns* (1988), *Alien Nation* (1988), and *The Limey* (1999). He is also the author of three best-selling books. Stamp was born in the London district of Bow in 1939, where he maintained an optimistic outlook on life despite the frequent bombings during World War II.

Lucas and Gurland chose Swedish actress Pernilla August to play the role of Anakin Skywalker's mother, Shmi. She became interested in acting as a young girl and pursued her dreams, not only becoming a successful stage actor, but also starring in many movies and working with director Ingmar Bergman. Unlike several of the cast members, she is not a long-time fan of the saga and admitted it is not quite as significant of a phenomenon in Sweden as it is in the United States. She first saw *Star Wars* one month before her screen test and only began to realize its impact on popular culture in the United States when she visited Denver, Colorado for the *Star Wars* Celebration in April and May 1999.

Although the *Star Wars* movies have always relied on lesser-known actors, they still feature talented professionals who portray the many characters populating the *Star Wars* galaxy. Unlike most directors, Lucas enjoys the freedom to choose only the most talented actors because he never has to worry about their public appeal or anonymity. After casting director Gurland, director Lucas, and producer McCallum assembled *Episode I's* impressive cast, Lucasfilm was prepared to begin the long and arduous filming process.

Filming Begins

On July 22, 1997, Lucasfilm began filming *Episode I*. Principal photography took place at Leavesden Studios just outside of London while location filming occurred primarily in Tunisia in Africa and at the Caserta Royal Palace in Italy. Lucasfilm also filmed all three previous *Star Wars* movies in England at Elstree Studios, located beyond the outskirts of London. Leavesden Studios, where Lucasfilm filmed most of *Episode I*, provided the ideal location to build more than 50 sets required for the movie.

The Rolls-Royce Company used Leavesden as an aircraft engine factory for years until the Millennium Group Ltd. bought the 286-acre site to convert it to a production studio for feature films. MGM Studios used Leavesden for filming the 1995 James Bond film, *Goldeneye*. The studio's 500,000 square foot main building provided an excellent space for Lucas and his talented crew to set up a multitude of sets required for *Episode I*. In addition, the cast and crew used several independent soundstages apart from the main building. Leavesden also boasted one of the largest studio backlots in the world with more than 100 acres for outdoor filming, but the Millennium Group Ltd. has since torn it down as part of a plan to build a larger, more impressive filming studio.

Producer Rick McCallum exclusively reserved Leavesden Studios in its entirety throughout the production and post-production stages of *Episode I*. Lucasfilm planned to re-shoot scenes long after the completion of principal photography, necessitating a longer reservation of Leavesden so *Episode I*'s sets could remain standing.

Many sets seen in *Episode I* incorporated both physical and digital elements. No team of filmmakers had succeeded in seamlessly integrating real sets and computer graphics as flawlessly as in *Episode I*. Lucas's effects house, Industrial Light & Magic (ILM), constructed entire sets using only computer graphics imagery (CGI). Whenever possible, George Lucas and his crew constructed actual, physical sets, but building some sets outside of the computer is often too difficult and too expensive. In an interview posted on June 2, 1997 on the Official *Star Wars* Website, McCallum said, "You have to understand that many of the scenes we're building just couldn't be done without the use of digital rendering."

ILM used blue screens and green screens extensively during the filming of *Episode I*. Blue and green screens are simply solid colored set pieces that aid computer graphics artists in post-production. On a partially built set, crews placed colored screens wherever graphics artists would later insert digital elements. Using computer graphics in post-production, ILM then substituted the missing elements, such as buildings, spacecraft, and characters, in place of the colored screens. Once completed, the shots show characters or ships appearing in front of a bustling city or other fanciful imagery instead of the colored screen used on set. McCallum said, "You can't just go and do a location shoot of Coruscant; there's nothing like it that people have ever seen." The complexity of many shots meant that "many of our 'locations' will exist only in digital form," McCallum said.

In addition to filming a large number of scenes on sets at Leavesden, the cast and crew traveled to several locations to film most of the movie's main sequences. One of the new filming locations for *Episode I* was the Caserta Royal Palace in Italy. Speaking of the palace during a press conference in Italy, Lucas said, "Caserta was one of the most beautiful palaces on the planet and once we saw this there was no question that we wanted to shoot here." The Caserta Royal Palace proved an excellent choice as Queen Amidala's own palace on the planet of Naboo in *Episode I*. Natalie Portman played the young queen and acted in most of the scenes filmed at Caserta.

Tozeur, Tunisia on the North African Sahara Desert became the planet Tatooine in 1976 when Lucas and his crew used the location for *Star Wars: Episode IV—A New Hope*, so Lucas chose to return for *Episode I* to film more scenes from the planet. Tunisia provided an excellent location for filming decades before, although temperatures reach highs of more than 140 degrees Fahrenheit. Lucas had initially planned for ten days of filming in Tunisia, but the cast and crew in the harsh desert faced more difficulties than just high temperatures.

On July 29, disaster struck the filming site in Tunisia. A rare desert storm devastated the sets and forced the Tunisian crew to begin reparations to prevent costly delays in the filming stage. At first the situation seemed dire. The desert was soaked and the sets appeared in tattered shape. The storm scattered hundreds of costumes across the desert landscape and damaged many props and set pieces, in addition to tearing the dressing room tents to shreds.

Crews feared the worst, but rebuilding began quickly and efficiently. A similar disaster occurred during filming of the original *Star Wars* more than twenty years earlier. Lucas remained optimistic and even joked that the disaster might be a positive sign considering the previous storm did not prevent the original *Star Wars* from becoming one of the most successful movies of all-time.

Lucas and the main unit managed to film several scenes in a relatively undamaged area, as did second unit director Roger Christian. Repair crews rebuilt the sets, mended the costumes, fixed broken generators, and restored the Tunisian set to working order. Everyone on location assisted in the rebuilding process and the hard work allowed production to remain on schedule. Despite the destructive storm, which caused an estimated $80,000 in damages, no production delays resulted.

On September 26, 1997, after 65 days of principal photography, filming wrapped at Leavesden Studios on phase I of production. The filming crews shot over 1.3 million feet of film, or roughly 246 miles of scenes that later required extensive editing. The cast and crew dispersed after the filming, although many of them returned the following year when Lucasfilm re-shot selected scenes. Lucas also required the filming of several new scenes as part of the additional shooting that occurred months later.

Rumors abounded that Lucas intentionally filmed bogus scenes just to confuse fans, preventing the spoiling of the movie in the event that overeager cast or crew members leaked plot details. The Official *Star Wars* Website even mentioned the possibility, although no official sources ever confirmed the existence of any such scenes. Regarding plot rumors, Lucas simply stated, "Don't count on it until you see the movie." Many rumors traveled the Internet, most of them inaccurate, but several of them proved correct. Nevertheless, until the release date neared, few people knew for certain which rumors were true, and which were merely the desires of anxious fans.

Despite the completion of phase I in the movie's production, the long phase of post-production had barely begun. *Episode I* still required eighteen months of post-production before its release. In addition to the special effects work that ILM had to complete, Lucas still required additional filming, which he had planned from the beginning of work on the prequel.

Just past the middle of March 1998, Lucasfilm once again began filming new scenes at Leavesden Studios. Many actors returned to complete short new scenes or re-shoots, often referred to as "pick-ups." The March pick-ups comprised a portion of the second phase of photography for *Episode I*. Initially, Lucasfilm scheduled an additional three weeks of pick-ups in August 1998, but Lucas and crew required less than one week of the planned period. "We had planned to do these pick-ups for about three weeks and we actually did it in about four days," McCallum said. The cast also had to complete additional dialogue recording sessions before Lucas and his crew returned to the United States to finish post-production.

Lucas prefers a non-linear style of filmmaking that allows him greater freedom to film scenes whenever convenient, rather than in order of the movie's events. Filming a movie from start to finish is not always practical and Lucas realizes the advantages of efficiency in moviemaking. When completed, he combines all of the separate shots to form the final cut of the movie. Regarding the production process for *Episode I*, McCallum said, "You look at the picture, you edit it, you see what is missing or what you need to make the film better, and you go back and shoot it." Lucas is never forced to consider a scene finished until the actual release of the movie, and even when it is in theaters, the possibility of a special edition still exists.

If Lucas wants to manipulate a scene, ILM can make almost any alteration or improvement. Throughout the making of *Episode I*, Lucas's crew combined the best versions of each shot to produce the desired results. For instance, if Liam Neeson performed six separate takes of the same scene, Lucas had the freedom to combine an element from one shot and a separate element from another. The completed scene was then a combination of the best elements from each of the original shots. Lucas also used other advanced technology during *Episode I's* production.

The time difference between London and California allowed Lucas to send film footage from each day's shooting to Skywalker Ranch in California for overnight editing. When Lucas and his cast and crew awoke the following morning, ILM had already worked on the previous day's shots. The advantages of such efficient time use proved invaluable. With a complicated movie such as *Episode I*, every hour saved gave Lucas and ILM more time to fine-tune the movie for its May 1999 release.

Although no company had perfected digital filming technology for *Episode I*, McCallum said Lucas and his crew shot several scenes digitally. Lucasfilm did not announce which scenes they shot digitally and company officials have given no indication of when, if at all, they might tell the public.

Early in the production of *Episode I*, Lucas indicated his desire to film *Episode II* entirely with digital equipment. Indeed, *Episode II* shot with entirely digital video cameras. Filmmakers enjoy many advantages in using the new digital technology, such as higher image quality and easier transfer to computers for editing. *Episode II* is the first movie ever produced entirely without film. Digital projection and digital filming represent the future of movies, but also mark a change in the way movies are made. Once again, Lucas is leading the film industry into a new era.

Prequel Toy 'Wars'

Mattel, Hasbro, and Galoob, the three largest toy manufactures in the United States, all fought for the valuable toy rights to the *Star Wars* prequels. Throughout the 1990s, Hasbro and Galoob both held *Star Wars* toy licenses. Analysts already expected the prequel toy rights would be costly, especially when Mattel entered the bidding along with the two former licensees. Never before had toy rights sold for as much money as they did for *Episode I*.

Star Wars is the most successful film-based licensing program in history. Since the release of the first *Star Wars* toys in 1978 after the success of *A New Hope*, toys based on the saga and its characters have enjoyed phenomenal success. "Since the original movie came out 20 years ago, there's hardly been any let up in demand for *Star Wars*' toys," said Frank Reysen, the editor of trade publication *Playthings* magazine. With the release of the *Star Wars Trilogy: Special Edition* in 1997, *Star Wars* once again held the title of best-selling boys toy line for the year. In 1996, *Star Wars* also ranked first among boys toys. "*Star Wars* is the biggest success story in the toy industry," Reysen said. Toy sales from the classic trilogy had exceeded $2 billion and overall merchandise based on the franchise had sold an estimated $4.5 billion. With three entirely new *Star Wars* movies upcoming, every major toy company wanted the toy license.

Several analysts speculated that the largest toy maker in the United States, Mattel, had no real interest in paying the high fees that Lucasfilm desired for the toy rights, but instead entered the bidding only to force rivals Galoob and Hasbro to pay higher prices for their licenses. Other analysts disagreed, insisting that Mattel had genuine interest in the prequel toy rights because they lacked a strong toy line for boys, such as G.I. Joe and *Star Wars*, both of which are Hasbro properties. Mattel produces Barbie, which remains the perennial leader in overall toy sales.

Insiders worried that if Galoob, the third biggest toy maker in the United States, did not acquire the rights to produce toys for the prequels, then the company would fall into serious financial trouble. Roughly one third of Galoob's sales during 1997 came from *Star Wars* toys, so the loss of the *Star Wars* license would have crippled the company. For Hasbro, the second largest toy maker in the

United States, *Star Wars* only represented six percent of their sales in 1997. Nevertheless, *Star Wars* is the best selling toy for boys, which is a distinction that made the toy rights extremely valuable to Hasbro. Lucasfilm's previous agreement with the two companies lasted through the end of 1998, but both toy makers desperately wanted to keep their licenses into the next millennium, when the last two prequels would play in theaters.

On Tuesday, October 13, 1997, Lucasfilm named Hasbro and Galoob the two *Star Wars* prequel toy licensees. Many analysts speculated that Lucasfilm chose the two companies again because of their experience with the *Star Wars* line, which both had managed successfully for many years. The triumph came at a steep price for both companies, but the deal extended their licenses through the release of all three *Star Wars* prequels. Analysts immediately labeled the deal the biggest in the history of the toy business. Never before had two major toy companies struck such a massive deal.

To retain their rights, Hasbro paid Lucasfilm an estimated $430 million in addition to royalties on every future *Star Wars* product sold. *Variety* estimated the royalties at 15-20%, which is nearly double the average royalty percentage paid for toys. *Forbes* estimated Lucas's take at 17%. In addition to the generous royalties, Lucasfilm received a 5% equity stake in the company. Despite informed estimates, neither company disclosed the exact terms of the deal, so the figures stated are only insider estimates.

In 1977, Kenner purchased the *Star Wars* toy rights, though in 1991 Hasbro acquired Kenner. Despite the fact that Hasbro merely retained their *Star Wars* license, company executives treated the deal as a major event. Losing the *Star Wars* license would have proved costly for the company, especially if a rival toy producer acquired it.

For the prequels, Hasbro once again owned the rights to produce core action figures based on the *Star Wars* movies, in addition to vehicles, games, electronic hand-held games, and many other products. "This is a major triumph for Hasbro," said Alan Hassenfeld, the chairman and CEO of the company. Hassenfeld said the *Star Wars* toy rights are "truly the crown jewels for the toy industry." Hasbro understood the importance of the saga to their continued success. Hassenfeld said, "We know the power of 'the Force,' and this agreement gives Hasbro the wonderful opportunity to develop the *Star Wars* brand over a broad range of categories well into the next millennium."

Hasbro managed their *Star Wars* license with exceptional care and excellence. Fans worldwide enjoyed the high quality of their products, as well as their dedication to the *Star Wars* franchise. Lucasfilm president Gordon Radley said, "Hasbro's proven creativity, passion for *Star Wars*, and its worldwide marketing expertise made them the compelling choice to be our key strategic partner in the toy and game arena."

Galoob's deal with Lucasfilm, though not as large as Hasbro's, was very lucrative for the studio. Under Galoob's deal, the company had to pay $140 million in advance plus royalties on future sales. Aside from the impressive sum of money that the toy maker paid to Lucasfilm, Galoob also offered the studio warrants for 20% of its common stock, or about 3.6 million shares, at a price of $15 per share. Even before the official announcement, which came at the close of the market, Galoob stock soared 12.5% in expectation of the deal.

Galoob initially became a *Star Wars* licensee in 1992 with their small vehicles and figures. For the new deal, Lucasfilm granted Galoob the right to make small-scale *Star Wars* toys based on the prequels and continue production of toys from the classic trilogy. "With the highly anticipated new *Star Wars* films, we expect growth of a magnitude greater than ever experienced in our company's history," said Gary Niles, the executive vice-president of Galoob.

Despite the triumph of retaining their *Star Wars* licenses, some insiders and analysts wondered whether the toy companies could sell enough merchandise to make their expensive deals financially rewarding. Few doubted that *Star Wars* toys based on the prequels would sell well, but would sales be enough to justify the massive contracts struck with Lucasfilm? Only time could determine the wisdom of the deals, but many analysts thought Galoob was running out of time. As early as February 1998, speculation began spreading that Galoob had overpaid for their *Star Wars* rights. Many analysts even thought the *Star Wars* deal would push the company into bankruptcy. Later in the year, however, Galoob received unexpected relief.

On Monday, September 28, 1998, Hasbro entered into a definitive agreement to acquire Galoob for $220 million in cash. For Hasbro, buying Galoob gave them a chance to eliminate some of the competition among consumers for their *Star Wars* product line. Galoob benefited from the deal because of Hasbro's size and their global marketing reach, in addition to the financial support that Hasbro could provide. Galoob's revenues fell 24% the previous quarter, which came almost entirely as a result of the smaller shipments of *Star Wars* toys for the quarter compared to the previous year, when the *Star Wars: Special Editions* drove company toy sales. Galoob needed a larger partner to continue their growth and success as a leading producer of quality toy products, so Hasbro provided a fitting solution to their financial woes.

Alan Hassenfeld said the addition of Galoob's "extensive *Star Wars* license will allow us to further develop this global brand franchise." Mark D. Goldman, president and CEO of Galoob, asserted that his company would benefit "enormously" as a result of "Hasbro's global reach and resources." Regarding the deal between the two toy giants, Lucasfilm said, "We congratulate Hasbro and Galoob on their agreement and are delighted that Hasbro will be able to include these additional toy rights in their overall *Star Wars* licensing program."

Galoob shareholders received $12 per share, an announcement that sent Galoob stock soaring 43% that Monday to close at $11.44. Hasbro stock did not immediately benefit from the announcement and closed at $30, down 3.2%.

With the acquisition of the nation's third largest toymaker, Hasbro closed the gap on Mattel's dominance in the industry. In the upcoming years, Hasbro hoped that the Force had enough power to bury Barbie and Mattel and claim the coveted title of the nation's number one toymaker. Despite the acquisition of Galoob, Hasbro did not own all of the *Star Wars* toy rights, much to their dismay.

Earlier in the year, on Thursday, April 30, Lego announced they had acquired *Star Wars* toy rights from Lucasfilm, which would enable the company to produce construction toys based on the classic trilogy and the prequels. The deal came as somewhat of a surprise to both Hasbro and Galoob, which at the time remained separate entities. Lucasfilm denied that it had caused any unrest with existing licensees, though. Howard Roffman, vice president of licensing for Lucasfilm, called such reports "seriously misinformed." Although Lucasfilm presumably informed Hasbro and Galoob that they sought a construction toy partner, Lego created greater competition for the consumers' money. Roffman claims, "We entered into agreements with each of these companies with the understanding that we would be pursuing a construction toy."

While Hasbro and Galoob worried that Lego could cut into their sales, Lego had no such worries about the other two toy giants. "I think we add a different dimension," said Peter Eio, president of Lego Systems Inc., based north of Hartford, Connecticut. Diane Cardinale, a spokeswoman for the Toy Manufacturers of America, did not think the market for *Star Wars* toys had even come close to saturation. She said, "Collectors of these items are a very committed group" and "they just can't seem to get enough."

Lego, founded in Denmark, had never entered into a deal with any external company since its creation in 1932. They had always designed and produced their popular construction toys within the company. Peter Eio said Lego had been seeking a long-term licensing partner for years, but had previously been unable to find one that would satisfy their needs. *Star Wars* provided the perfect toy property for Lego. Eugene Gilligan, executive editor of *Playthings* magazine said, "I don't see how you could get a better property than *Star Wars*. It's just an automatic sell."

Toy properties with long-term prospects are rare. Most toys based on movie properties provide a short flurry of sales immediately following the movie's opening and throughout the year of release, but toy sales dwindle as the movie leaves theaters. Even worse, toy companies face many risks when producing products based on a movie because the success of the toy line often depends heavily on the success of the movie itself. *Star Wars* is one of the few toy properties based on a movie series that has enjoyed continued success long after the movies exited theaters. The longevity of the *Star Wars* franchise proved irresistible for Lego.

Eio said, "Obviously, we see it as a substantial opportunity globally." Lego's annual sales at the time neared $1.3 billion, but the company expected the *Star Wars* license to add substantially to revenue. Neither company, Lego nor Lucasfilm, disclosed the financial terms of the deal, although insiders speculated that Lucasfilm received far less from Lego than they had received from either Galoob or Hasbro. The reason for the smaller payment allegedly stemmed from Lucasfilm's desire to see a more complete toy line for the prequels. In their May 17, 1999 issue, *Newsweek* claimed Lego spent $50 million for the toy rights, but estimates on the exact value of the deal remain pure speculation.

Regardless of the price, Lego gained a powerful alliance. Their president and CEO Kjeld Kirk Kristiansen said, "The alliance with Lucas Licensing Ltd. represents a major step for the LEGO Group worldwide." Radley said, "We are very proud to have our *Star Wars* construction toys designed and marketed by a company that is renowned for quality, creativity, and imagination."

With the completion of the final toy deal, Lucasfilm had awarded all of the major licenses. Before the first customer purchased the first ticket for the first prequel, the new trilogy of movies had earned a profit for Lucasfilm. The anticipation for the movies did not just come from the fans and the avid moviegoers. Companies such as Hasbro, Galoob, and Lego became involved in the wave of anticipation surrounding the prequels, but the difference between the two interested groups, fans and companies, could not have been more pronounced. While the companies tied their future financial success to the new *Star Wars* films, fans merely enjoyed the ride.

Fox Has The Force

Every major studio in Hollywood hoped to gain the rights to distribute George Lucas's prequels, but insiders questioned whether or not Lucasfilm would award distribution rights to any studio at all. Many analysts believed Lucasfilm would release and promote the movies independently, eliminating the need for an out-side distributor. Lucas decided against the option, though, choosing instead to find a major studio with experience handling widespread distribution and pro-motion of event movies. The right to distribute all three prequels was potentially extremely lucrative, even though Lucasfilm only intended to award a small per-centage of the box office gross for each film to the distributor. Every studio exec-utive understood the potential windfall of a deal with Lucasfilm, so the quest for the prequel rights began.

Although Lucas distributed *The Empire Strikes Back* in 1980 and *Return of the Jedi* in 1983 with Twentieth Century Fox, no contract bound him to distribute the prequels with the studio. Lucas included a "key man" clause in his initial con-tract with Fox, meaning he no longer owed loyalty to the company. The key man clause freed him from any obligation to distribute *Star Wars* movies with Fox once Rupert Murdoch acquired the studio from Marvin Davis, a Texan oil bil-lionaire.

Lucas's strong friendship with Steven Spielberg led to rumors that Lucas would ally himself with his friend's studio, DreamWorks SKG. The studio, formed in 1994 by Steven Spielberg, Jeffrey Katzenberg, and David Geffen, appeared to be one of the front-runners in the race for the prequel rights, but did not receive them. Instead, Lucas chose an older, more established studio.

On Thursday, April 2, 1998, Twentieth Century Fox Studios and Lucasfilm Limited announced that Fox would distribute the next three *Star Wars* movies. In addition, Fox gained broadcast rights to the first prequel, which Lucas planned for an early summer release the following year. Fox did not immediately disclose the terms of their broadcasting agreement with Lucasfilm, but *Variety* later reported the studio paid $80 million, which was one of the highest fees ever.

As part of the deal, Fox transferred the rights to the original *Star Wars* movie, *A New Hope*, to Lucasfilm. The company has always owned all rights to *The*

Empire Strikes Back and *Return of the Jedi*, but Fox entirely funded the first *Star Wars* and thus owned the rights to it. The deal Lucas struck with Fox in the 1970s for *A New Hope* assured him sequel and merchandising rights. Despite Lucas's gain, historians consider it one of the largest gaffes in Hollywood history because the deal eventually cost Fox more than $5 billion in lost revenue. The man who made *Star Wars* successful should own his creation, so the prequel negotiations placed the movie in rightful hands. Finally, after more than twenty years, Lucas officially controlled all rights to *Star Wars: Episode IV—A New Hope*.

Lucasfilm chose Fox again largely because of the effective job their studio did in working with Lucas and his companies to restore the classic trilogy just a few years prior. "We've enjoyed working very closely with Bill [Mechanic], Tom Sherak and their talented colleagues on the worldwide theatrical and video releases of the *Special Edition*," said Lucasfilm president Gordon Radley. In addition, Fox oversaw the worldwide distribution of *Titanic*, the most successful film of all-time in international box office receipts. "Fox has proven to be an outstanding worldwide film and video distributor," Radley said.

The *Star Wars* rights guaranteed Fox three major blockbusters from 1999 through 2005. Lucasfilm scheduled the release of *Episodes II* and *III* in 2002 and 2005, but the dates remained tentative. Fox received a lower than average gross participation for the prequels, mostly because Lucas planned to finance all three movies himself, meaning Fox enjoyed nearly no financial risk. The studio took an estimated ten-percent of the box office gross from *Episode I*. In exchange for participation in the gross revenue, Fox agreed to manage the worldwide distribution and marketing of the three movies, while Lucas would entirely oversee the productions.

"This is truly an historic day for this company, this studio and its employees," Peter Chernin, Fox Group chairman and CEO, told *Variety*. Chernin said, "It is one of the privileges of my career that Fox will once again join George Lucas and Lucasfilm to bring the first three chapters in this incredible saga to the world." Seeing the Fox logo before each *Star Wars* movie and hearing the famous fanfare has become a major part of the viewing experience. Fans did not want inconsistency between the two *Star Wars* trilogies, so Lucasfilm's decision pleased enthusiasts of the classic trilogy around the world.

Although nearly every movie studio wanted the distribution rights to the *Star Wars* prequels, Lucasfilm only ever met with Fox. Tom Sherak, chairman of Twentieth Century Fox Domestic Film Group said, "The bottom line is the Lucas people are probably the most loyal people you'll ever meet." Nevertheless, the negotiations required a significant amount of time to complete. Fox had planned to announce the partnership at ShoWest in Las Vegas, a convention of theater owners and studios that occurred just days before the announcement, but Lucasfilm and Fox did not complete the deal until Thursday afternoon on April 2.

"We feel like *Star Wars* is part of the fabric of Fox," said Bill Mechanic, Chairman of Fox Filmed Entertainment. Many fans also feel Fox is a significant part of *Star Wars* history. With *Episode I* in post-production, the wait for the first prequel neared the one-year mark. After Lucasfilm had chosen the distribution studio for *Episode I*, fans waited anxiously for the next important announcement.

The Phantom Menace

On Friday, September 25, 1998, Lucasfilm finally announced the official name of *Episode I*. The first of three prequels, and the beginning of the saga, *Episode I* was named *The Phantom Menace*. Lucasfilm released the title through the Official *Star Wars* Website, ending the long wait for the first prequel name, but not according to many fans.

Initially, the fan community shunned the title. Many people said it made no sense and sounded too much like a comic book title, or that it lacked the grandeur that a new *Star Wars* movie should possess. The backlash largely stemmed from the preconceptions many fans had about the title, rather than the meaning and quality of the name itself. For many years, enthusiasts had speculated about the name of the first prequel. Many people believed it would be called *Balance of the Force*, *Guardians of the Force*, *The Clone Wars*, or other fabricated titles too numerous to list.

Despite the rumored names, George Lucas only had two working titles for *The Phantom Menace*, which were *Episode I* and *The Beginning*. People primarily referred to the first prequel as *Episode I* because Lucasfilm placed emphasis on the episode name so the public and the media understood that the events in the movie precede those of the classic trilogy.

After the title announcement, many fans even insisted that Lucas intended to confuse them with what they thought of as an unusual title. Adamantly arguing that Lucas would change the title only weeks before the release of the movie, a sizeable group of fans ignored the announcement. After all, Lucas had renamed *Return of the Jedi* from *Revenge of the Jedi* before it entered theaters in 1983. A poll conducted on the largest unofficial *Star Wars* fan site, TheForce.net, found that an alarming 48% of 502 voters did not believe *The Phantom Menace* was truly the title of *Episode I*.

Nevertheless, Lucasfilm spokeswoman Lynne Hale insisted, "*Phantom Menace* is the title." In March 1999, when asked in an online chat if Lucasfilm intended *The Phantom Menace* title to serve as a decoy, Rick McCallum responded, "Absolutely not. That is the title of the movie." Lucasfilm had nothing to hide; *Episode I* had a name, whether or not fans liked it.

In *Star Wars Insider* issue 41, published in December 1998, McCallum said, "The title definitely reflects the subject of the movie." Although many fans did not initially approve of the title, McCallum, and especially Lucas, knew its significance to the movie. McCallum said, "Once you see the movie, you'll understand the title." True to his word, most fans understood and appreciated the title upon the movie's release.

The backlash over the prequel's name only foreshadowed further backlash when the film arrived in theaters. The absurdity of bashing a movie's title before its release did not occur to many fans as they became engaged in the hype and anticipation of a new *Star Wars* film. Despite the initial negative sentiment about the title, most fans who criticized it later realized its meaning. One poll on TheForce.net, taken months after the title announcement, indicated that 40% of 5,329 voters liked the title more than when they first heard it. Only 3% liked it less, while 16% hated it, and 25% said they still loved it.

After a sizeable percentage of fans expressed their disapproval of the title, the inevitable disappointment of many fans with the movie itself should have become apparent. When people expect one story, but receive another that differs from their preconceived notions, disappointment and resentment often follow. Regardless, excitement over the movie reached new peaks as the months progressed, so nobody stopped to consider the implications of a backlash against just the title of the movie.

If fans showed disappointment over the title without having actually seen the movie, what would happen if they saw it and not every event occurred as they had hoped or expected? One could only hope the prequel would satisfy fans regardless of the events in its story, but most importantly, that it would satisfy Lucas and his desire for perfection.

Despite the backlash, the wait for *The Phantom Menace* continued with fans receiving their first glimpse of the movie just a few months later. The outcry over the title ended and many fans forgot their criticisms. The first film preview of *The Phantom Menace* finally arrived when Lucasfilm released Trailer A to theaters in November; fan excitement had never been as intense.

Trailer A

Since the first rumors of a prequel trilogy began stirring in the media, fans wanted even just the smallest glimpse of George Lucas's prequel. Despite the eagerness of millions of fans, Lucas did not show any footage of his movie until 1998, when fans flocked to Trailer A, which was the first official film preview of *Episode I.*

A trailer, one of the primary tools used to promote new movies, is a movie preview that studios create to impress moviegoers with quickly cut footage from the advertised film. Decades ago, previews trailed the movie, thus their name, "trailers." In modern theaters, previews for upcoming productions precede the featured attraction, so the name is misleading yet traditional.

Rumors traveled the Internet throughout the early months of 1998 concerning which movie the first *Episode I* trailer would play alongside first. Anonymous Internet sources indicated that *The X-Files: Fight the Future* would be the first movie to feature Trailer A. The rumors seemed plausible. *The X-Files*, a Twentieth Century Fox release, arrived in theaters on June 20, 1998. The trailer, however, did not arrive with it, so the rumors never materialized and the wait for the first trailer continued.

Later in the summer of 1998, rumors persisted as supposed insiders claimed the first trailer for *Episode I* would appear before the *Titanic* VHS, which arrived in retail stores in early September. Many fans scoffed at the absurdity of the rumor. As they expected, Trailer A did not appear before *Titanic* on its September 1 release.

Finally, on November 6, 1998, Lucasfilm announced through their Official *Star Wars* Website that Trailer A would enter selected theaters for a special preview on Tuesday, November 17 only. In 75 locations in 26 states, D.C., and Canada, Trailer A played three days earlier than its national release. Fans who had the opportunity to see Trailer A on the 17th could see it twice, both before and after the featured attraction. The trailer later premiered in nearly every theater in North America on Friday, November 20.

Lucasfilm determined the states in which Trailer A would play on November 17 based on the number of *Star Wars Insider* subscribers in each area of the country. The *Star Wars Insider* is the official *Star Wars* magazine, which Fan Media printed bi-monthly, though Wizards of the Coast, a Hasbro-owned company, acquired Fan Media after *The Phantom Menace's* release.

Lucasfilm's trailer announcement from the Official *Star Wars* Website was "a present to the fans," said Lucasfilm spokeswoman Karen Rose. For all of the loyal fans who followed the Official *Star Wars* Website since its creation, and who eagerly awaited even the most trivial news about *The Phantom Menace*, Trailer A was a worthy present. "We really want to do something special for our fans who have been so patient and yet so enthusiastic about this new movie," Lucasfilm spokeswoman Jeanne Cole told *USA Today*.

The first trailer for a movie is commonly referred to as a "teaser trailer" because it contains very few plot details. Instead, teaser trailers attempt to create interest in an upcoming movie through impressive visuals or a memorable concept. Sometimes, they do not even contain more than a few seconds of actual footage, but still serve to inform moviegoers of the film's release up to a year in advance. While *The Phantom Menace* did not need a teaser to create interest, it helped further raise awareness of the movie. The marketing department chose to focus the trailer primarily on Anakin Skywalker to emphasize his importance in the new trilogy. Lucasfilm also wanted to continue their pursuit in informing casual moviegoers that the prequels are set many years before the original *Star Wars Trilogy*.

The teaser poster for the film, referred to as a "one-sheet," featured Anakin Skywalker, whose shadow appeared as the outline of Darth Vader. The image largely succeeded in informing uninitiated individuals that Anakin Skywalker becomes Darth Vader. The security surrounding even the printing of the one-sheets surprised many people. According to reports in *Variety*, Fox officials oversaw the printing to prevent eager employees from taking any posters for themselves. In addition to the extra security precautions, Fox printed the one-sheet using a counterfeit-proof, five-color process.

"The trailer works together conceptually with the advance one-sheet and theatrical banner," said Jim Ward, Lucasfilm's director of marketing. Trailer A ran two minutes and eleven seconds long, which is a fairly average length for a teaser. The music accompanying the first trailer came from the original trilogy because no new music was ready for integration into the footage at the time Lucasfilm constructed it. Also, the classic music helped provide familiarity for the public and the fans.

Fans wanting to see the early preview of George Lucas's first prequel on November 17 had to attend one of three films, which were *The Waterboy*, starring Adam Sandler, *Meet Joe Black*, starring Brad Pitt, or *The Siege*, starring Bruce Willis. Another method of seeing the trailer soon became available, though, and more than ten million people chose the more viable alternative.

On November 18, one day after Trailer A played in theaters, Lucasfilm uploaded the teaser trailer to the Official *Star Wars* Website. Several journalists and fans speculated that Lucasfilm offered the trailer through their site in an effort to discourage fans from illegally recording it at theaters. Although Marc Hedlund, Lucasfilm's director of Internet development said, "We had planned to post the trailer on Tuesday night but we wanted to wait until after it hit the cinema." Nevertheless, many camcorder copies of the trailer became available through fan sites despite the noticeably inferior sound and picture quality.

Although one might assume that such illegal recording would frustrate Lucasfilm, Hedlund said, "Only a hard-core fan is going to sneak a video camera into a theater, film our preview, digitize it and put it online. And only an extreme fan is going to want to see that poor quality." Although, downloading the trailer from the Official *Star Wars* Website was not easy at peak hours of the day and night. Even fan sites received such heavy traffic that sometimes seeing the trailer required more extreme measures.

Lucasfilm tried to prevent illegal copies of the trailer from circulating by telling theater owners they must return Trailer A to receive the next *Star Wars* trailer at a later date. Although theater owners knew that selling promotional materials from the film violated copyright laws, a few trailers became available to buy. On eBay, a leading online auction house, several copies of Trailer A sold for more than $400. Tom Sherak, chairman of Twentieth Century Fox's domestic film group said, "We've asked exhibitors to send the trailers back to keep them from being sold," but he conceded, "Sometimes there's only so much you can control."

After three days of release, "Between three and four hundred thousand people" downloaded the trailer, according to Hedlund. Many fans chose to download the trailer from fan sites such as TheForce.net, so the actual number of downloads after three days likely exceeded 500,000. The Official *Star Wars* Website experienced such an overload of visitors that Lucasfilm had to increase their bandwidth capacity from 70 T1 lines to 81. An estimated 350 people visited the official site every second, according to Lucasfilm administrators.

In addition to theaters and the Internet, fans could also watch Trailer A on TV, where it played on nearly every major station multiple times for days after its release. From *Entertainment Tonight* and *CNN* to local news stations around the country, Trailer A was ubiquitous.

Although fans could stay at home and see the new trailer for *The Phantom Menace*, theaters remained the ideal place to witness its visual splendor. News media across the country watched and reported as die-hard fans paid the full price of admission to see the first footage from a new *Star Wars* movie in nearly sixteen years. From Los Angeles to New York, movie attendance increased as fans flooded theaters. After the trailer played in front of the feature attraction, regardless of the theater, wild applause and standing ovations followed.

In Los Angeles, *Variety* noted that nearly 500 people showed up for the 1:00 p.m. showing of *The Siege* at the Mann Village Theatre in Westwood, but almost two-thirds of them walked out of the movie after the trailer ended. Nevertheless, many fans returned for the encore showing of the trailer immediately following the movie. According to the *Los Angeles Times*, the theater experienced an 85% increase in ticket sales from the previous day because of fans crowding their theater to see Trailer A. Overall, Sherak said attendance was up 140% in theaters playing the trailer on its first night.

Fan reaction to the trailer bordered on complete satisfaction. Excited fans hailed the special effects as revolutionary, like nothing they had seen before. They also appreciated the lack of spoilers in the trailer, meaning it gave away few plot details, but instead moved from scene to scene, showcasing the movie's incredible visuals. Trailers are designed to entice viewers through visuals and sometimes a unique concept, but they are not supposed to ruin the plot of the film they promote. After the trailer, fans and casual moviegoers alike waited in breathless anticipation for the film's release.

The level of excitement surrounding the first trailer for *The Phantom Menace* had no precedent. In the history of the motion picture industry, never had a mere preview for an upcoming movie inspired such enthusiasm and mass public response. In addition to satisfying eager fans, Trailer A helped establish *The Phantom Menace* as the must-see movie of 1999.

George Lucas also expressed his satisfaction about the reaction to the teaser trailer. "It has been so gratifying to hear that people have enjoyed the trailer," he said. Lucas said he was "really overwhelmed at the response" he received from all of the fans.

Throughout the world, foreign countries waited for their opportunity to obtain a glimpse of Lucas's vision, which happened when Trailer A began playing in countries around the world. Unfortunately, many international fans had to wait months before the trailer arrived in their nation. In Japan, Trailer A did not appear before a movie until April 17, 1999. In Germany, fans waited until May

20, 1999, which was after the film's North American release date. In France, *Star Wars* fans could not see Trailer A in theaters until June 23, 1999.

After the hype surrounding Trailer A finally subsided, it had set an Internet record as the biggest download event in history with more than ten million copies downloaded. The trailer seemed to be a more important event than many actual movies. Never before had such a sizeable number of people paid just to see a movie trailer. Although speculation about the next trailer commenced immediately after the release of Trailer A, most people assumed that nothing could compare in size and scope to the excitement generated by the first trailer. *Star Wars* is an unpredictable phenomenon, though, and months later, media, fans, and industry analysts watched in disbelief when Trailer B duplicated the success of its predecessor.

Toy Fair

The American International Toy Fair is a major annual event in the toy industry. The convention of more than 1,200 buyers and manufacturers takes place in Manhattan, New York and is closed to the public. It is the biggest tradeshow in the toy industry and has a major impact on the selection of products that consumers see on the shelves as far ahead as the holiday shopping season at the end of each year. At Toy Fair, the manufacturers have to gauge the demand for each product on display. From their analysis of the demand, they decide how much supply to make available. Any product shortages throughout the year are because of miscalculations at Toy Fair. "Holiday season shortages go all the way back to Toy Fair," said Diane Cardinale, a spokeswoman for the Toy Manufacturers of America. Likewise, if demand for a product is limited and too much supply exists, Toy Fair is likely the cause of the discrepancy.

On Monday, February 8, 1999, the 96th annual Toy Fair began, lasting through the following weekend. *Star Wars*, of perennial importance at Toy Fair throughout the decade, was especially significant in 1999. Despite the frenzy over the toy line, Hasbro only allowed the retailers to see toys for *The Phantom Menace*. Retailers interested in seeing *The Phantom Menace* toy line had to sign secrecy agreements while a security guard protected a locked door that prevented the media or anyone else from seeing the toys.

The secrecy surrounding the toys closely paralleled the secrecy surrounding the movie's plot and filming. While George Lucas had not revealed many secrets about his anticipated prequel, Hasbro had not uncovered their prequel toys for the public either. The reason for secrecy surrounding the toys for *The Phantom Menace* arose from Lucas's desire not to spoil the movie's plot, which would ruin the experience for many fans. "We want them to go see the movie and have a little bit of a surprise and don't want to spoil the fun for the fans," said Holly Ingram, a spokesperson for Hasbro.

While many fans wanted to know every detail about *The Phantom Menace*, others preferred to walk into the theater with limited knowledge of the film's plot and characters. Seeing the movie without knowing many details would make the experience more surprising, and thus fulfilling, many fans believed. Hasbro officials said the company signed a pact with Lucasfilm not to reveal the prequel toys until just before the movie's release in May, so fans attempting to protect themselves from spoilers were mostly safe.

While trying to obtain an early glance at toys for *The Phantom Menace* was nearly impossible at Toy Fair, the Internet provided a much more viable alternative. Various websites, including TheForce.net, offered leaked pictures of many toys from *The Phantom Menace*. Although people are often skeptical about the validity of unofficial pictures, upon seeing them nobody could deny their authenticity. Once again, the Internet uncovered *Phantom Menace* secrets, much to the chagrin of official sources. The availability of the pictures was not the first or the last time insiders posted unauthorized, accurate information on the Internet regarding the anticipated movie.

Analysts already knew *The Phantom Menace* toys would boost Hasbro sales significantly. Nobody doubted *Star Wars* would reign as the number one toy for boys for a fourth consecutive year. For the 1998 holiday season, despite the absence of a new movie, *Star Wars* toys held the number two spot overall behind Barbie and the top spot among boys toys. Saying that analysts expected *Star Wars* toys to become the top selling boys toy line again in 1999 is similar to saying *Star Wars* is popular; neither statement was ever in question.

While the movie's complicated special effects sequences prompted the creation of new digital technology at Lucas's Industrial Light & Magic, Hasbro also had to create new technology for the movie's toys. At the Toy Fair on February 8, Hasbro announced an entirely innovative, new technology called COMMTech, or Communication Output Memory Module Technology. The toy giant licensed the COMMTech Reader from Innovision, a company based in the United Kingdom, and it served as the newest enhancement for action figures.

The COMMTech Reader adds an entirely new dimension to action figures by allowing for talking toys. Each figure came packaged with a COMMTech chip, which allowed for the toy to interact with other ones in the same product line. After moving a COMMTech chip over the reader, the reader emits a line of dialogue the character spoke during the movie. Each chip usually holds three separate lines of dialogue, although chips with four also exist. COMMTech "gives children a new way to play with action figures," said Alan Hassenfeld, Hasbro's Chairman and CEO.

In addition to interpreting the chips, the COMMTech reader can also store up to three entire chips of the users' choosing within its memory system. The reader also has several built-in sounds, such as blaster and lightsaber sound effects. Every action figure for *The Phantom Menace*, at least in the first line of toys, included a COMMTech chip, although customers had to purchase the reader separately. Because of the higher production costs, the toy prices increased slightly. Still, the suggested retail price of $8.99 per figure kept them affordable.

Lego also planned impressive products for *The Phantom Menace* that they revealed during Toy Fair. One of the toys, the Droid Developer Kit, allowed consumers to create their own R2-D2 units. The droid actually senses light and then reacts to it by moving one direction or another. "Children at a certain age, say around 10, start to put their Legos aside," said John Dion, public relations manager for Lego. The availability of innovative products that use advanced technology keeps kids playing with Legos even longer than before when such products did not exist. Unfortunately, the Droid Developer Kit was not available until the holiday season in 1999, which meant thousands of other products related to *The Phantom Menace* flooded the market prior to its release.

With the multitude of products scheduled for release, licensed companies wanted to avoid saturating the market, though they had to gauge the demand based on limited knowledge. Three separate companies produced the majority of *Star Wars* toys, including Kenner, Galoob, and Lego. Although Hasbro owned Galoob and Kenner, both companies had planned extensive product lines. Because of the wealth of merchandise in development, licensed companies had to plan their product rollouts carefully during a longer period of time, instead of immediately before or after the movie's release.

Previous to the Toy Fair, Hasbro and Galoob released three preview toys for *The Phantom Menace*. At the end of 1998, Hasbro released their STAP (Single Trooper Aerial Transport) product, which featured a vehicle from *The Phantom Menace* that included a droid riding it. In addition to the STAP, which sold well in stores, fans could send in six proofs of purchase from *Star Wars* action figures and $2.99 to receive a Mace Windu preview toy. Hasbro produced a limited number of Mace Windu toys, so the demand far outstripped the supply initially. Its value increased dramatically before the *Star Wars* Fan Club made the action figure readily available.

Galoob released the Gian Speeder and Theed Palace Play Set, which featured Queen Amidala's palace from *The Phantom Menace*. The play set also quickly became a popular item and gave fans a preview of Galoob's prequel toy line.

At Toy Fair, Hasbro displayed more than 300 products from *The Phantom Menace* that only a limited number of people saw. *Star Wars* toys were especially important at the 96th annual Toy Fair because rather dismal 1998 sales overshadowed the industry, forcing analysts to pin their hopes on *Star Wars*. In 1998, action-figure sales declined 13.3 percent, so *Star Wars* once again needed to revive an industry and reverse a negative trend, which insiders expected *The Phantom Menace* would accomplish. Similar expectations of the prequel in every facet of its release largely prevented honest reporting of the movie's success throughout the year because of unfairly high expectations.

Trailer B

Although the madness over the first trailer for *The Phantom Menace* seemed impossible to surpass, the second *Star Wars* trailer succeeding in becoming an even more impressive event. Major media sources such as *Variety* had concluded that a new four-minute long trailer would arrive at theaters on January 24, 1999. Regardless, Lucasfilm indicated the trailer would come out much closer to the actual release date of the film, which was then scheduled for May 21, 1999.

On January 28, 1999, the Official *Star Wars* Website reported that Lucasfilm would release Trailer B sometime in March. The company had not yet set a date, although the site also confirmed the planned release of another poster to coincide with the release of Trailer B.

On February 16, 1999, the Official *Star Wars* Website confirmed that Trailer B had a running time of roughly two minutes and 30 seconds, and also assured fans the trailer would arrive in theaters shortly. The announcement stated that the trailer contained entirely different footage from Trailer A and focused more on the plot of the film, not just on Anakin Skywalker.

In early March, media sources such as *E! Online*, *USA Today*, and *The New York Post* quoted unnamed sources stating Trailer B would appear in theaters on March 12, 1999. On March 8, within a week of the reports, the Official *Star Wars* Website announced that Trailer B would premiere in theaters nationwide on March 12, just as the unofficial sources previously claimed.

Although many reports stated *Wing Commander* would feature the newest *Star Wars* trailer, Lucasfilm said Trailer B would play with several films. They also warned fans that Trailer B might not always appear before each copy of *Wing Commander,* but most people looking to see Trailer B in theaters on its first weekend of release attended the space movie, which was loosely based on the computer game series of the same name. Although Fox wanted Trailer B to play only in front of their movie, *Wing Commander,* Lucasfilm wanted the studio to release the trailer independently so it could be seen before many films.

Just after 9:45 p.m. on Wednesday, March 10, 1999, George Lucas showed Trailer B to more than 4,000 anxious theater exhibitors and other industry professionals at the annual ShoWest conference in Las Vegas. Pepsi hosted the special screening while Fox sponsored it. As with Trailer A, security greatly concerned Fox and Lucasfilm. Guards checked every bag and Tom Sherak, chairman of Twentieth Century Fox Domestic Film Group, asked people to stop anyone trying to record the trailer illegally. "If you see a person to your left or right holding up a video camera while we're showing you what we're about to show you, stop them," Sherak reportedly pleaded with the audience.

Lucas announced at ShoWest that the prequel had a new release date. He stated that on May 19, 1999, *The Phantom Menace* would premiere in theaters nationwide, not on the previously planned date of May 21. The release date moved from a Friday to a Wednesday, so just as the original *Star Wars* in 1977 opened on Wednesday, May 25, 1977, the prequel also enjoyed its first day of release in the middle of the workweek.

The decision to move the release date up two days for *The Phantom Menace* stemmed from Lucasfilm's desire to enable fans to see the movie on Wednesday and Thursday, thereby hopefully allowing families to see it during the weekend. Lucasfilm thought that by moving the release date up to a Wednesday, die-hard fans would have seen it before the weekend and families not willing to wait in extremely long lines would have a chance to see it over its opening weekend. Lucas said the announcement was intended "to give fans a head start and give families a chance to see it on the weekend."

Despite the shortening of the wait until opening day, the announcement angered several fans, specifically ones flying in from foreign countries to attend the premiere. International fans who had already booked flights to the United States to see *The Phantom Menace* either had to rethink their plans or cancel their trip altogether. Fortunately, most fans had already planned to fly into the states several days early to wait in line, so Lucasfilm's decision had minimal negative impact. Most fans reveled in the announcement and were glad that Lucasfilm shaved two days off the long wait. Before fans concentrated on the final stretch until the movie's release to theaters, they wanted to see the final trailer for the most anticipated movie of all-time.

Although fans who wanted to see Trailer A had to venture to theaters to see it first, Trailer B became available first on the Internet. On Thursday, March 11, 1999, Lucasfilm uploaded Trailer B to their Website for fans worldwide to view one full day early. Speaking of Trailer B, Jim Ward, director of marketing for Lucasfilm said, "We wanted something that would both blow the fans away and sustain them during the last stretch before the movie opens." Trailer B succeeded on both fronts.

Making the trailer announcement even more exciting for fans was Lucasfilm's statement revealing that Apple's newest QuickTime technology would be the sole means by which to see Trailer B on the Internet. QuickTime offers the best available quality in video presentation for Web users. Trailer A played only in lower quality formats, but Apple's QuickTime was superior for the presentation of the second trailer on computers around the world, regardless of the platform. Steve Jobs, CEO of Apple Computers said, "Lucasfilms' exclusive choice of Quick-Time over its rivals—RealNetworks RealPlayer and Microsoft's Media Player—is a real coup for QuickTime." QuickTime had already won many industry awards, so users recognized and appreciated its superior sound and video quality.

Lucasfilm strived to ensure the quality presentation of Trailer B as engineers at the studio worked diligently to create a special sound mix for the trailer that worked especially well for the online copy. Jim Ward said, "George Lucas wanted to create the highest quality Internet viewing experience for our new trailer, so we turned to QuickTime because it sets the standard for Internet video quality." Interested moviegoers could download the trailer from either the Official *Star Wars* Website at www.starwars.com or the Official Apple Website at www.apple.com. In addition to the two official sources, numerous fan sites posted the trailer, just as they had with Trailer A.

Accompanying Trailer B to theaters was the final poster for *The Phantom Menace*, which artist Drew Struzan had finally completed. Fans are familiar with Struzan's work on the covers of many *Star Wars* novels. In addition to his artwork for the novels, he created three *Star Wars: Special Edition* drawings in 1996 that served as the primary posters for the re-releases. The poster for *The Phantom Menace* closely resembles the posters he drew for the *Special Edition* releases as it has the same tone and style. *The Phantom Menace* poster features each of the main characters in vibrant color and shows the element of adventure and excitement present in each *Star Wars* movie. The movement away from photographs on posters provides an excellent opportunity for artists such as Struzan to display their talent.

Trailer B played in theaters around the nation in generally high sound and visual quality that people can only experience in theaters, so many fans still paid for tickets to other movies just to see the trailer. In addition to playing in theaters and on the Internet, Trailer B played on every major media station, just as its predecessor had months earlier. The event was no less newsworthy than the first trailer, allowing Trailer B to duplicate the earlier success.

Profit-seekers began selling copies of Trailer B on eBay, so the problem still existed despite earlier efforts to eliminate illegal sales with Trailer A. Sales of

Trailer A became a problem in November 1998, so continued sales of the next trailer again worried Fox officials, who tried diligently to halt the illegal activity. "What they're doing is an illegal act, and we will do anything we can possibly do to protect our copyright," Tom Sherak said. Online auction company eBay acted very cooperatively with Fox and Lucasfilm in dealing with the illegal sales. "If they requested that we take down the bidding sites, we would do so immediately, no questions asked," said Kevin Pursglove, a spokesperson for eBay.

Trailer A held the record for the most downloads on the Internet, giving Trailer B a considerable challenge in trying to re-write history. While many fans expected a close competition, Trailer B easily triumphed. After 24 hours, Internet users had already downloaded more than one million copies of Trailer B. Apple called the first day results the "biggest online download event in history." Although Trailer B still had millions of downloads remaining before it trumped the teaser trailer, the demand for it was unprecedented. Anticipation for *The Phantom Menace* had reached a new level. Trailer B also jumpstarted burgeoning software QuickTime as more than 600,000 people downloaded the program within the first day of the trailer's release.

Within five days, more than 3.5 million people had downloaded the newest trailer for *The Phantom Menace*. The five-day download mark set an Internet record, which was the second speed record that Trailer B smashed. Jobs said, "Over three and a half million downloads in five days makes this the biggest Internet download event in history." Just a week after its release, Trailer B's download pace assured it the coveted title of the biggest overall online download event in history. After three weeks had elapsed, 6.4 million people had downloaded the trailer, but the number continued to rise. Apple's partnership with Lucasfilm was a success for both companies. "Apple is proud to have participated in this online experience of the new *Star Wars* movie," Jobs said.

Trailer B created the same frenzy in theaters nationwide as Trailer A had months earlier. Fans paid to see it in theaters despite sometimes having to sit through poor quality films. Attendance increased for many movies on the strength of the *Star Wars* trailers alone. The long wait for *The Phantom Menace* had nearly ended. With just months remaining before the movie's debut in theaters nationwide, Trailer B provided the last major preview of the movie. "This is the last trailer before the release of *Episode I*," Jim Ward confirmed.

Prior to the release of Trailer B, most fans did not imagine it had any chance of topping the success of Trailer A because no trailer in history had received as much attention as the first for *Episode I*. Although most people anticipated the excitement over Trailer B, few people expected it would best its predecessor. By the time the movie arrived in theaters, more than ten million people had downloaded Trailer B, solidifying its position as the most successful download event in history. After more than fifteen months in release, visitors to the two official websites had downloaded the trailer 35 million times.

The public's desire for any information related to *Star Wars* became even more apparent with Trailer B. Remembering that the enthusiasm surrounding the trailer came from the fans is important because the hype did not stem from the studio that released the movie. Ward said, "We're thrilled with the fans' response. Apple's QuickTime software provided us with the highest quality and enabled us to push Internet video to its limits." Lucasfilm only created two trailers for *The Phantom Menace*, which is a standard number even for lower budget movies. Sony created four separate trailers for *Godzilla* (1998), which is the most fitting example of a studio-hyped movie that did not stir much public enthusiasm. When Sony finally released their movie in theaters, the consumer interest was weak and the movie performed significantly below expectations.

Lucasfilm never created the interest in *The Phantom Menace*; it all stemmed from eager fans and an interested public. Fan excitement and public curiosity with *The Phantom Menace* helped both Trailer A and Trailer B become impressive successes; Lucasfilm and Fox did not artificially create the interest. In a culture dominated by companies and corporations convincing consumers what they should like, and consequently what they should buy, seeing the consumers creating the hype was refreshing.

Phantom Fan Sites

The Internet played an important role in promoting *The Phantom Menace* through both official and fan created Websites. Lucasfilm used their Official *Star Wars* Website to provide fans with information about the movie's production, theatrical release, and product tie-ins. It also hosted both trailers for the prequel, but the unofficial fan sites posted most of the interesting rumors and many breaking news stories. Three main Websites, TheForce.net, Jedinet.com, and Countingdown.com, provided fans with their daily fix of *Star Wars* news and information.

Scott Chitwood founded TheForce.net in 1996 along with Darin Smith, his roommate at Texas A&M University. His team of more than ten staff members reported daily news and rumors collected from fans all around the world. TheForce.net has an established network of reliable sources that keeps its readers knowledgeable about the latest *Star Wars* information.

Paul Ens, a staff member for the site, said at the time, "We have two movies left to go, so I don't want to say too much about how we find our spies, and of course for some people their jobs are at stake." Ens even obtained a copy of the script for *The Phantom Menace* well before the film's release, although he refused to read it, unlike fellow staff member Brian Linder. "I did read it. It was the Holy Grail, and I had been chasing it for awhile," Linder said. He added, "Obviously, there were very few people with access to the entire thing. It's marked in a way it could be linked to the source if it got back to George Lucas."

TheForce.net has established a spy network that ranges from die-hard fans to industry insiders. Ens said, "Some contacts we've made at conventions or we have friends at Lucasfilm who will make unofficial comments. We also have spies who are directly involved with the production, and they come to us." Although the media often criticizes the Internet for spreading inaccuracies, TheForce.net finds and reports a wealth of information about *Star Wars* movies in advance of their release dates.

Joshua Griffin, the main editor at TheForce.net for many years said, "When someone comes to us with information, the hard part is telling whether or not they are truly who they say they are—or complete fakers." He admits, "I would say that at this point, we probably get several imposter sources each day, trying to pass off information that is not completely accurate, or complete works of fiction." Nevertheless, TheForce.net's staff members attempt to discern possibly accurate information from ridiculous rumors. When asked why employees at Lucasfilm would risk their jobs to provide a fan site with information, Griffin said, "It's a game really, and there is a certain thrill to leak information out on a production." He said a large percentage of their information comes from "folks who have signed no waivers and non-disclosure agreements." Griffin wants "to maintain the reputation for the most reliable rumors on the Internet for *Star Wars*," but he admits, "We've been duped before."

TheForce.net attracts tens of thousands of visitors every day, but traffic steadily increased from its inception in 1996 through the release of *The Phantom Menace* in 1999. Griffin said shortly after the release of the film, "Right now we receive around 50,000 daily unique computers visiting the site, which translates into over 5,000,000 ad impressions each week." As the release date for the movie approached, traffic rose each month "and after a major promotion or interview," Griffin said. The fan-created video *TROOPS*, which is a spoof of both *Star Wars* and *Cops*, also attracted heavy traffic because of major media organizations such as *Entertainment Weekly* featuring stories on it. The video even entered TheForce.net and *TROOPS* director Kevin Rubio into The Guinness Book of World Records for "Greatest *Star Wars* Tribute."

The high traffic to TheForce.net caused many problems for the Website over its first several years. While the site began as a fairly inexpensive hobby at $40 per month, monthly costs quickly ballooned to between $2,000 and $3,000. The site has changed hosting companies more than six times, including working with Imagine Media, a banner advertising company based in San Francisco, California. The company publishes magazines such as *PC Gamer* and *Mac Addict*, as well as hosting a popular entertainment Website called The Daily Entertainment Network, or The DEN. Ens said, "At first, it was barely covering our costs, but now we're starting to see a very small profit." Since his comments, though, The DEN became IGN, the Internet Gaming Network, which became part of Snowball.com. "We entered [into] an agreement with IGN that makes us no money at all, but covers all hosting and nearly unlimited expansion," Griffin said.

TheForce.net donates any excess money from banner ads to charity, which is part of Lucasfilm's expectations for fan sites because profiting from their licensed pictures and characters violates copyright laws. "In 1999 alone, we gave just short of $10,000 to the staff's favorite charities," Griffin said. The site also set up a charity system through Amazon.com, which is called the "Honor System," where fans can donate money to TheForce.net, which the site then donates to chosen charities in different countries. The charitable donations from fan sites along with Lucas's strong interest in contributing to worthy causes demonstrate a genuine interest among *Star Wars* fans and Lucasfilm to help people in need of assistance.

Although many studios have become involved in legal battles with fan sites and their Webmasters because of copyrighted photographs posted on the sites, such as Paramount with *Star Trek* fan sites, Lucasfilm maintains a healthy relationship with fans and Webmasters. Part of a statement that Lucasfilm issued on April 25, 1996 read, "Lucasfilm appreciates *Star Wars* fans support and we want you to be able to communicate with one another. Your energy and enthusiasm makes [sic] you an important part of our *Star Wars* family."

Although Ens said of Lucas, "There's always a worry that he might sue us," TheForce.net is on favorable terms with Lucasfilm. Lynne Hale, director of communications for the studio said, "We love TheForce.net. It's pretty much our policy that as long as they are using the copyrighted images and materials to show their enthusiasm and not making money, then that is fine." She adds, "As long as they are just fans having fun, then that's great. Remember, our fans have stuck with us for 20 years." Marc Hedlund, director of Internet development for Lucasfilm added, "The fan sites celebrate the trilogy, so we don't view them as a threat. If anything, they're a benefit." Griffin also said, "We do keep in frequent contact with the Official Site and Lucasfilm representatives," though he emphasized, "There have been few complications with Lucasfilm, for which we are truly thankful."

TheForce.net requires many hours of work each week from its staff members and provides almost constant coverage of *Star Wars* news and events. Ens said, "Between us [the staff members] and the times of day we work, we have almost 24-hour coverage of the site." Linder added, "It's like trying to work one full time job, manage my personal life, and work a second job as a professional *Star Wars* fan." Their hard work makes TheForce.net the best fan site on the Internet.

Joshua Griffin, who has since retired from his duties, spent more than twenty hours each week on the Website and considered it a hobby just as "some people ride horses, others build model airplanes or watch TV, and I work on the largest unofficial *Star Wars* Internet Website," he said. Griffin said, "If anything happens in the *Star Wars* universe, you can read about it on TheForce.net almost immediately and with thoughtful comments." He said in an interview shortly after *The Phantom Menace* came to theaters, "Fans visit on a daily basis to speak out in the forums, keep up to date on *Star Wars* news, and truly experience the journey to these next two movies." Despite the hard work that Griffin had to put into the site, he admitted, "I love the thrill of writing a news article and knowing that in just a few minutes hundreds if not thousands of people will see it." Although TheForce.net is the most extensive and frequently updated fan site, several others are also popular among fans.

The newest fan site at the time of *The Phantom Menace*'s release was Countingdown.com, which just began to become a major attraction for fans in late 1998. The site featured an exact countdown until the movie arrived in North American theaters, but like TheForce.net it also offered daily news and rumors. Unlike the TheForce.net, though, Countingdown.com's *Star Wars* site was run almost entirely by one person, Lincoln Gasking. According to an article in the *Washington Post* on April 17, 1999, the site regularly received 100,000 visitors per day.

Gasking's native land is New Zealand, where his parents own a bed and breakfast at which he stayed while running Countingdown.com and organizing lineups for the movie. Speaking about the creation of the site, Gasking said, "In 1998 I met Tim Doyle of countdown2titanic.com and we expanded it to a more general movie site, Countingdown.com, together with Phillip Nakov." The Countingdown site grew to include many other movies, but the *Star Wars* site was by far the most popular.

Although the site had few staff members, it had many contributors and spies. Unlike TheForce.net, Countingdown's *Star Wars* site peaked from early 1999 up until the movie's release in the United States, but the site quickly lost its appeal as the updates declined. Gasking was extremely busy planning international lineups, so without people to answer e-mails and post news, the site was no longer able to compete with the other fan sites. Nevertheless, its primary purpose was counting down until the release of the film. During the final months leading up to release, Countingdown.com not only competed with other fan sites, but often provided the best, most accurate, and most interesting news and rumors on the Internet.

As Gasking and his fellow dedicated fans lined up outside of Mann's Chinese Theatre, the Website even offered streaming, live video footage of the fans in line. Also, visitors to the Website could talk to the people standing in line, either through calling them on the nearby payphone or typing to them in a special online chat room established for Gasking and fellow fans from around the world.

A third major fan site, Jedinet.com, also provided news, rumors, and information about *The Phantom Menace*. Although Jedi Net is the oldest *Star Wars* fan site, their coverage of *The Phantom Menace* was not quite as impressive as TheForce.net or Countingdown.com. Nevertheless, the site is well designed and includes numerous features on the entire *Star Wars Saga*. Jedi Net, while not always as frequently updated as TheForce.net, is nevertheless one of the most impressive *Star Wars* sites on the Internet. Many people choose to visit all of the major fan sites, which is a decision that serves die-hard fans with abundant time better than selectively visiting a single one for their daily *Star Wars* needs.

The sense of community that exists between *Star Wars* fans does not spread to the fan sites, which fiercely compete for the most recent rumors and news. "There's lots of infighting among the fan sites," said Carl Cunningham, who runs the Prequel Watch section of Jedi Net. Cunningham's site was guilty of contributing to the feud when staff members posted a crossed out logo of TheForce.net on their front page, expressing their opposition to the rival site. "When we posted prototype action figures, TheForce.net posted them the next day with their watermarks on them, and no accreditation to us," Cunningham said in defense. He added, "There's a fair amount of flame mail" that Jedi Net receives.

TheForce.net's Joshua Griffin said, "There is a sense of competition between sites, but to be honest I rarely visit other *Star Wars* sites." He added, "When I get online, I do the news, spy reports and direct the staff and make things happen." He has a positive attitude about any rivalries, saying, "I find any rivalry with other sites pointless and anything like that would only distract me from making TheForce.net the place fans will want to visit."

Many of the staff members at TheForce.net have far more important priorities in their lives than pointless rivalries. Griffin said he spends his free time "working with the youth in our church, my relationship with God, family, and coaching football." He also said, "If I get some extra time, I usually visit the Jedi Council Forums, where over 5,000 messages a day are posted by the fans. I love talking directly with them and being accessible to the people who are just like myself—they have a passion for TheForce.net and *Star Wars*." Paul Ens is a self-employed computer programmer who lives in Saskatchewan, Canada and also runs local church youth groups in addition to spending several hours on the site each day. He is married and has one son.

Another fan site, StarWarz.com, which the media did not often mention among the major *Star Wars* sites, also received many visits. Lou Tambone, who fans know as T'Bone Fender, his nickname, runs the Website, which offered numerous "spoilers" about the movie before its release. While many fans wanted the surprise of walking into theaters not knowing about the events that would unravel on screen, other fans preferred to learn anything they could about the film. Details about a film's plot or characters are known as spoilers; many fans visited StarWarz.com just to find the newest ones about *The Phantom Menace*.

When the British Broadcasting Company asked Tambone how many times he had seen the *Star Wars* movies, he responded, "If you think I can actually give you a number—you are nuts." He finally said, "Hundreds and hundreds…Sound OK?"

Aside from being prominent on the Internet, the fan sites also received mainstream media attention through television shows, magazines, and newspapers. For instance, *Newsweek* published an article on several notable fans and their Websites in their February 1, 1999 issue. The article even received a mention on the cover of the magazine. It offered commentary from several of the Website owners and featured photos of important fans such as Terence Daniels, Brian Linder, and Steve Head of TheForce.net, Lou Tambone of StarWarz.com, and John Benson of Jedi Net.

Besides the numerous fan sites, the Official Website also offered *Star Wars* enthusiasts a wealth of information about *The Phantom Menace*. Lucasfilm's site at www.starwars.com launched on November 26, 1996, before the *Star Wars: Special Edition Trilogy* arrived in theaters, but quickly transformed to provide fans with exclusive pictures, interviews, and announcements about *The Phantom Menace*. Lucasfilm used their official Website to announce the title of the film, which many people thought would come from a more traditional press conference or official press release to the media. Instead, Lucasfilm chose to thank the visitors to their Website by making the announcement available to Internet surfers.

When Lucasfilm first launched StarWars.com in 1996, Internet marketing was in its infancy, but two movies helped permanently change the importance of the medium as a tool for selling movies to the public. *The Phantom Menace* was the first movie to make the Internet the primary source for information about a film. Both Trailer A and Trailer B set Internet download records, establishing that the new medium is not only a powerful marketing tool, but a popular one. Millions of visitors checked the site weekly for updates on the film's casting, production, and post-production progress. While the site began as a simple headquarters for *Star Wars*, it gradually became a powerhouse of information and pictures.

A second movie, which competed with *The Phantom Menace* in theaters, also helped drive Internet marketing into prominence. *The Blair Witch Project*, a tiny independent movie produced for less than $100,000 and acquired by Artisan for $1 million, used the Internet to reach tens of thousands of potential fans. The Internet site tried and often succeeded at convincing moviegoers that *The Blair Witch Project*, in addition to being one of the scariest movies ever, was also based on a true story. The film, however, is pure fiction and its status in the horror genre, along with its quality, is debatable. The Website was realistic enough to fool thousands of moviegoers into believing the story was true, which helped stir a frenzy of interest in the movie.

Aside from informing fans of the latest prequel news, Lucasfilm also used the Official *Star Wars* Website to let them know about Internet chats with the stars, which TalkCity hosted immediately before the film and throughout the first few months of its theatrical release. The chats featured guests such as producer Rick McCallum, animatics artists Kevin Baillie and Ryan Tudhope, casting director Robin Gurland, special effects veteran Dennis Muren, actress Pernilla August, and actors Liam Neeson and Jake Lloyd.

In addition to the Official *Star Wars* Website, Hasbro also launched an impressive site, which prompted *Wired* to write an article titled, "Web-Site Force Is With Hasbro, Not Lucas." While the Hasbro site may have impressed visitors more than the official one when *Wired* published the article in early 1997, Star-Wars.com improved drastically between its launch and the release of *The Phantom Menace*. The date of the article is important to understanding the discrepancy between the film saga's official site and the site of a licensee. At the time, Hasbro's *Star Wars* license was set to expire within months and the company wanted to send a clear message to Lucasfilm that they were "committed to the license," said Sean McGowan, a toy analyst at Gerard Klauer Mattison.

The Hasbro site offered impressive features such as movie clips, QuickTime video views of *Star Wars* action figures, and a Shockwave interface, which made the site visually more sophisticated than most other Internet sites. The Quick-Time videos are meant to show "how the technology in the production in action figures has increased exponentially since the '80s," said Rick Ruskin, the marketing manager for Hasbro's *Star Wars* products. Hasbro continued to offer impressive Websites for their products, even after the release of *The Phantom Menace*.

On May 20, 1999, Hasbro published a press release about the launch of their Tiger Electronics *Star Wars* Website, which was "the first Website dedicated to *Star Wars: Episode I* electronic toys." The site features Flash plug-in technology, which allows for higher quality sound and improved animation. It also featured playable demos of Tiger Electronics *Star Wars* games, message boards for fans to discuss the games, and *Star Wars: Episode I* e-cards (cards sent through e-mail).

The Internet played a significant role in promoting *The Phantom Menace* to moviegoers, but most importantly it connected people who share a common interest in the saga. The fan sites informed readers of the newest rumors, the latest news, and provided many of the most intriguing pictures, but they also provided forums for fans to meet each other and discuss their common interests. Lucasfilm helped pioneer Internet marketing through their clever and controlled release of information on StarWars.com. While studios rarely considered the Internet part of their marketing plan in 1997, today every major new release has a Website dedicated to it.

The fan sites helped increase the interest in *The Phantom Menace* and also served as additional free advertising for Lucasfilm. The Official *Star Wars* Website kept enthusiasm strong and did not cost Lucasfilm much money to maintain for the considerable benefits it provided. Although the fan sites contributed to the hype and anticipation, the unprecedented coverage of the movie from almost every media empire in the world made *The Phantom Menace* an historic movie.

Strict Terms

One of the most contested issues over *The Phantom Menace* began in early April 1999, when Twentieth Century Fox announced the terms by which theaters must abide to play the movie in their theaters. As with many announcements surrounding *The Phantom Menace*, the terms requested had few precedents. Because of the anticipation preceding the movie's release, almost every theater exhibitor agreed to Fox's conditions. *Variety* first published the specifics of the terms on April 6.

First, *The Phantom Menace* had to play on the largest screen in the theater for the minimum length of its theatrical run. Fox required all theaters to play the movie for eight or twelve weeks, depending on the marketplace. If a theater wanted to play the movie for a lesser number of weeks, it had the option to begin playing the prequel on June 18 and hold it for a minimum of four weeks. If the exhibitor committed to playing the movie on two or three screens in their multiplex, it had to play on the same screens for the entire duration of its release.

In competitive zones with more than one theater chain present, *The Phantom Menace* had to play on at least three screens at each theater complex. Fox also prohibited interlocking, which is the act of using one print to show a movie on two screens. Although theaters hired more employees than normal during the movie's release to ensure order, they could not deduct security expenses from the rental fees. Theaters could not honor any passes for at least the first eight weeks of the movie's release. Theaters and other companies often distribute free movie passes, but Fox wanted to prohibit their use while demand for tickets was strong. Although free passes are often denied for new movies, the eight-week duration seemed unusually long to many exhibitors.

Theaters had to make their revenue payments to Fox within seven days during the first several weeks of *The Phantom Menace's* release. Typically, studios allow thirty to sixty days for payment. Fox also prohibited any paid on-screen advertising for the first two weeks. In addition, Fox allowed only eight minutes of trailers preceding the movie, yet the studio had already included two and a half minutes of their own promotional film footage.

In addition to the terms that Fox established, Lucasfilm wanted *The Phantom Menace* to play in quality theaters equipped with the most advanced sound systems and speakers. Lucasfilm did not want the movie playing in theaters that lacked digital sound equipment. Tom Sherak, chairman of Twentieth Century Fox Domestic Film Group said, "Fox will be looking to play the film in digital sound in every market that digital is available." After years of perfecting technical aspects of the film ranging from minor sound effects to painstaking visual details, Lucasfilm wanted fans to experience the movie in optimal viewing conditions. In smaller markets, Lucasfilm had to be content with the best theaters available. "In markets that do not have digital sound, although we believe digital sound is important, it is more important for our fans to be able to see the movie," Sherak said. The quality presentation of *The Phantom Menace* concerned Lucasfilm even before the negotiations with exhibitors.

Fox and Lucasfilm fined any theater that failed to meet the terms and conditions they established. In addition to fines, theaters risked having their print or prints of *The Phantom Menace* confiscated. The threat of being unable to play the most highly anticipated movie of all-time, and consequently a likely box office hit, deterred most theaters from ignoring the terms that Fox established.

Theaters often made special arrangements with Fox, allowing them to stop playing *The Phantom Menace* prematurely in some cases. Also, Fox allowed many theaters to downsize *The Phantom Menace* from two screens to one screen in the middle of the required run. The studio executives did not want to upset theater owners, considering they have to negotiate with them for each movie they release.

Many exhibitors complained about the strict arrangements, although they realized that *The Phantom Menace* would bring amazing business to their theaters. "There are often conditions put on (theaters), but this is pretty unusual," said Paul Dergarabedian, president of Exhibitor Relations Co., the primary box-office tracking firm. The conditions, though unusual, did not strangle theaters nearly as much as they insisted.

Almost everyone agreed that Fox could have asked for nearly any condition from theaters and had it granted. The anticipation surrounding the movie at the least assured a massive opening weekend. Add a sizeable opening to *Star Wars'* proven record at the box office and most analysts expected *The Phantom Menace* to perform extremely well, possibly becoming the highest grossing movie of all-time. After Fox announced the terms, the studio still had to negotiate with theaters, though they did not expect many problems. "Fox feels that with this type of product they can make these demands and the exhibitors will agree to them,"

Dergarabedian said. He said, "Who wouldn't want to have their theater playing this movie?"

While a segment of the media tried to portray Lucas as the evil emperor, bullying the helpless theaters, the truth is far from their misconception. By requiring theaters to hold *The Phantom Menace* for eight or twelve weeks, he gave every fan nationwide a chance to see the movie multiple times. Lucas and the talented crew at Lucasfilm worked nearly five years making *The Phantom Menace*, so he rightly refused to let theaters use his movie as a cash cow only to discard it promptly for the newest competing summer blockbuster. Fans who enjoyed watching the movie many times during the summer appreciated his insistence that theaters play it for at least two months.

When the original *Star Wars* premiered in 1977 on only 32 screens nationwide, it opened in a vastly different movie marketplace. In the 1990s, most movies played in theaters for an increasingly short number of weeks and quickly exited theaters in favor of other, newer films. Whereas popular movies once played all summer and into the fall, now only the most successful blockbusters enjoy the luxury of extended theatrical releases. Theaters continue to push quality movies out of the marketplace prematurely, making way for the newest and most heavily advertised films. Instead of holding onto consistent performers, theaters eliminate the older movies in favor of new releases that promise massive openings, but usually fade quickly. Moviegoers often have to see a movie within the first few weeks if they intend to see it at all. By requiring theaters to continue playing *The Phantom Menace* during most of the summer, Lucas assured fans a chance to see the movie and prevented theaters from profiting from it in the first several weeks, then dumping it like any other film.

By eliminating annoying, non-movie advertisements from playing before *The Phantom Menace*, Lucas improved the viewing experience for anxious fans. In addition to eliminating the ads, he forced rival studios to shorten their trailers so fans did not have to bother watching long trailers in which they had no interest. Although trailers are a fun part of the movie experience, anxious *Star Wars* fans at a midnight screening of *The Phantom Menace* did not want to see ads; they wanted to see the movie.

Lucas wanted *The Phantom Menace* to be a fun experience for the fans and the public because *Star Wars* is largely supposed to be about having fun. He wanted the fans to experience *The Phantom Menace* in the best possible theaters without having their experiences ruined by obnoxious advertisements and excessively long trailers. According to a study that the market research and box office tracking firm ACNielsen EDI conducted, 64% of frequent moviegoers would rather have less than seven minutes of trailers before a movie than more than eight minutes.

Most studios figured that cutting their trailers from two minutes to less than one minute would improve their odds of having the trailer positioned with *The Phantom Menace*. Jeff Blake, president of Sony Pictures Releasing said, "Any situation which would increase the chances of 100 percent placement on *Star Wars* is something we have to consider." Analysts expected tens of millions of people to see *The Phantom Menace* within just weeks of release, so every major studio wanted their trailer to play in front of the movie.

Several studio executives reacted negatively to the required shortening of their trailers. "I didn't ask anyone to cut their trailer in half to play with *The Matrix*," said Dan Fellman, the head of Warner's distribution. Mr. Fellman seemed to miss the importance of the event. No movie had ever been as eagerly anticipated as *The Phantom Menace*. While *The Matrix* became very popular, before its release the movie had no special significance and no guaranteed blockbuster status. Tom Sherak insisted, "This is *Star Wars*. It's a special movie."

One New York exhibitor, however, did not feel the prequel deserved any special consideration. One of the only disagreements between Fox and exhibitors came in New York City, where Manhattan theater chain Loews Cineplex did not play *The Phantom Menace* on any of its theater screens in the New York area. Fox and Loews never came to an agreement on the rental terms for the prequel, which resulted in the movie playing on far fewer screens than Fox desired in New York, which is a key market for movies because of its high population density.

The dispute occurred because Fox demanded that Loews, as well as every other exhibitor, pay a "floor" on *The Phantom Menace*. A floor is a guaranteed minimum percentage of the box office receipts for a movie. Lucasfilm president Gordon Radley told *Variety*, "It's not like no one in New York wanted to play this movie. Why should (Loews) be given an exception?" Loews has never given a floor for any movie in its Manhattan area sites; even for *Star Wars*, the theater chain was unwilling to yield to pressure from Fox. "We play hardball…if you roll over on this, then we have to roll over for everybody else," said Loews Cineplex Entertainment CEO Larry Ruisi. Instead, Loews opted not to play the movie at all in New York City.

On Thursday, April 15, Fox and Lucasfilm announced which theaters would play *The Phantom Menace* upon its release. The announcement inevitably did not please all of the theater chains, but Lucasfilm and Fox attempted to give the best quality theaters in each market the chance to play the movie, although theater companies often disagreed with their decisions. AMC, for instance, did not receive *The Phantom Menace* in key Southern California markets such as Century City, Santa Monica, and Pasadena, among others. One veteran film buyer said, "You can never go into a situation like *Star Wars* and expect anything like 100% coverage."

One last-minute change came in Los Angeles at the Mann's Village Theatre in Westwood and the Mann's Chinese Theatre in Hollywood. Outside of the famous Chinese Theatre, Lincoln Gasking and the Countingdown.com crew had created a lineup for *The Phantom Menace* that lasted a total of 42 days. Fox had initially scheduled the movie to play at the theater for nearly the entire summer, but instead negotiated a four-week deal that allowed the prequel to play at both theaters through June 17. The arrangement, called a "four-wall" deal, allows the distributor to pay the theater a guaranteed sum of money to play the movie for four weeks. Many people familiar with the negotiations speculated that Fox only bothered to secure the theater because of the eager fans already waiting outside since early April, which was roughly when Fox announced the theater arrangements. Fox offered no official comments about their decision.

With the strict terms and conditions set for exhibitors, Fox and Lucasfilm did not intend to take advantage of theater owners; instead they aimed to ensure the best possible experience for the consumer. Sherak said:

> We're not trying to make things impossible. We're trying to be as consumer-friendly as possible—any onscreen advertising they do for the first two weeks is going to draw boos anyway. What we're doing is asking our partners to come along on this very special ride.

Theater owners complained about the arrangement with Fox, wishing they could have a larger slice of the box office pie than they received. *Star Wars* fans, however, appreciated what Fox and Lucasfilm accomplished in their negotiations. The efforts of individuals at Lucasfilm and Fox helped make *The Phantom Menace* a special experience for fans nationwide, who enjoyed the movie in the nation's best theaters throughout the entire summer in many cases. After the sixteen-year wait, fans at least deserved a full summer of *Star Wars*, especially the die-hard fans who camped in line for months outside of Mann's Chinese Theatre.

Star Wars Celebration

Lucasfilm held the first *Star Wars* celebration on the tenth anniversary of the original *Star Wars* movie in 1987. Prior to the anniversary celebration, Lucasfilm had never authorized a fan event or convention. The release of *The Phantom Menace* encouraged fans to discuss the highly anticipated return of *Star Wars* with other die-hard followers from across the United States, and even around the world. The second *Star Wars* Celebration, which took place just weeks before the release of *The Phantom Menace*, gave fans a unique opportunity to share their passion for the saga and share in the anticipation of the first new *Star Wars* movie in sixteen years.

The first official *Star Wars* fan event was in Los Angeles, California, the entertainment capital of the world. During the years leading up to *The Phantom Menace's* release, many fans speculated that Lucasfilm would authorize a second fan event, but nothing materialized for many years. The rumors were inaccurate until the end of 1998, when they became reality as Lucasfilm announced the second official *Star Wars* convention.

In the October/November issue of the *Star Wars Insider*, Fantastic Media, the magazine's publisher, announced the coming of the second Lucasfilm authorized fan event. The announcement stated that the event would take place in Denver, Colorado during the spring of 1999, just prior to the release of *The Phantom Menace*. The editor of the *Star Wars Insider*, Jon Bradley Snyder, stressed that Lucasfilm intended the event as a gathering for fans, so he requested suggestions for it from the magazine's readers. Many science-fiction conventions focus primarily on selling merchandise and obtaining autographs, but the *Star Wars* Celebration in 1999 had a different focus. Lucasfilm intended the event to serve as a "thank-you to the fans," a Lucasfilm spokesperson later said.

Lucasfilm actively collaborated with Fantastic Media to ensure that the *Star Wars* Celebration would be a memorable event for fans of the saga. In fact, the notion of another fan event, later known as the *Star Wars* Celebration, came from Lucasfilm. Dan Madsen, *Star Wars* Fan Club President said, "It was Lucasfilm who first contacted us." The idea for a new fan event first surfaced in fall 1997, although actual work did not begin until spring 1998. Lucasfilm spokeswoman

Jeanne Cole said, "We have a long relationship with Fantastic Media, and we'll be cooperating in every way on this convention." She added, "We'll be sending cast members from *Phantom Menace*, crew members, stunt people, everything." The effort that both Lucasfilm and Fantastic Media invested in the event made it memorable and unique.

The first official *Star Wars* fan publication, called *Bantha Tracks*, existed for almost ten years, from 1978 through 1987. Through 35 issues, *Bantha Tracks* kept fans of the *Star Wars Trilogy* informed about news relating to the saga and also provided exclusive information and interviews. Factors, Inc., an outside licensee, began the publication in July 1978 following the amazing success of the first *Star Wars* movie. Nine months after *Return of the Jedi's* release, membership reached a peak of 184,046. Just a few short years later, however, membership dwindled to about 5,000. By 1987, *Bantha Tracks* ceased publication.

The discontinuation of *Bantha Tracks* only marked the end of one era of *Star Wars* fever as another publication quickly filled its place. Shortly after the end of *Bantha Tracks*, Lucasfilm authorized Fantastic Media to publish the *Lucasfilm Fan Club Magazine*, which focused on Lucasfilm properties in general, as opposed to just the *Star Wars* franchise. Nevertheless, a massive and exciting *Star Wars* revival began in the early 1990s, so the magazine name changed to reflect the restored interest in the space saga. In 1994, Fantastic Media renamed the magazine on its 23rd issue and the *Star Wars Insider* began.

At the beginning of the new millennium, the *Star Wars Insider* is one of the most popular fan club publications in the world as no other science fiction related publication even claims close to the impressive number of subscribers that the *Insider* boasts. By the end of 1998, membership in the *Star Wars Insider* had swelled to more than 150,000 subscribers, though by March 1999 it reached 300,000. Dan Madsen predicted the number would increase to roughly half of a million by the end of May 1999. Fantastic Media expanded its employee base from about 25 in 1997 to about 90 by early 1999. The company's excellent handling of the official *Star Wars* magazine was a delight to fans while the *Star Wars* Celebration in 1999 offered an excellent opportunity for many of those fans to meet.

In *Star Wars Insider* issue 42, Snyder expressed delight at the fans' enthusiastic response to the *Star Wars* Celebration. Many suggestions proved too difficult to attempt, although Fantastic Media considered and implemented quite a few of them. Snyder announced that Lucas would be unable to attend the event, but prequel producer Rick McCallum had cleared room in his schedule to make a special appearance. Also, Snyder confirmed that autograph signing would not be part of the *Star Wars* Celebration, at least for the actors. Although the announcement disappointed many fans, the decision helped make the *Star Wars* Celebration more informative and organized, rather than a mass of eager fans stampeding for autographs. Instead of autographs, cast and crew members spoke to eager fans about their careers and the making of *The Phantom Menace*, in addition to answering questions from audience members.

Fantastic Media wanted the event to serve as a fun celebration of *Star Wars'* past and an exciting and informative look into its future, beginning with the first new movie in sixteen years, *The Phantom Menace*. Despite the fans' pleading, Lucasfilm did not show the prequel at the *Star Wars* Celebration. Jeanne Cole said, "To see that you'll have to wait like everyone else."

The *Star Wars* Celebration lasted from Friday, April 30 through Sunday, May 2 at the Wings Over the Rockies Air and Space Museum, located roughly fifteen minutes away from the Denver International Airport. Fantastic Media chose Denver because the company is also based in the city, making the event a lot easier to organize. A sizeable number of people chose to attend for a single day, though only a limited number of passes were available for people without reserved tickets. Most fans chose to buy the three-day pass for $34, which allowed them entry into the event for all three days. BTC Travel even offered special lodging and transportation arrangements to fans flying in from other states. Rick McCallum and Anthony Daniels (C-3PO) had already agreed to appear at the event, but many additional members of the cast and crew also attended.

In the months leading up to the release of *The Phantom Menace*, the Official Website posted many announcements about cast and crew members attending the *Star Wars* Celebration. On February 12, Lucasfilm confirmed that Ray Park, the talented martial artist who played Darth Maul, would attend the Celebration. On February 17, Lucasfilm announced that Brian Blessed, the voice behind Boss Nass in *The Phantom Menace*, would attend the event. Then on February 22, Terry Brooks, author of the novelization for *The Phantom Menace*, confirmed that he would attend the Celebration. By March 29, actress Pernilla August joined the growing list of people scheduled to appear, in addition to actor John Morton, who played rebel fighter pilot Dack in *The Empire Strikes Back*. Besides cast members, costume designer Trisha Biggar, visual effects supervisor John Knoll, sound designer Ben Burtt, and famous *Star Wars* fan and author Steve Sansweet all attended the event.

The growing list of celebrities attending the Celebration undoubtedly spurred ticket sales. By late March, Fantastic Media had sold more than 7,500 tickets for the event, of which 90% sold to fans living outside of the Denver area. Even international fans flew in to attend the *Star Wars* Celebration, including fans from Argentina, Australia, Germany, and the United Kingdom, among others. "There is a huge pent-up desire for an official *Star Wars* event," Snyder said. "This is going to be a major, major deal for *Star Wars* fans," he added. His comments proved even more accurate as ticket sales soared higher than expected in the weeks leading up to the three-day event.

Lucasfilm expected more than 30,000 fans to attend the event in Denver, which is a massive gathering for any convention. Speaking in February about the hype surrounding *The Phantom Menace*, Madsen said, "It's even more dramatic as we watch the clock tick down…It's probably the most anticipated movie of all-time." The Smithsonian Exhibit in Washington, D.C., another major *Star Wars* attraction, showcased props and costumes from the classic trilogy and drew more than one million visitors in its first fifteen months.

As the release date for *The Phantom Menace* neared, fan anticipation reached new heights. On April 30, 1999, the *Star Wars* Celebration began. The weather on Friday, April 30 gave fans a cold and rainy opening to the huge event, but could not dampen the enthusiastic crowds. Rain poured down upon the Wings Over the Rockies Air and Space Museum as fans prepared to enter, but the weather conditions did not deter the *Star Wars* faithful.

As staff members and exhibitors made the final preparations, thousands of fans waited outside of the gates. Finally, at 12:30 p.m., staff members opened the gates and the Celebration began. The most popular locations on the Celebration grounds became sheltered areas such as Auditorium A, where the opening ceremonies unraveled, and within the hangar, where fans could preview the merchandise cramming store shelves throughout 1999. Anthony Daniels, known to moviegoers as C-3PO, greeted fans and played a video presentation that included the teaser trailer and special greetings from actors Ian McDiarmid and Ewan McGregor, in addition to composer John Williams and George Lucas. The Denver community had not recovered from the Columbine High School tragedy, so for one minute fans stood in silence in memory of those people who lost their lives at the tragic shooting. Organizers also set up a fund for attendees to donate money to the families of victims of the Columbine tragedy.

A unique greeting from Tokyo welcomed the fans to Denver for the *Star Wars* Celebration. Just weeks before, more than 5,000 fans at a convention in Tokyo, Japan had insisted on sending their greetings to the North American fans attending the Celebration. Jim Ward, marketing director for Lucasfilm, presented the videotaped "hello" to fans in Denver, who emphatically cheered their approval. *Star Wars* is truly a worldwide phenomenon, but in Japan many eager fans had to wait until July 10 to see the movie in theaters. Japanese moviegoers have always appreciated *Star Wars*, so the excitement for the first prequel in Japan rivaled the hype in North America.

Jim Ward also introduced the *Episode I* music video at the opening of the Celebration called "The Duel of the Fates," produced by Lucasfilm and Sony Classical and featuring music composed and conducted by John Williams. After the four minute and fifteen second presentation, the introduction ended and the *Star Wars* Celebration had officially begun.

Giant, inflatable replicas of Pepsi cans with *Star Wars* characters on them stood more than ten feet tall between the hangar and the giant exhibition tents. Pepsi intended the inflatable versions of the soft drink cans to remind fans of the twenty-four different collectible cans available from the company throughout the summer and into the fall.

Everyone present at the *Star Wars* Celebration wore a pass to distinguish event organizers from fans; each pass featured a character from the film. Lucasfilm used ten different passes, including C-3PO (staff members), Sebulba (all access), Darth Maul (three day), Obi-Wan Kenobi (Friday), Qui-Gon Jinn (Saturday), Anakin Skywalker (Sunday), Queen Amidala (VIP guest), the Pit Droid (backstage), Jar Jar Binks (exhibitors), and the Battle Droid (volunteer). The passes hung from a yellow band featuring an imprinted message that advertised Sony Classical's May 4 release of *The Phantom Menace* soundtrack.

The *Star Wars* Celebration offered fans many experiences and activities, so most fans had to choose which ones they wanted to see and which ones they felt they could skip. At the *Star Wars* Celebration, fans could obtain autographs from several writers and artists, including Hugh Fleming of Dark Horse Comics. Several costumed *Star Wars* characters gave fans a chance to have their picture taken with their favorite heroes and villains from the *Star Wars* universe. Decipher held daily trivia contests in which fans could participate in hopes of wining prizes. Mark Tuttle of Decipher directed the trivia contest three times daily.

The Lucasfilm THX Group held a demonstration of their cutting edge home theater sound technology in addition to playing the Smithsonian documentary film, *The Magic of Myth*, several times daily. The film previously only played at the Smithsonian in Washington, D.C., and other museums that had the opportunity to host the Magic of Myth exhibit on its traveling tour. In addition to the activities described, nearly every licensee for *The Phantom Menace* set up booths within the hangar to give fans an early look at their products.

Licensees with booths at the event included Hasbro, Lego, Applause, Rawcliffe, Estes, Decipher, TriCon (which is comprised of KFC, Pizza Hut, and Taco

Bell), Colgate, Hallmark, WestPoint Stevens, DK Publishing, Dark Horse Comics, Scholastic Publishing, Del Rey/Randomhouse Publishing, and several others. Fans could also buy entirely new *Star Wars* merchandise at the Celebration Store, located on the perimeter of the building. People wanting to purchase merchandise from the store had to wait in a very long line outside of the Main Hangar. Sometimes, fans wanting access to the *Star Wars* Celebration Store had to wait upwards of four hours in line, and often in the rain. Nevertheless, the wait was worthwhile for fans eager to purchase the new merchandise.

People attending the event also had the opportunity to buy the novelization of *The Phantom Menace*, written by best-selling author Terry Brooks, in a specially signed and leather-bound edition limited to only 5,000 copies. Besides the quality and collectible value of the book, the standard hardcover novelization of the movie was not available in stores until May 3. Fans who purchased the book at the *Star Wars* Celebration had the advantage of being among the first people to read the story of the newest installment of the saga.

All of the licensees used the Main Hangar to display their products. The massive Main Hangar measures 330 feet in width throughout most of its structure and 266 feet at the Southwest part of the building. The Hangar is 450 feet long and provided well more than 100,000 square feet of space for throngs of fans to admire the newest *Star Wars* products. Lucasfilm granted the most space to Hasbro, Pepsi, and Decipher, in addition to their own LucasArts gaming center, which was located at the North of the building.

Lego's booth displayed their upcoming products based on *The Phantom Menace* in addition to showcasing their toys related to the classic trilogy. Lego MindStorm's Droid Developer Kit quickly became one of the most popular toys at the *Star Wars* Celebration. Company employees at the Celebration eagerly showed curious fans the electronic toy, which allows customers to create R2-D2, the STAP (Single Trooper Aerial Platform), or other vehicles seen in *The Phantom Menace*. Although Lego did not release the Droid Developer Kit until the holiday season, fans still enjoyed seeing the innovative product. Lego also built entire characters and vehicles out of their building blocks, such as the Naboo Fighter from *The Phantom Menace*. Hasbro displayed their products in numerous showcases, where fans marveled at the planning involved in creating such an extensive toy line for a single movie. Event organizers never intended for the merchandise to become the focus of the *Star Wars* Celebration, so fans could participate in many activities and events.

In addition to receiving an early preview of the movie's merchandise, fans could learn more about the actors and actresses in *The Phantom Menace* by listening to them speak at scheduled times each day. Seeing the actors and actresses in person was one of the most interesting and enjoyable aspects of the Celebration because it provided the opportunity to learn more about them and their experiences on the set of *Star Wars*. Ahmed Best spoke of his stage experience in *Stomp*, and of his first major role in a feature film as Jar Jar Binks in *The Phantom Menace*. Although many people waited in line to hear Ahmed Best speak, Ray Park was the most popular actor at the *Star Wars* Celebration.

Large lines preceded every scheduled event with Park, who played the fan favorite villain, Darth Maul. Park reveled in the attention he received and seemed very excited about his role in *The Phantom Menace*. He spoke of the hours of make-up required daily to turn him into the Sith Lord and even posed for people in his classic, menacing look that fans saw in the movie's previews. After he answered questions from his audience, he shook hands with many of the fans, although organizers prohibited autographing.

The skies cleared and the sun returned for fans on the final day of the *Star Wars* Celebration in Denver. The lines even shortened considerably as people enjoyed the final day of the event before returning home to prepare for the final few weeks of the long wait for *The Phantom Menace*. The *Star Wars* Celebration ranks among the top fan events ever, mainly because of the polite and courteous people who attended. No violent incidents occurred during the Celebration and almost everyone treated their fellow fans with respect and kindness. Despite an expected 30,000 fans in attendance, nearly 10,000 more actually arrived at the event.

Star Wars unites people like no other movie or movie series aside from *Star Trek* has ever done, allowing for thousands of enthusiasts to gather in one location and feel a connection with the rest of the fans, despite not knowing anything about them. The success of the *Star Wars* Celebration encouraged Lucasfilm to consider future celebrations, such as for *Episode II and Episode III*. On the first day after the *Star Wars* Celebration ended, the toy rush began in retail stores nationwide.

Toy Rush

A significant aspect of being a *Star Wars* fan for many people is collecting the toys associated with the movies. The widespread interest in *Star Wars* toys led to a major battle between toy companies to acquire the elusive toy rights from Lucasfilm years earlier. The same interest that led major toy companies to pay hundreds of millions of dollars in licensing fees made fans rush to retail stores on May 3, 1999, which became a major event in the history of merchandising, and *Star Wars* fandom.

On April 14, a press release from Toys "R" Us announced plans to open most of its 703 toy stores at 12:01 a.m. in anticipation of unprecedented demand for toys from *The Phantom Menace*. Although other toy lines were massively successful before the *Star Wars* prequel toys arrived, Toys "R" Us had never opened early to accommodate the demand. "Wherever we can open at 12:01 a.m., we will," said Toys "R" Us executive Denny Williams in a statement from the company. In some areas, blue laws prevented the stores from opening at just past midnight, although the vast majority of Toys "R" Us stores nationwide opened early in the morning for fans to purchase their merchandise. "Our customers are big *Star Wars* fans, and they deserve first crack at the tremendous amount of product on our shelves," Williams said.

Wal-Mart, the largest purchaser of merchandise from *The Phantom Menace*, also planned to prepare their stores for the rush of *Star Wars* fans. Unlike Toys "R" Us, however, about 1,100 of its 2,400 stores already offered 24-hour service. Nevertheless, Wal-Mart had to pay additional staff members to accommodate the midnight shoppers. "When customers enter the store on May 3, they will feel a *Star Wars* presence," Wal-Mart spokesman Les Copeland told *USA Today*.

In addition to retail giants such as Wal-Mart and Toys "R" Us, many stores also made special plans for the first day of sales. Kmart's plans paralleled those of Wal-Mart, while Musicland Stores Corporation treated May 3 "almost like a holiday," a spokesperson said. Musicland Stores Corporation includes the popular stores Sam Goody, Suncoast Video, Musicland, and Media Play. FAO Schwarz also opened some of their stores at midnight for two hours.

The Internet once again contributed to the mania. Amazon.com and eToys.com opened their online *Star Wars* sections at midnight, allowing fans to place their orders promptly when the products became available for purchase in stores.

Products on sale May 3 included not just action figures, but almost every other item imaginable. Merchandise featuring characters from *The Phantom Menace* ranged from toothpaste, soap, and T-shirts, to inflatable chairs, action figures, and skateboards, among many other products. Denny Williams of Toys "R" Us said, "We have an incredible range of products surrounding *Star Wars*. Our assortment is so vast, we should be able to please both kids and collectors alike looking for *Star Wars* merchandise." Hasbro continued to ship many more products to stores nationwide throughout the summer and holiday seasons, and even into the following years.

On Monday, May 3, just after 12:01 a.m. at toy stores nationwide, products for *The Phantom Menace* finally became available to consumers. Fans across the nation lined up late the previous night to buy the new merchandise and eagerly rushed stores when the doors opened. Although most fans knew that the stores stocked plenty of merchandise, the experience of lining up for toys excited most fans and gave them practice for the real line-up, which was the line for the movie itself just weeks later.

Rebecca Caruso, a Toys "R" Us spokeswoman said, "We had 700 trailer trucks of merchandise delivered to our stores last week." Shoppers not wanting to participate in the midnight madness still had a favorable chance of finding the products they wanted later on the same day, but for many *Star Wars* fans, being part of the madness was all part of the fun.

Reports of fans buying every single toy released penetrated the media on the following day. Some avid collectors even purchased multiple copies of each toy, so they had one figure with which to play, and the other to keep unopened as a collectible. The collectible value of such mass-produced items is questionable, but some toys from the classic trilogy sell for more than $1,000 in the current toy market. Almost all of the old toys, if unopened, are worth hundreds of dollars. Some major collectors spent more than $1,000 on merchandise from *The Phantom Menace* on the morning of May 3 alone.

At an FAO Schwartz in Boston, the employees cheered as customers rushed in to the sound of the *Star Wars* main theme, which played in the background throughout the store. At a Toys "R" Us in Milwaukee, Wisconsin, store managers marveled at the madness, claiming they had never seen anything like the rush for *Star Wars* toys. In Modesto, California, where George Lucas grew up, at least 150 shoppers arrived at the local Toys "R" Us at midnight.

FAO Schwarz's flagship store opening in New York City was one of the busiest. The store opened for the special event at 12:01 a.m., like many stores nationwide, and remained open until 3:30 a.m. More than 1,500 shoppers visited the store during its special opening to buy the newest *Star Wars* toys. Alan Marcus, a spokesperson for FAO Schwarz New York said, "I can safely say that, in our 137 years, we have never seen an entertainment property create anything near this much excitement." The store itself, which had "everything from life-size R2-D2s to a giant screen that runs the *Phantom Menace* trailer as a nonstop loop," was "breathtaking," Marcus said. At 10:00 a.m. on Monday morning, the line-up outside of FAO Schwarz for the normal opening was almost equally busy. Marcus said that when they opened the doors, it "sounded just like you hear at the ballgame when someone hits a home run." Bill Miller, executive vice-president of marketing and planning for FAO Schwarz said, "The response has been phenomenal. Sales so far have been tremendous."

Other retailers reported high sales also, including Zellers Incorporated. Vice-president of marketing Peter Housley said, "Within five minutes they completely cleaned the whole peg-wall of action figures." The six Zellers stores that opened on midnight reported sales of $100,000 for the first day, which the company reported on May 4. George Gross of G Squared Promotions Ltd. said, "The retailers are on electric selling programs, so you know exactly how many pieces are sold in each store by the minute of the day."

Many stores offered special incentives for *Star Wars* shoppers. A Toys "R" Us in southeast Oklahoma City hosted a costume contest as well as a tent where customers watched the classic *Star Wars Trilogy*. A Toys "R" Us in Omaha, Nebraska served cakes shaped like *Star Wars* characters to greet midnight shoppers.

The twelve-inch figures, specifically Darth Maul, proved especially difficult for shoppers to locate. Despite the efforts of many stores to limit fans to two of the items per person, the oversized figures sold quickly. Although hundreds of people lined up at many locations for toys from *The Phantom Menace*, most stores received less than ten of each twelve-inch figure. Hasbro made most items readily available, but the twelve-inch figures were always a challenge to find. On eBay, they sold for sometimes two and three times their retail price. A few lucky shoppers who acquired twelve-inch Maul figures actually received cash offers for their figure even before leaving the store with the product.

Nobody could reasonably estimate how much money shoppers spent on *Star Wars* during the morning of May 3 and throughout the rest of the day, although some other estimates surfaced. By 7:00 a.m. on Monday morning, Toys "R" Us had already sold more than 800,000 pieces of *Star Wars* merchandise nationwide, Rebecca Caruso stated. Total sales for Toys "R" Us on May 3 came in around 1.25 million units of merchandise from *The Phantom Menace*, including more than 50,000 Lego sets. Although first day sales do not always serve as an indicator for overall performance, Hasbro's toys for *The Phantom Menace* enjoyed an encouraging start. Soon after fans lined up late at night and into the morning for *Phantom Menace* toys, the real lineup began for the film's tickets.

Advance Ticket Sales

From the day Lucasfilm revealed plans for producing *Episode I*, eager *Star Wars* fans worried about acquiring their opening day tickets. When Lucasfilm announced that *The Phantom Menace* would play only in carefully selected theaters, similar to the *Special Editions* in 1997, fans realized that finding a seat during opening weekend would prove difficult. Although, when *The Phantom Menace* actually opened, it played in significantly more theaters than the *Special Editions*. Nevertheless, with the hype sweeping the nation and the world, fans everywhere worried about buying opening day tickets, especially ones to the first showings at 12:01 a.m. For many past blockbusters, advance ticket sales ensured enthusiasts a seat in the theater opening day, but Fox and Lucasfilm did not agree to sell advance tickets for *The Phantom Menace* without theater chains' prodding.

On March 24, 1999, through the Official *Star Wars* Website, Fox and Lucasfilm announced they would not make advance tickets available for *The Phantom Menace*. Tom Sherak, chairman of Twentieth Century Fox Domestic Film Group said, "Our biggest fear is that if we sell tickets in advance, scalping will take place." Fox and Lucasfilm did not intend to inconvenience fans by denying advance ticket sales. Instead, they worried that a few unscrupulous individuals would buy entire auditoriums and sell the tickets at inflated prices.

Although many fans did not agree with Fox's decision, Tom Sherak said, "We understand and regret that waiting in line may cause some inconvenience, but we feel scalping or auctioning off of tickets would create a greater disservice to families and fans." The studio planned to deny advance ticket sales only for the first two weeks, after which they would become available for the duration of the film's release. Fox said they would still allow same-day ticket sales in all locations, meaning that moviegoers could purchase tickets to night showings in the morning of the same day, but no earlier.

Fox's announcement disappointed MovieFone, the largest movie guide and ticketing service in the United States. In its eight-year history, no studio had prevented MovieFone from selling tickets to an upcoming movie before its release date. Despite the initial announcement, *The Phantom Menace* did not become the first movie to break the company's streak.

Before most fans had a chance to begin their line-up plans, Fox and Lucasfilm reversed their decision. On April 23, the two companies announced that they would allow advance ticket sales for *The Phantom Menace*, but with several restrictions. The Countingdown crew had already begun to line up outside of Mann's Chinese Theatre in Hollywood, California, so the announcement mattered little to them, but the news excited other eager fans nationwide. After Fox, Lucasfilm, and the National Association of Theater Owners (NATO) discussed the ticket sales issue, they found an alternative to barring advance ticket sales completely. Their plan called for theaters across the United States and Canada to begin selling tickets for *The Phantom Menace* on May 12 at 3:00 p.m. Eastern Daylight Time. Fans had a new date to anticipate, and in many cities lines formed days before theaters began selling their tickets. In an effort to prevent scalping, theaters agreed to sell a maximum of twelve tickets per person.

Because Fox felt that theaters could enforce the twelve-ticket limit well enough to prevent heavy scalping, the studio decided to allow for advance ticket sales. "The theater owners promised sellers would watch so that some guy doesn't buy tickets and then get right back in line," Sherak said. Though he admitted, "If somebody wants to do it bad enough, they will." The announcement came as somewhat of a compromise between the studios and the theater chains. "It's a bit of a compromise for us, but the theaters have invested a lot of equipment and money into providing the advance ticket service to their customers," Sherak said. The reversal of Fox and Lucasfilm's earlier decision did not affect some *Star Wars* fans, though.

Lincoln Gasking, leader of the line-up outside of Mann's Chinese Theatre, said he would "prefer there were no advance sales," citing the speed at which theaters would sell out of tickets at a rate of twelve per person. Nevertheless, considering he already had a place in line, the decision hardly mattered. Lorie Drabik, also in line for *The Phantom Menace* said, "Hopefully, Mann's Chinese is going to take care of us. Hopefully, they're going to make sure we get our tickets." Officials assured fans who had lined up already that they would be the first moviegoers to receive their tickets. At least for the die-hard fans lined up outside of Mann's Chinese Theatre, the line-up continued. Accurately summing up how most fans felt about the movie, line member Lorie Drabik said, "It's so much more than just a movie...it's an experience."

MovieFone president Russ Leatherman stated, "As always, we will ensure that moviegoers who use MovieFone and moviefone.com have instant access to listings and tickets for this eagerly anticipated movie." MovieFone allows moviegoers in 46 states to purchase tickets over the phone at 777-FILM, or through their

Internet site at www.moviefone.com. MovieFone profits by charging a minimal service fee on each ticket sold.

In anticipation of the May 12 early ticket sales date, MovieFone increased its Internet capacity to allow for ten times as many people to access their site at any given time as had been previously possible. In addition to the massive increase of bandwidth, the company increased their telephone capacity by thirty percent. "In this case, everyone's going to start coming after tickets at the same point in time," said Andrew Jarecki, MovieFone's chief executive officer. He remained optimistic about MovieFone's ability to serve customers, stating the simultaneous demand "presents a challenge to us, but it's one we think we can handle."

MovieFone attempted to allow customers to purchase their tickets for *The Phantom Menace* easily once they reached the service by creating a comprehensive letter system for the movie. When calling MovieFone, customers are asked to input the first three letters of the movie's title for which they want to purchase tickets. Although with the prequel, guessing the first three letters of the movie's long title provided more of a challenge than for most films. Because the movie's full title is *Star Wars: Episode I—The Phantom Menace*, customers might be confused and enter an invalid combination, MovieFone reasoned. To combat the problem, the company allowed customers a variety of options for the letters, including "Sta," "War," "Epi," "Pha," and "Men."

Regal Cinemas, the largest theater chain in the world, reported that fans had already begun camping out Tuesday, May 11 in numerous cities, including San Antonio, Las Vegas, Cleveland, Philadelphia, and Portland, Oregon. In an unusual reversal of roles, Carmike Cinemas chose not to offer advance ticket sales for *The Phantom Menace*. Although nobody could reasonably estimate how many tickets moviegoers would purchase on May 12, most analysts agreed that at major locations nationwide, tickets for most showings on May 19 would sell out.

When May 12 finally arrived, few people could believe the event occurring at theaters across the United States and Canada, and at MovieFone, which had underestimated the ticket demand for *The Phantom Menace*. Fans crammed both their website and phone lines for hours following the official start of sales. "We are serving as what I can best quantify as zillions of users right now," said Movie-Fone spokeswoman Christine Fakundiny on the afternoon of May 12. Instead of reaching anyone at MovieFone, frustrated fans instead heard a busy signal that left them without the tickets they desired. A spokesperson said MovieFone received more than four million calls within the first 24 hours of *Star Wars* tickets being for sale, although five percent of the calls were for other films.

Despite the failure of the Internet site and the phone lines, MovieFone worked diligently to provide the best possible service for moviegoers, but demand for *Phantom Menace* tickets exceeded expectations, leaving the company unprepared for the unprecedented demand. Officials attempted to solve the problem by increasing their serving capacity, although nothing could sufficiently quell the excitement for *The Phantom Menace*.

When discussing the number of tickets sold over MovieFone, both online and over the phone, Fakundiny said, "We know it's a lot," and "we know it's more than we've ever served in a single day." After further inquiry, a spokesperson for MovieFone said only that the company could not disclose any exact ticket sales information.

Despite Fox and Lucasfilm's attempts to prevent scalping, sales of rather ridiculous proportions resulted from the frenzy over the prequel. On leading online auction house eBay, some tickets for the first screenings of *The Phantom Menace* in New York sold for more than $200. Other scalpers sought even more money. For instance, one seller in California requested $600 per ticket. The prices were high, but in one instance of sheer insanity, a seller offered six tickets for *The Phantom Menace* at a theater in Columbia, Maryland for $99,000. The tickets remained unsold, but anxious fans often bought high-priced tickets, fearing they would not otherwise have the opportunity to see the film on opening night. "You laugh, but *Star Wars* is the biggest event movie ever," said one scalper based in Manhattan.

Theater owners around North America reported advance ticket sales for *The Phantom Menace* were spectacular and completely unprecedented. While Movie-Fone became a popular alternative to venturing into crowds at the multiplex, most fans still chose to visit their local box office for tickets.

On May 12, hundreds of thousands of anxious fans nationwide snatched up tickets for prime show times, such as the very first screenings of the movie, which most theaters offered at 12:01 a.m. *USA Today* reported that in two hours of advance ticket sales, a Loews Cineplex in East Brunswick, New Jersey sold more than 3,500 tickets. A Detroit theater from the same chain sold more than 10,000 tickets in a similar timeframe.

In San Francisco, almost every theater sold all of their tickets to the 12:01 a.m. shows. At the Coronet, a famous theater in San Francisco, all of the 1,200-plus seats for the first screening sold in advance. Despite impressive early sales, most theaters reported tickets were available for other showings, such as the 1:00 p.m. and 4:00 p.m. screenings. Even the less popular times sold out at most theaters as May 19 neared, though. The AMC theater chain reportedly sold more than $2.5

million in advance tickets through Sunday, May 16, but most chains never disclosed their advance ticket sales information.

Never before had audiences displayed such boundless enthusiasm for a movie they had not even seen. A spokesperson for Century Theaters said the early sales were "phenomenal, a record breaker." Other industry professionals throughout North America gave similar comments. In the history of advance ticket sales, no movie had generated as much early interest as the *Star Wars* prequel. Records fell on May 12 as *The Phantom Menace* set a new precedent for advance ticket sales, but the movie's record-breaking theatrical release had yet to begin.

Early Charity Screenings

With the hype for *The Phantom Menace* still building, most avid moviegoers wanted to see the movie immediately. Although long lines and waits seemingly would be the only way to see the movie near its opening date, a better alternative arose. In selected cities across North America, charities screened *The Phantom Menace* for fans and corporations. Although the high prices deterred many people, die-hard fans showed up in droves.

In late March 1999, rumors of an early charity screening began to surface in major media outlets. On Thursday, March 18, *The Denver Post* published an article about the event, although further details were not available until March 24 when *Variety* ran an article on the charity screenings. The trade paper reported that twelve cities would offer a special screening of *The Phantom Menace* to benefit children's charities on May 16, three days before the national premiere.

Finally, on April 12, the Official *Star Wars* Website announced the specifics of the charity screenings. As *Variety* had reported weeks earlier, Lucasfilm scheduled the special screenings for May 16. Eleven North American cities held a charity screening, not the previously reported twelve, including Boston, Chicago, Dallas, Denver, Los Angeles, New York, Philadelphia, San Francisco, Seattle, Toronto, and Washington, D.C.

In Los Angeles, the Elizabeth Glaser Pediatric AIDS Foundation benefited from the charity screening. Foundation executive director Janis Spire said to *Variety*, "George Lucas has a gold mine, and he shared it with charity. We really appreciate that." Spire had no doubt that tickets would sell briskly. "I have a feeling we're not going to have a hard time selling tickets to this event," she said. The event took place at Westwood's Avco Theater on three screens at 1:00 p.m. Unfortunately for fans in the area, sponsors of the Los Angeles event chose to make it an invitation-only screening. Tickets for the event sold at $500 each.

All of the money collected from each event directly benefited the selected charity while corporate sponsors covered all expenses. Tom Sherak, chairman of Twentieth Century Fox Domestic Film Group said, "Each of these events will have an underwriter who insures that all of the money raised from ticket sales directly benefits the charity." Concerning Fox's goal for the event, Sherak said,

"This is all about trying to raise as much money for the charity as possible." Additionally, Lucasfilm required that all tickets be sold for the event, meaning that even executives at Fox had to pay for their own tickets.

Prices for the tickets varied from city to city, although they typically ranged from $250 to $500. The ticket price also usually included a party after the screening. Corporate packages available at higher prices also helped raise money for children's charities around the continent.

In Dallas, tickets started at $300 with all proceeds benefiting the Children's Medical Center of Dallas. The charity held the fund-raising event at the United Artists Plaza at 4:00 p.m. Event coordinators expected sales of around 700 tickets, which were sold to anyone interested.

In Boston, tickets started at $500 each and benefited the Joey Fund. Pam Spritzer, a spokesperson for the fund said, "We're grateful—overwhelmed—by this opportunity." The Joey Fund, which Cambridge businessman Joe O'Donnell established in 1986 in memory of his son, works with the Cystic Fibrosis Foundation in supplying financial support for research and patients.

In Philadelphia, demand for the *Star Wars* tickets proved too great for the local charity to manage. Instead, the Big Brother Big Sister Association of Philadelphia had to hire a local ticket agency, Upstages, to handle the demand. Tickets started at $500. Even the mayor, a self-proclaimed *Star Wars* fan, attended the event. "I'm so excited I'm going to buy a ticket, and the mayor rarely buys anything," Mayor Rendell said. The charity screening took place at the United Artists RiverView Plaza at 4:00 p.m. In Philadelphia, the ticket did not include the party after the showing, which cost an additional $100.

In New York, the charity event benefited The Memorial Sloan-Kettering Cancer Center. "It's going to be the most sought-after ticket in town," said Peggy Siegal, an organizer for the event. Speaking of Lucasfilm's ticket policy, Siegel said, "All the money is going to a good cause, so everyone is going to have to buy a ticket."

The charity event proved remarkably successful. At the Los Angeles premiere, 1,462 people attended the charity event, raising $1.25 million. The charity had only expected to raise $700,000, according to published reports. Many stars attended the event, including two actors from *The Phantom Menace*, Jake Lloyd and Samuel L. Jackson. In addition to the two *Star Wars* stars, Brian De Palma, Drew Carey, Magic Johnson, Lisa Kudrow, Melanie Griffith, and Danny DeVito attended the event. A live webcast at www.ReelPreviews.com allowed fans worldwide to see the stars arrive at the charity premiere. The movie itself drew overwhelming praise from celebrity guests and other people fortunate enough to attend the screening.

The San Francisco charity event benefited The San Francisco Boys and Girls Club, collecting roughly $560,000 from 1,300 moviegoers. The event took place at the Galaxy Theatre. Once again, people who attended the event marveled at the movie and expressed their distaste with early critical sentiment. Lucas also went to the event, making the San Francisco screening especially noteworthy and helping sell all tickets within 72 hours. "I wanted to do it because I live here," Lucas said. He added, "The audience reaction today was great. I'm interested in audiences."

In New York, Natalie Portman attended the charity screening at the Loews Astor Plaza. In addition to Natalie Portman, *Star Wars* stars Liam Neeson and Ahmed Best were also present. Other famous people at the New York premiere included Sarah Michelle Gellar, The Backstreet Boys, Donald Trump, Christian Slater, David Spade, Barbara Walters, Kevin Spacey, and many others. More than 1,000 people saw the charity premiere in New York.

In Dallas, a sell-out crowd of 700 people attended the event, raising an estimated $200,000. Early reviews did not dampen the audiences' anticipation for the screening. Once again, the movie received rave reviews from most people in attendance.

The early screenings in eleven cities around the United States and Canada raised $5.3 million for local charities, an unprecedented achievement in movie history. Lucasfilm and Twentieth Century Fox did not receive any of the money. Furthermore, Fox did not include the charity figure into the reported box office gross of *The Phantom Menace*.

Children directly benefited from the charity event because sponsors reserved a portion of the seats at each screening for disadvantaged children. The charity event demonstrated Lucas's desire for everyone to benefit from his work. For a movie to open first for charity and then for the public is a rare occurrence. "I wanted to provide this opportunity to benefit children in at least this small way," Lucas said. Although the announcement angered some fans who cared only about when they would see the film, the charity premiere came only three days in advance of the film's national premiere.

In the history of motion pictures, few movies have helped charities across the nation as much as *The Phantom Menace*. Although the event on May 16 helped raise millions of dollars, other charity events relating to the prequel preceded it and others followed. One can safely say that *The Phantom Menace* raised more money for charity than almost any movie ever released, which an important and honorable distinction.

New Technology

When George Lucas wanted to create the visual effects that amazed audiences in 1977, he had to create his own visual effects company, Industrial Light & Magic. No existing company had the technology or the knowledge to create the effects that Lucas needed to tell his story. When he founded Industrial Light & Magic in 1975, he effectively created the modern visual effects industry. Although *The Phantom Menace* could not change Hollywood as monumentally as the original *Star Wars*, it nevertheless began an important revolution in movie presentation.

In high-quality theaters across the nation, movies are presented in 5.1 channel digital audio using Sony Dynamic Digital Sound (SDDS), Dolby Digital, or Digital Theater Systems Digital Surround Sound (DTS). In a 5.1 channel digital sound system, speakers surround the moviegoer on the left and right sides of the auditorium. In addition to the side speakers, front speakers also project sound into the theater. In all, theaters equipped with 5.1 channel surround sound have five full-range channels and one low-frequency channel to play deep bass frequencies. While many theaters have rear speakers, in 5.1 channel systems the sound that emanates from them is often indistinct. The distortion results from rear speakers combining sounds from the left and the right, rather than having a unique channel from which to play the sounds.

On October 20, 1998, The Lucasfilm THX Group and Dolby Laboratories Inc. announced a breakthrough in quality sound presentation at ShowEast, an exhibitor's convention. The two companies introduced the co-developed and jointly owned system known as Dolby Digital—Surround EX. Surround EX allows theater owners to present movies in 6.1 channel full surround sound. Gary Rydstrom, Director of Creative Operations for Skywalker Sound said, "I wanted audiences to be completely encircled by surround, as well as hear sounds played directly behind them."

Dolby Laboratories, a private company based in San Francisco, California, is the world leader in digital and analog sound. Lucasfilm's THX Group is dedicated to ensuring quality sound presentation in commercial theaters around the world as well as home theaters. The THX certification is a symbol of excellence given to theaters that are renowned for superiority in both sound and visual presentation. The certification is also awarded to home theater sound systems and computer audio equipment.

With Surround EX, the THX Group and Dolby Laboratories wanted to create a technologically advanced sound system that enables audiences to hear movies such as *The Phantom Menace* in the full splendor that their creators had intended. Surround EX adds a rear channel to the auditorium that allows for better "fly-over" and "fly-around" sound effects. The speakers at the rear of the theater accurately reproduce the back surround sound information, which gives moviegoers smooth and accurate sounds instead of the choppy and unnatural ones typical of rear speakers in 5.1 channel systems. Rydstrom said, "I wanted to develop a format that would open up new possibilities and place sounds exactly where you would hear them in the real world."

Lucas has been concerned about the quality of sound in movies throughout his career. Audiences typically do not hear the same sounds that the filmmakers intended them to hear when they made the movie, which presents a problem for the talented individuals who worked diligently to create those sounds. Discontentment with the existing sound systems influenced Lucas's decision to debut the THX system in conjunction with *Return of the Jedi* in 1983. "This new surround technology provides filmmakers with a powerful new creative tool for producing realistic soundtracks," Lucas said. He added, "I'm proud that THX and Dolby joined forces to develop this new technology and bring it to the industry."

For many filmmakers, one of the most frustrating aspects of a movie's release is having audiences not see and hear the movie as they had intended. "With the new format, we've taken the technology to an additional level that makes an amazing difference in sound possibilities," said Dolby Laboratories President Bill Jasper. The new sound system allowed audiences to witness the sounds that the filmmakers intended them to hear.

Fans had another reason to celebrate when Lucasfilm announced that Surround EX would premiere with *The Phantom Menace*. The *Star Wars Saga* is renowned for its sound and sound effects editing. The first *Star Wars* movie, *A New Hope*, won a Special Achievement Award for Sound Effects Creation from the Academy of Motion Picture Arts and Sciences as well as winning the Best Sound Oscar. *The Empire Strikes Back* won the Best Sound Oscar at the 1981 Academy Awards while *Return of the Jedi* received nominations for both Sound and Sound Effects Editing.

The sound for *The Phantom Menace*, created by five-time Academy Award winner and ten-time nominee Ben Burtt, benefited from the Surround EX enhancement in many theaters. The prequel received an Oscar nomination for both Sound and Sound Effects Editing. Rydstrom said, "If any movie has the power to demonstrate the technology, it's *Star Wars*." He added, "All three previous *Star Wars* films pushed the envelope in terms of sound and really pushed earlier sound technologies like Dolby Stereo and 70mm six-channel into more theatres."

Surround EX requires that filmmakers create a special soundtrack mix, but the improved presentation quality is considerable in properly equipped theaters. "With 6.1, sound mixers will be able to place very specific surround sounds in the left, right and rear speakers," said Kurt Schwenk, Director of Professional THX. Many movies released after *The Phantom Menace* have already taken advantage of the system, including *The Haunting*, a 1999 DreamWorks production. Monica Dashwood, General Manager of Lucasfilm THX said, "THX took the opportunity to develop with Dolby a system that raises the bar on quality." Countless future movies will use a 6.1 channel digital audio mix, prompting theaters worldwide to take advantage of the superior system.

Adding Surround EX capabilities to an already THX-approved theater requires minimal effort and not too much money either. Although, theaters that are not already equipped with high quality sound systems must invest a more significant amount of money to add the Surround EX upgrade. For most theaters, the upgrade to Surround EX requires only the purchase of an SA10 adapter, approved by Dolby.

Sales for the innovative sound system were brisk. On December 8, 1998, *Variety* reported that Dolby had already sold more than 1,000 Surround EX units. Famous Players, a Canadian theater chain, purchased 700 units for their theaters. John Bailey, Famous Players president said, "Surround EX ensures that our guests will continue to have the best and most thrilling out-of-home entertainment experience possible."

By March 8, 1999, sales of Dolby Laboratories' Surround EX system reached nearly 2,500 units in the United States alone, according to *Variety*. After less than six months of release, the sales pace that Dolby Digital Surround EX set put the system on course to become one of the most rapidly adopted cinema sound products ever.

Dolby Surround EX made $12 million for Dolby Laboratories on sales of 4,600 Surround EX adapters, *Variety* reported on October 19, one year after the format's introduction. "As part of our ongoing effort to make the movie-going experience even more attractive, Dolby Digital Surround EX provides a new tool for movie sound mixers to add further involvement and excitement for film fans around the globe," Jasper said to *Variety*.

Although the premiere of the new sound system with *The Phantom Menace* further demonstrated the importance of the movie as a showcase for new technology, an even more significant achievement arrived at several theaters along with the movie. Digital sound premiered in 1990, although digital projection lagged behind. For years, movie industry pundits insisted that digital projection would be the wave of the future, although audiences had yet to notice. The movement needed a powerful and influential figure to push the digital format. Lucas, always a frontrunner in technological advances, became the voice for digital projection and digital filming. "What better PR is there than for him to show *Phantom Menace* in this format? It gives it some teeth," said Paul Dergarabedian, president of the box office tracking firm Exhibitor Relations Company.

On March 10, 1999 at ShoWest in Las Vegas, Lucas announced that four selected theaters in the United States would begin projecting *The Phantom Menace* digitally on June 18. The announcement meant that the prequel would become the first major studio release projected with entirely digital technology. "I wasn't sure how inevitable [digital] was until Lucas spoke up at ShoWest," said William Kartozian, president of the National Association of Theater Owners (NATO).

Both CineComm Digital Cinema and Texas Instruments had separate agreements with Lucasfilm to project the movie in two cities at two theaters each. Both companies are leading forces in the digital projection of movies. CineComm, formed in 1998, took advantage of Hughes-JVC ILA (Image Light Amplifier) projection technology, while Texas Instruments used their own projectors based on micro mirror technology. Gordon Radley, president of Lucasfilm said, "We went to CineComm and Texas Instruments because we wanted to bring the reality of digital projection to the eyes of the public as soon as possible." With digital projection becoming a reality, film could become nearly obsolete within a decade of *The Phantom Menace's* release.

The magnitude of the announcement cannot be overemphasized. For one hundred years, theaters have projected movies using film, but finally digital projection is changing the quality of movie presentation. Leading technology companies made many other advances in digital equipment, such as digital theater sound, digital cameras, and digital video discs (DVDs); digital projection was the next logical step. Paul Breedlove, DLP Cinema Program Director for Texas Instruments' Digital Imaging division said, "We believe that people will look back on this digital electronic cinema demonstration as the event that started the transition to digital electronic projection in theatres."

The Lucasfilm THX Group also created cinema specifications for digital cinema projection that include resolution, screen light levels, color uniformity, color temperature, and warm-up time to optimum performance. Dashwood said the specifications underscore "our pledge to ensure that the public enjoys the highest quality film presentation."

Die-hard fans across the nation, as well as industry professionals, closely observed the event that occurred on June 18. "The whole industry is going to be keying on what happens at those four theaters," said Dergarabedian. If the public response to digital projection proved overwhelmingly favorable, many filmmakers hoped that it would speed up the technology's arrival in mainstream theaters.

On Friday, June 18, four theaters in two cities played *The Phantom Menace* using the newest digital technology. Lucasfilm chose the two biggest markets, New York and Los Angeles, to test the Texas Instruments and CineComm digital projection systems. CineComm handled the projection of the movie at Pacific's Winnetka Theater in Los Angeles and the Loews Route 4 Paramus in the New York area. Texas Instruments held the projections at AMC's Burbank 14 Theater in Los Angeles and the Loews Meadows 6 in Secaucus, New Jersey. Radley said, "We are proud that *Star Wars: Episode I—The Phantom Menace* will be the first movie digitally projected for moviegoers." The digital version of the movie played in theaters for four weeks.

Rick McCallum, producer of *The Phantom Menace* said, "This is a milestone in cinematic history." Further stressing the importance of keeping the filmmakers' vision intact, McCallum said, "For the first time ever, a filmmaker can be certain that the audience will see and hear the film in the way the filmmaker intended it to be seen and heard." He added, "All any filmmaker wants is to be able to show a film that is free of scratches and which has all the qualities of image brightness, focus and color that everyone has struggled and spent so much time and effort to create." McCallum's desires came true for the fans in both cities who were fortunate enough to attend a digital screening.

Ben Earl, a *Star Wars* fan who attended a digital screening of *The Phantom Menace* on its first day at the AMC 14 Theater in Burbank, California, shares some of his thoughts about the new format. "The biggest difference that was easily noticeable was in the printed words. In the digital format, they were incredibly clear-cut and crisp," he says. Earl also enjoyed the brightness of images on screen. He says, "When there was any type of light such as a lamp or sun, it looked as if there was actually a lamp or sun right there in the theater." Although he praised the digital format, he also pointed to several trouble areas that must be alleviated before the widespread use of digital projection. "One of the two times that I saw

Star Wars, the movie 'hung' a little bit due to the computer," but he adds, "I will look forward to always seeing movies in the digital format," once the problems are corrected.

The advantages of seeing a movie presented digitally rather than by standard film projection are numerous. With a digitally presented movie, the quality remains constant throughout the entire theatrical run, unlike film prints, which typically deteriorate within a few weeks. Moviegoers are discouraged when they see a film print that a theater has played too many times, rendering it void of the visual quality it once possessed. The deterioration also frustrates filmmakers, who work hard on making their movie visually appealing, only to have audiences see a battered film print weeks after its arrival in theaters. With most of the new technology being developed, the goal is to give audiences an experience closer to the filmmakers' initial vision. "The digital version is the film we made," McCallum said.

The color and resolution of movies projected digitally is far superior to standard film prints. The most surprising aspect of a digitally projected movie is the sharpness of the picture, although McCallum admitted, "The quality is going to get better, but we're doing it now because, as George says, 'Why not push it now?' It's inevitable anyway." Also, the digital picture remains steady throughout the screening as opposed to the slight shaking that sometimes occurs with film projection. Movies presented digitally also have twelve information tracks that filmmakers can use to store foreign subtitles, or a multitude of other special features that are not available in theaters lacking digital equipment.

"The change [in moviemaking and distribution] is going to happen," assured Jeff Blake, president of Sony Pictures Releasing. Although several problems must be corrected, digital projection will eventually become a reality at nearly all theaters nationwide. "Now...it's just a matter of how we make the changeover and who pays for it," said William Kartozian. "I can't think of a better time to be in the motion picture business," Lucas said to exhibitors at ShoWest.

Although moviemakers have shot their movies using film for the past century, they can transfer the film into the digital medium by a process known as "telecine." Eventually, the majority of filmmakers will shoot their movies digitally, but the technology is still new and relatively untested. *Star Wars: Episode II—Attack of the Clones* was the first movie shot using digital cameras for the entirety of the production, meaning that Lucas and his crew did not use any film. When projected at digital theaters, *Attack of the Clones* never left the digital format. It went straight from digital cameras to digital computers to digital projectors, allowing for no quality loss at any juncture of the process.

The long-term goal for digital theater technology is sending movies via satellite to theaters nationwide for projection. Then, following the movie's theatrical run, exhibitors could eliminate it from their databases. Encryption codes would hopefully prevent large-scale piracy of movies by cutting out the middleman and the physical movie itself. Some industry players are skeptical, however. "What makes you think that the same guys cloning cellular phones at LAX aren't going to be doing the same thing with *Star Wars*?" said Robert Gibbons, spokesman for Eastman Kodak's professional imaging group. Although, considering Kodak and other film companies would lose millions of dollars each year if theaters projected movies digitally, his comments are understandable. Still, he may have a valid argument.

While industry professionals considered the encryption code for DVD nearly unbreakable, hackers finally cracked it. Furthermore, if pirates managed to intercept a satellite transmission and crack the encryption code for a movie, they would have a perfect copy that they could upload onto the Internet, available for unscrupulous individuals to download within a day.

In addition to the superior quality of digitally presented movies, studios would save hundreds of millions of dollars in expenses per year by distributing their movies digitally, instead of on film prints. Since the inception of the movie industry, studios have shipped film reels weighing nearly 60 pounds to theaters across the nation for projection. Creating thousands of film prints costs millions of dollars for studios. Multiply the number of film prints by the sizeable number of movies released each year by each studio and the expenses are astronomical. If studios could eliminate film print costs, they could see an immediate savings of $1.2 billion annually, according to some analysts.

One major problem has arisen over digital projection. Who should pay for the equipment theaters use to project the movies? Theaters say the studios should pay the price, insisting that if the studios save the money, then they should have to pay the expenses. The studios contend that giving theaters money to buy digital projection systems is not economically beneficial. Also, deciding which studios would pay for which theaters would be a hassle, especially if some studios refused to participate. The cost of fitting a single screen with a digital projection system is roughly $100,000. Steven Friedlander, the distribution chief at Fine Line said, "This isn't just an upgrade; it's a complete retrofit." Nevertheless, analysts expect all of the nation's top theaters to use digital projection systems within a decade. "The technology is ready. The industry just has to make its business arrangements and figure out how it will be put together," said Paul Breedlove.

Despite the financial savings for studios, there are also advantages for theater owners. One such advantage is flexibility. Assuming satellite transmission becomes standard, theaters could receive a new movie on a moment's notice. In addition, theaters could project any movie on as few or as many screens as they needed to accommodate audience demand. Essentially, the supply becomes flexible and theaters could mold it to meet the demand, which is especially convenient in a market where consumer interest is often difficult to gauge.

Another important advantage of digital movies makes the transition even more appealing for studios. Instead of keeping film vaults, studios could keep entirely digital archives. After several decades, film prints deteriorate, just as the original *Star Wars* had faded immensely in the twenty years between its initial release and the *Special Edition* re-release. The restoration of the film prior to its return to theaters in 1997 saved the movie from permanent damage. In the future, studios will store their movies in digital archives, rendering the prospect of losing them negligible.

"We at CineComm are quite certain that historians will one day write about the June 18th opening of the digital release of *The Phantom Menace* with no less excitement than was given the opening of *The Jazz Singer*, motion picture's first talking movie," said Russell Wintner, the Co-Founder and Chief Technology Officer of CineComm Digital Cinema. Maybe Mr. Wintner is already correct.

The premiere of two major technological advancements with *The Phantom Menace* made the movie event itself even more monumental. Few movies ever premier with new technology to enhance their presentation, but *The Phantom Menace* required superior means of presentation to complete the theatrical experience. After a sixteen-year wait for the new *Star Wars* movie, *The Phantom Menace* arrived with the newest and most advanced technology.

Unprecedented Media Coverage

In the history of cinema, no movie had received as much media attention and fan anticipation as *The Phantom Menace*. Television stations and entertainment shows around the country offered reports of fans paying the full price of admission to see the film's first two trailers while the print media published thousands of stories about the unprecedented frenzy. The United States media is incredibly adept at creating hype for major entertainment events, so their reporting often supplanted paid advertising for the first *Star Wars* prequel.

Despite the engulfing media coverage, a small backlash began early in 1999, which later became a greater menace to *Star Wars* fans. On January 18, *Newsweek* published an article titled, "Buzz Wars, Episode One: The Backlash Menace." The brief article declared that a backlash against the film had already begun and the deafening hype could damage the prequel's success. Most importantly, the magazine stated, "Insiders call 9-year-old Jake Lloyd (who plays Anakin Skywalker) 'Mannequin Skywalker'—word is he stinks."

Former child actor Ron Howard, who is also close friends with George Lucas, came to Lloyd's defense in a letter published in the February 1 issue of *Newsweek*. He called the earlier article "snide and insipid," but was especially offended by the publication's comments about the young actor. He wrote, "The potshot at [Lloyd] was downright irresponsible. I seriously doubt the 'insiders' you mention are inside enough to have seen an edited version of the new *Star Wars*, because I have, and in my opinion, Jake is terrific in the film (which, by the way, is truly amazing)." He further condemned the magazine by stating, "For *Newsweek* to attack a child's performance based on rumor and without even having seen the movie is shameful." Though the backlash was minimal, more criticism and negative media followed, but not before hundreds of media organizations published thousands of positive articles about *The Phantom Menace*.

While the media closely watched the making of *Episode I* years in advance of its release, the notable beginning of the deafening hype came with *Vanity Fair's* cover story of the film in their February 1999 issue, titled "The Force is Back." The article featured exclusive pictures by Annie Leibovitz, as well as an interview with George Lucas conducted by David Kamp. The article discussed the intense enthusiasm surrounding the film. During the interview, Lucas also revealed the prequel's opening text scroll. The pictures included were very high quality and offered some of the best early previews of the film from any magazine. *Vanity Fair* benefited greatly from covering *Star Wars* as their February 1999 magazine became the fifth best-selling issue ever. The February 1998 *Vanity Fair* sold 292,000 copies, but the *Star Wars* cover in the same month of the following year sold 541,000 magazines.

Lucas even contributed to the media's coverage of *The Phantom Menace* by writing his own article in the February issue of *Premiere* magazine. The article focused on the coming of the digital era in Hollywood and the significance of new technology in storytelling. He explained that he is a storyteller primarily, but communicating his story to audiences requires advanced technology because of the complexities of his *Star Wars* universe. The most important aspects of filmmaking remain the same, but the increasingly advanced technology that filmmakers can use makes the process less frustrating in many ways.

Following his article in *Premiere*, Lucas gained publicity for his film through two exclusive segments on CBS's *60 Minutes* television show. Lesley Stahl interviewed Lucas about two different subjects, one for each segment of the show. The first segment concentrated on Lucas's work with *The Phantom Menace* and how the newest technology allowed Lucas to create a movie that is closer to his original vision than the past films. Stahl visited Lucas at the Skywalker Sound mixing stage at an Industrial Light & Magic (ILM) visual effects screening. The second portion of the show focused on Lucas's personal life and the issues that occupied his mind as the release date neared. Both segments premiered on the March 28 edition of *60 Minutes*.

The March 26 issue of *Entertainment Weekly* featured Obi-Wan Kenobi on the cover and included an "exclusive" first look at the prequel. The article focused on the power of *Star Wars* as an almost religious part of the culture and discussed the likely success of the first movie. The magazine included many pictures directly from the film and several of alien characters who have very limited roles in the prequel. The issue, which was #478, set a new sales record for *Entertainment Weekly*, outselling all 477 previous issues.

In April, *Vogue* joined the growing list of magazines to feature a *Star Wars* story. The cover declared, "Exclusive *Star Wars* Style." Inside of the magazine, a brief article explained the difficulties of creating the costumes for *The Phantom Menace* and featured commentary from Trisha Biggar, the costume designer for the first film. The magazine compensated for the short article with exquisite, full-page pictures of Queen Amidala's dresses, some of which took more than a month to craft. The article was most notable because *Vogue* rarely ever devotes space to feature films, but *The Phantom Menace's* penetrating coverage led to stories in almost every magazine nationwide. According to *Forbes*, if the article were billed as advertising for the film, it would have cost Lucasfilm and Fox $433,380.

Also in April, *InStyle* magazine featured a story on Lucas's Skywalker Ranch, which is the headquarters of Lucasfilm's operations. The article offered pictures of the Main House at Skywalker Ranch, Lucas's personal 15,000-volume library, his writing nook, and some miniatures of characters appearing in *The Phantom Menace*. The article included information about Skywalker Ranch, which boasts its own twelve-person fire department, a small inn for visitors, and Lucas's impressive art collection.

Cinefantastique's April issue had George Lucas on the cover in an artistic rendition alongside other *Star Wars* icons. Lawrence French's article in the magazine discussed aspects of the making of the film and also the known plot details at the time of publication. *Cinefantastique* also offered several color photos taken directly from the movie.

While most newspapers and magazines aimed to sell their publications to fans because of strong stories, exclusive interviews, or never-before-seen pictures, other journalists decided to create controversy to gain attention. On April 11, the *Detroit Free Press* printed an article written by Mitch Albom titled, "*Star Wars* Geeks Need to Get a Life." Albom criticized all *Star Wars* fans, including Lincoln Gasking, who was preparing to line up outside of Mann's Chinese Theatre for the movie's premiere. He also stated that the only purpose of *Star Wars* is to make money, called all fans "sheep," said that fans who talk about the movie online lead empty lives, and generally displayed a pompous, arrogant attitude.

Albom, a sports writer who wrote the best-selling book <u>Tuesday's With Morrie</u>, loses much of his credibility from his comments about people who were merely enjoying a hobby, much like sports fans. A sports writer has no business writing about movies that he does not understand. He criticized fans for counting down the days until the release of the movie, paying to see the trailer, and lining up for tickets. He failed to make the connection between *The Phantom Menace* and every single Super Bowl.

Sports fans often arrive at the Super Bowl shirtless with paint on their faces and all over their bodies. They often wait days for their tickets, sometimes paying thousands of dollars for airfare and admission to "The Big Game." Albom said that most *Star Wars* fans "are young people in their early 20s," which he finds pathetic because they should have "lives." Since when are grown men who wear face paint and drink beer at football games more worthy human beings than movie fans wearing *Star Wars* clothing items and awaiting the release of a new film? Albom demonstrated through his poorly conceived article that he is not mature enough to understand that there is nothing wrong with passionately enjoying one's hobby, whether that hobby is sports or movies. Nevertheless, his article created controversy, and thus attention, both for the writer and for the publication.

Magazines played an important role in promoting the new movie to a variety of moviegoers, but newspapers provided more consistent, daily coverage of the film and its stars. While smaller newspapers around the country covered events ranging from the frenzy of the first trailer to the mass consumer interest in the toys for the movie, *USA Today* launched the hype to a new and unprecedented level.

Beginning 50 days in advance of the film's release, *USA Today* featured a daily countdown until *The Phantom Menace* arrived in theaters. Each day, the paper printed a special box in the *Life* section that stated the days until the film's launch and also included one interesting fact about the prequel. Every week, the weekend edition of the paper featured a full story on the movie, which informed fans of the latest products and news relating to it. The inclusion of a daily countdown did not preclude the paper from running other articles about *The Phantom Menace*, when a story arose.

USA Today was not the only paper to offer guaranteed daily articles about the film, however. The *New York Post's* Bill Hoffman wrote a daily article on *The Phantom Menace* beginning in early April. Each article focused on different aspects of the phenomenon, ranging from the innovative special effects of the first prequel to the new products arriving in stores in early May. The articles were typically between 300 and 400 words long, so the *New York Post* upstaged even *USA Today* in pure coverage of the film, which is not entirely surprising considering that Rupert Murdoch, owner of Twentieth Century Fox, also owns the *Post*. The *San Jose Mercury News* began a weekly column on the prequel in late February, nearly three months in advance of its opening.

The print media offered excellent stories about *The Phantom Menace* and everything relating to it, but the Internet also provided some legitimate reporting from respectable Websites. *E! Online*, the Website for the popular entertainment channel *E!*, began a weekly newsletter containing the newest information about *The Phantom Menace*. Published every Saturday beginning in early February, *The Phantom Memo* provided fans and visitors to the Website weekly updates about the movie in addition to frequent articles posted throughout each week.

The most significant magazine cover story arrived when the April 26 issue of *Time* came to newsstands. Richard Corliss wrote an informative article on the movie's hype and the intense anticipation leading up to its release, but the article also featured a detailed foldout of the characters, vehicles, and weapons appearing in the movie. The magazine included many pictures taken directly from the film, but the main portion of *Time's* coverage of the prequel was an interview between Lucas and Bill Moyers about "the meaning of the Force and the true theology of *Star Wars*." Lucas revealed his desire for the *Star Wars* movies to incite questions about each person's faith and he explained the nature of *Star Wars* as an amalgamation of many different religions.

While the media frenzy intensified in April, the climax of the hype occurred in May with the release date of the movie rapidly approaching. Characters from the movie appeared on tens of covers, but the stars also collected many cover appearances; Lucas even made the front of *Wired*, a computer and technology magazine. On magazine covers, television screens, Internet sites, and over the radio, *Star Wars* was ubiquitous.

Rosie O'Donnell declared all of May "*Star Wars* Month." Almost every day on the show, she featured clips from *The Phantom Menace*, with the permission of Lucasfilm. The *Star Wars* creator even appeared on her show on Wednesday, May 5. Actors from the first prequel appeared on the show throughout the month. O'Donnell also gave away merchandise from the movie throughout the month. On the same day that Lucas appeared on *The Rosie O'Donnell Show*, he spoke with Leonard Maltin of *Entertainment Tonight* on a syndicated question and answer segment.

Entertainment Tonight joined O'Donnell in helping promote the film and provide exclusive segments for fans and moviegoers. On Monday, May 3, *Entertainment Tonight* started their "*Star Wars* Week." The show offered a variety of features on *The Phantom Menace* each day, including behind the scenes footage, costume fittings, star interviews, and new footage from the movie.

Several Fox television stations also offered special shows for *The Phantom Menace* in an example of effective cross-promotion between the company's film and television divisions. On Saturday, May 15, Fox News aired a special on the movie, which the Fox on Entertainment team of Dana Kennedy and Bill McCuddy hosted. Their *Full Force* special included interviews with Lucas and several of the cast members as well as clips from the film and behind the scenes footage.

Not wanting Fox to be the sole beneficiary of the *Star Wars* phenomenon, other networks attempted to benefit from the *Phantom Menace* frenzy. CBS created "Prequel Monday," which fell on May 17, just two days before the film's opening. Craig Kilborn hosted Prequel Monday, which featured all new episodes of *Cosby*, *The King of Queens*, *Everybody Loves Raymond*, and *Becker*. NBC did not want to miss out on the increased ratings, so they joined CBS and Fox with their all-week "Jay Takes a Swing at *Star Wars*," which featured star appearances, exclusive clips, *Star Wars* comedy, and "Force-filled Surprises!" Aside from NBC's *The Tonight Show with Jay Leno*, ABC benefited from the saga with *The Rosie O'Donnell Show's Star Wars* Month.

The main Fox network also featured a special on the film, which premiered on Tuesday, June 15 from 9:00-10:00 p.m. Samuel L. Jackson hosted the special, called *From Star Wars to Star Wars*, which focused on the groundbreaking special effects in the saga. The special, written and directed by Jon Kroll, explained the technical aspects of creating a *Star Wars* film and also recalled the past 25 years of special effects. Lucas, James Cameron, and Steven Spielberg provided commentary for the show.

In addition to the *Star Wars* special on Fox, earlier in the year the network's *That '70s Show* concluded its season on March 14 with an episode centering on the 1977 opening of *Star Wars*. Eric, played by Topher Grace, dreams that he is Luke Skywalker while the rest of the cast members from the show appear as other characters from the film.

The media not only provided the hype for *The Phantom Menace*, but also provided commentary about the frenzy they created. CNN's Jim Moret said, "I don't look at our function as being a marketer of the film. But if it's being embraced enough by moviegoers to obsess over seeing a trailer, if people are going to camp out to get the first tickets, that's a story." Cultural commentator and author Douglas Rushkoff said, "My definition of hype is when the intensity of the publicity is greater than the value of the actual event." He also said *The Phantom Menace* was worthy of its hype to an extent because the fans and the public were genuinely interested in the film.

Besides articles that examined the hype surrounding the film, offered interviews with actors and crew members, and discussed the plot of the movie, comic strips also humorously examined the public's intense enthusiasm for *Star Wars*. The staff of popular humor paper *The Onion* contributed to the humor, including an article about Bill Clinton joining the lineup for the movie outside of Mann's Chinese Theatre. Tim Harrod, a staff member for *The Onion*, writes most of the *Star Wars* related stories. Even though he satirizes the saga, he is an admitted fan. He even stood in line for hours to see *The Phantom Menace*, though *The Onion* was not the only publication to provide *Star Wars* humor before the movie's release.

Fox Trot offered some of the best and most frequent comic strips. Bill Amend, who created the comic strip, is a *Star Wars* fan himself. His comics provided cultural commentary on the events leading up to the release of the movie. Dave Barry also joined the frenzy with his April 28 article, which discussed the appeal of the saga and "the very real risk that [Lucas] will make billions of dollars."

In May, almost every major magazine featured a cover story on *The Phantom Menace*. *Premiere* offered a special "*Star Wars* Spectacular" and printed four separate covers of their May issue. The first featured Liam Neeson as Qui-Gon Jinn, the second pictured Natalie Portman as Queen Amidala, the third showed Ewan McGregor as Obi-Wan Kenobi, and the final cover displayed Jake Lloyd as Anakin Skywalker standing just in front of Lucas. The cover was not designed just to sell copies, though; the magazine featured more than 30 pages of impressive information about the first prequel. The magazine included an exclusive interview with Lucas, a feature on the making of the movie, and interviews with the primary cast members pictured on the magazine's different covers. The special collector's issue was extremely popular with the public and required the magazine to order an unprecedented 150,000-copy second printing.

TV Guide borrowed from *Premiere's* four-cover idea and released four different versions of their May 15-21 issue, each featuring characters from *The Phantom Menace*. When all four issues are placed side-by-side, one large picture is formed that artistically depicts the movie and its characters. Inside of the undersized magazine, several articles focused on the primary stars of the film and creator Lucas. The issue also boasted several full color photos from the prequel.

Many magazines attempted to outdo the competing publications' *Star Wars* coverage, although each one usually offered at least several new facts or useful quotes from people who worked on the movie. *Wired* magazine's cover for May declared, "Believe the Hype" and pictured Lucas on the cover with a yellow and orange colored background. Two articles in the magazine focused on *The Phantom Menace* with the first one detailing the revolutionary special effects and the second featuring another interview with Lucas.

Many magazines did not offer an actual *Star Wars* cover for their May issues, but instead chose to place one of *The Phantom Menace's* stars on the front. *Movieline* put Liam Neeson on the cover and featured an interview with the talented actor, but also offered an interview with James Earl Jones and an article on *Star Wars* collecting. Natalie Portman occupied the cover of *Vanity Fair's* May issue, which included an interview with the young actress, but no *Star Wars* pictures or articles. Ewan McGregor, not to be upstaged by his fellow cast members, appeared on the cover of the May *GQ* issue. In his interview with the magazine, he talked about everything from *Star Wars* to his reputation for partying and drinking.

Time beat its closest rival publication in delivering a *Star Wars* cover, but a *Newsweek* cover story on the film arrived on newsstands with the May 17 issue, which featured an artist's rendering of the film and its characters. The cover story read, "The Hyping of *Star Wars*: Behind the Marketing Machine," and also included "David Ansen's Verdict" of the film. Ansen's review of *The Phantom Menace* was fairly negative and played a role in the continuing rise of backlash against the hype and the movie itself.

Entertainment Weekly featured more exclusive coverage of *The Phantom Menace* in their May 21 issue, which placed Jake Lloyd, Liam Neeson, Ewan McGregor, and Natalie Portman on the cover. The issue, like many others, offered information about the various cast members, including some of the lesser-known ones such as Pernilla August. It also included a short guide to some of the finer details in *The Phantom Menace*, including information on how casual moviegoers can sound as though they are *Star Wars* experts.

Aside from the major magazines, even obscure publications featured stories on *The Phantom Menace*. For instance, *Metropolis*, the magazine on "architecture, design, and a changing world," featured a two-page spread on some of the technology in the movie. The article offered commentary about the aesthetics of several of the viewscreens in *The Phantom Menace* from Peter Walpole, a set decorator on the prequel.

Almost every major video game magazine covered the new games based on *The Phantom Menace* that hit store shelves concurrently with the film's release. Media company Ziff-Davis placed the prequel on the covers of all three of its publications in the same month, which was without precedent in their publishing history. *The Phantom Menace* appeared on the covers of *Computer Gaming World*, *Electronic Gaming Monthly*, and *The Official U.S. PlayStation Magazine*.

The magazines covered two new LucasArts video games, which were available on the PC and on several console systems, depending on the game, including Nintendo's N64 and Sony's PlayStation. George Jones, editor-in-chief of *Computer Gaming World* said, "In our minds, these two LucasArts' *Star Wars* titles are the next best thing to the movie itself and we're happy to be able to provide our readers with a chance to get an inside look." Interestingly, *The Official U.S. PlayStation Magazine* chose to place *The Phantom Menace* on their cover instead of the official announcement of PlayStation 2, which is the system that eventually replaced the original version. "The two *Episode I* trailers have already captured the imaginations of *Star Wars* fans everywhere, and ZD's publications will only build on that fanatical interest by delivering the most in depth info on the *Phantom Menace* games," said Joe Funk, editorial director of the Ziff-Davis Video Game Group.

Other video game magazines rode the *Star Wars* publicity wave besides the Ziff-Davis publications. *Next Generation* boasted in capital letters on their cover, which featured Obi-Wan Kenobi and Qui-Gon Jinn, "Exclusive Screens and Info." *Nintendo Power* placed a scene from the pod race on the cover in advertising their recent release of *Star Wars: Episode I* Racer. *Computer Games Strategy Plus* also featured a scene from the pod race on the cover and offered information about both of the first games based on *The Phantom Menace*. *Gamers' Republic* did not devote an entire cover to the movie, though it mentioned *Star Wars: Episode I Racer* prominently just below the title.

Traditional sci-fi publications also covered the prequel, which was not too surprising because of the movie's status as the most revered saga in science fiction history. The July issue of *Sci-Fi Entertainment*, which is the official magazine of the Sci-Fi Channel, pictured the two Jedi Knights, Obi-Wan Kenobi and Qui-Gon Jinn, on the cover. *Cinescape*, which published many *Star Wars* covers in the years leading up to the film's release, partially pictured Kenobi on their May/June cover, which mainly focused on Mike Myers and *Austin Powers: The Spy Who Shagged Me*.

The summer 1999 issue of *Sci-Fi World* featured a computer rendered Darth Maul on the cover and offered a "Kliffs Notes" article on the *Star Wars* characters. The summer issue of *Sci-Fi Flix* put Darth Vader, Anakin Skywalker, and C-3PO on the cover in front of an old production painting of a building on the planet Alderaan, which the first Death Star destroyed in *Star Wars: Episode IV—A New Hope*.

The May issue of *X Posé* followed many other magazines by featuring the two Jedi Knights on the cover and contained an article titled, "20 Reasons Why *Star Wars: The Phantom Menace* is Going to be Incredible!" In addition, the May issue of *DreamWatch*, which claims to be "The Best in Popular Science & Fantasy Entertainment," also featured the two Jedi Knights. Even more unoriginally, *Starlog*, a well-known sci-fi publication, placed the exact same picture on their June issue. Originality among many media publications was drastically lacking.

Sci-Fi Universe offered a *Star Wars* special for their August issue and boasted "behind-the-scenes" information and photographs. The cover had many smaller pictures from the movie, but one of them also happened to be the exact same one that both *Starlog* and *DreamWatch* prominently placed on their covers. *Starburst's* August issue included 22 pages of interviews and photos along with a cover primarily featuring Obi-Wan Kenobi, but also four other characters from the movie to the left side. Aside from their regular issues, the publication offered a *Starburst Summer Special* with the Jedi Knights and Sith Lord Darth Maul on the cover. In addition to the aforementioned two issues, the magazine had before covered *The Phantom Menace* many times, including an artistic rendering of the movie and its characters on the cover of the February issue during the same year.

The media frenzy surrounding *The Phantom Menace* came to a climax in May. According to NewsTV Corporation, based in Lawrence, Kansas, *Star Wars* was the second most-discussed subject in May on primetime news magazines and morning news programs behind only the tornadoes in the Midwest. An article that *The Boston Globe & Mail* published in May 1999 revealed several startling statistics about the media hype for the prequel. According to their research from *Dow Jones*, 33 articles appeared in major English print media during September 1998, 70 in October, 235 in November, 165 in December, 312 in January 1999, 286 in February, 611 in March, and a whopping 1,423 articles during April. Starting in February, the article count began to double each month with May surpassing even April's massive total.

Besides the deluge of magazines arriving on newsstands in May, the media continued its onslaught of coverage throughout the summer. In June, adding to the list of *Star Wars* stories in unexpected publications, *Popular Mechanics* featured technology and vehicles from *The Phantom Menace* on the cover. Their article focused on the machines in the first prequel and offered detailed pictures explaining the interior workings of the spaceships and vehicles that appear in the movie. All of the illustrated pictures, though, are the same as those from Dorling Kindersley's book titled *Star Wars: Episode I* Incredible Cross-Sections by David West Reynolds.

Rolling Stone placed Jar Jar Binks on their June cover, where the alien was reading an old copy of the August 25, 1977 issue from when the first *Star Wars* movie appeared on the front. The June *Rolling Stone* featured one of the only articles focusing on Ahmed Best, the actor who played and voiced Jar Jar Binks, who later became an entirely computer generated character. Peter Travers, head film critic for *Rolling Stone*, earlier trashed *The Phantom Menace* for its "bad dialogue" and supposedly poor plot, but his negative review did not stop the publication from trying to profit from the phenomenon with their cover story.

Cinefex also put Jar Jar on the cover of their July issue and, unlike many magazines, offered new and exclusive information. The publication devoted their entire July issue to the special effects of *The Phantom Menace*, which made it the best and most detailed magazine focusing on the movie. The issue, which included more than 150 pages of text and pictures, offered a detailed and thoughtful behind-the-scenes look into the most impressive special effects ever created for a movie. In addition to the informative writing and numerous photos, many companies included special congratulatory messages to George Lucas and his companies. Also, several companies placed ads thanking Lucasfilm for choosing to use their technology in the movie's production. *Cinefex* also included a list of every person who worked at ILM on the first prequel.

Film Score Monthly used the same picture as *Starlog* and *DreamWatch* on their June cover, although for some reason it is flipped horizontally. Thankfully, famous composer John Williams was pictured prominently in front of the overused scene. The article emphasized the importance that George Lucas places on music in his films and his trust in Williams to help communicate the mood of the scene and the characters through his music. Williams faced some difficulties with recording the film's music when Lucas changed the final twenty minutes of the film after consulting with his close friend and fellow filmmaker Steven Spielberg. The magazine also included a guide to some of the most widely known musical themes in the *Star Wars Saga* in addition to awarding the newest soundtrack four stars, continuing a string of rave reviews for the musical score.

Premiere already featured multiple stories about *Star Wars* throughout 1999, including their four special edition covers, but that did not deter the magazine from featuring another story in their July issue. The article gave a shot-by-shot look at the pod race, which required years of work from the visual effects artists at ILM. The terrain that Lucas wanted to use for the pod race does not exist on earth, so visual-effects supervisor John Knoll used Arches National Park and other western landscapes to help picture the terrain on the desert planet of Tatooine, where the pod race takes place in *The Phantom Menace*. The magazine also offered an article titled, "*Phantom* Legacy," which outlined some of the ways that the movie will permanently change filmmaking, and to an extent the ways in which it has already made its impact.

Natalie Portman enjoyed the most cover appearances and media attention of the *Star Wars* stars after her role in *The Phantom Menace*, although the other actors also remained prominent in the media. In September, *Jane* magazine placed Natalie Portman on the cover and featured an interview between her and Susan Sarandon, which included details about how Portman was handling her stardom. In November, she appeared on the cover of *Mademoiselle*, which contained an article with many quotes from the young actress. It explained her serious nature as an intelligent student, but also tried to change her image from merely an overachieving workaholic to an interesting and fun young actress. *Anywhere But Here* (1999) and *Where the Heart Is* (2000) helped Portman remain active between the release of *The Phantom Menace* and filming on the second *Star Wars* prequel.

Several magazines featured cover stories on *The Phantom Menace* well after its release in May. *Parabola*, which focuses on "myth, tradition, and the search for meaning," placed Darth Maul on the winter 1999 issue, which examined the presence of evil in the world. Considering that *Star Wars* is a modern mythological story, the publication was justified in placing the Sith Lord's visage on their cover. In the four-page article, writer Shanti Fader shows more knowledge of the saga and of the prequel than any of the critics demonstrated in their reviews of the film. The article explains the disappointment of many fans at Darth Maul's lack of screen time, but accurately states that he is not the main villain, rather Darth Sidious, otherwise known as Senator Palpatine, is the true force of evil.

Not all publications placed *The Phantom Menace* on their covers to praise the film. A few magazines, such as *The Door*, which is "the world's pretty much only religious satire magazine," chose to criticize the movie in an apparent attempt to create controversy. The publication's November/December issue pictured Jar Jar Binks on the cover and asked, "Meeza the Anti Christ?" Nearly all media groups felt that Binks was an appropriate target of their ridicule, so *The Door* was only one of many publications to criticize the character.

During 1999, *Star Wars* appeared on eight covers of *Entertainment Weekly*, either through pictures relating to the movie or information about an enclosed article. Besides the numerous cover appearances, the magazine mentioned the saga in almost every single issue throughout the year. Leading up to the film's release, almost all of their articles were positive, but as other media outlets began to turn against the prequel, *Entertainment Weekly* vehemently attacked Jar Jar Binks and the film whenever possible, even in mostly unrelated articles.

For years, the film received a wealth of coverage from hundreds of media outlets, all heralding the coming of the new *Star Wars* movie. In early May, though, the sentiment towards the movie in the press began to sour. A limited hype backlash, which began in early 1999, quickly turned into an onslaught of mixed to negative reviews of the film from major critics. Before the film even arrived in theaters, several critics accused Lucas of rampant racism in his prequel. After the release, numerous articles inaccurately painted the movie as a commercial failure.

While many reporters and journalists quickly attempted to demean the film they had spent years declaring as the Second Coming, more respectable and objective publications continued to report the facts about the movie and its success. The public voiced its opinion through *The Phantom Menace's* astronomical ticket sales and the commercial success of most related merchandise. Several journalists, such as Tad Cronn in the *Seattle Post-Intelligencer*, even wrote impressive articles in defense of the film and its plot.

The media used *The Phantom Menace* for its own commercial benefits, but simultaneously derided Lucas for the shrewd marketing deals that he secured for the film. Howard Roffman, vice president of licensing at Lucasfilm said, "If there's any hype at all, it comes from the media." He added, "They see this as an important story that will get viewers and sell newspapers and magazines. It has resulted in a level of attention we frankly are not seeking ourselves." Lucasfilm attempted to control the hype surrounding the film, but they could not stop the media from running thousands upon thousands of stories on the prequel and everything related to it.

Lucas triumphed over the media and its cynicism by using it to his advantage, saving tens of millions in advertising dollars. The media's struggle to bury the prequel and declare it a commercial failure did not succeed. *Star Wars'* reputation remained intact for the next two prequels to the most popular trilogy of all-time.

Critical Reviews

When the first *Star Wars* movie premiered in theaters nationwide in 1977, most of the nation's top critics praised the film for its visual flare and timeless appeal. *Time* magazine called it the best movie of the year, *Variety* gave it a glowing review, the *New York Times* called it the greatest movie serial ever, and similar sentiment followed in the vast majority of the film's reviews. Despite mostly great critical reaction, several reviewers could not understand the appeal of the movie, saying that it lacked depth and character development. *Star Wars* received eleven nominations at the Academy Awards in 1978 and won seven of them, but lost to the uproarious Woody Allen comedy *Annie Hall* for Best Picture.

After more than twenty years, criticisms of *Star Wars: A New Hope* from professional critics are rare. When *Star Wars: Special Edition* opened in theaters on January 31, 1997, the critical reviews almost unanimously hailed the return of one of the greatest movies of all-time. There are always several dissenters, but the overall percentage of positive reviews increased drastically. Despite the critical success of the first *Star Wars* movie, no sequel or prequel in the saga has enjoyed great reviews.

According to many polls, *Star Wars* is the most popular and appreciated movie of all-time. In a 1997 poll that *Mr. Show Biz* conducted through their website at MrShowBiz.com, more than 3,000 people chose *Star Wars: A New Hope* as the greatest movie of all-time, beating *The Godfather* (1972) in second place and *Pulp Fiction* (1994) in third. *The Empire Strikes Back* placed ninth and *Return of the Jedi* finished 23rd. Other polls also confirm the public's love of *Star Wars*.

In a series of polls that the *Washington Post* conducted in 1998, the publication pitted the American Film Institute's top twenty greatest films against each other. They began with the twentieth film, *One Flew Over the Cuckoo's Nest* (1975), versus the nineteenth film, *Chinatown* (1974). The process continued until a winner of the bottom fifteen entries in the list of twenty was decided. The winner of the top five films then faced the underdog from beyond the upper echelon. *Star Wars*, named the fifteenth best film by the American Film Institute, defeated ten movies before facing *Casablanca* (1942) in the finals, where the sci-fi film triumphed by receiving 25,546 votes to an embarrassing 2,467 for the decades old romance film. Not only is *Star Wars: A New Hope* considered the greatest movie of all-time in America, but also in the United Kingdom, where Lucasfilm produced all four of the first movies.

In BSkyB's Millennium Movies Poll, which the satellite company conducted among roughly 162,000 British moviegoers to find the best films of the millennium, *Star Wars: A New Hope* again topped the list. The space epic collected more than a third of all votes cast, defeating *Titanic* (1997) in second place and *Gone With the Wind* (1939) in third. The poll sponsors feel that the results represent the entirety of Britain because everyone had ample opportunities to vote. George Lucas even commented about the poll, saying, "I'm amazed and surprised that *Star Wars* was picked as the number one film of the millennium." The British love for *Star Wars* did not end there, however.

In another poll that *Empire Magazine* and the HMV retail chain conducted just weeks later, moviegoers also picked *Star Wars: A New Hope* as the greatest movie of all-time, ahead of *Jaws* (1975) in second place and *The Empire Strikes Back* in third place. If the first two polls did not make *Star Wars: A New Hope* the clear choice for favorite movie among British moviegoers, then a third one cemented its position beyond any doubt. The British Broadcasting Company's Film 99 Viewers' Movies of the Millennium poll, with more than 25,000 votes, also witnessed the original *Star Wars* seize first place. Perhaps most impressively, viewers named *The Phantom Menace* the fifth best movie of all-time, *The Empire Strikes Back* the seventh, and *Return of the Jedi* the 28th greatest ever.

Aside from the numerous successes in polls that varied organizations conducted in the United States and the U.K., several additional surveys also demonstrate that *Star Wars: A New Hope* is the most popular film. In a 1999 poll among Amazon.com visitors, more than 250,000 people voted to declare the first *Star Wars* movie the greatest video. Although all of the original three *Star Wars* films have since gained the status of classics, the two sequels to *A New Hope* did not fare as well initially.

Three years after the first *Star Wars* movie premiered, *The Empire Strikes Back* opened in theaters to mixed reviews from critics. Overall, more critics praised the movie than criticized it, but many of them felt that it did not compare favorably to the first movie. A few critics called it the best movie sequel of all-time, while others called it a poorly crafted film with no plot, limited character development, and poor acting. *The Empire Strikes Back* received five Academy Award nominations, in technical categories, and won two statues.

When *The Empire Strikes Back: Special Edition* opened in theaters on February 21, 1997, the movie received a higher percentage of positive reviews than even the first *Star Wars*. Easily more than ninety percent of critics nationwide gave the movie a positive review, with many voicing their opinion that it is the best of the original *Star Wars Trilogy*. The majority of *Star Wars* fans also declare *The Empire Strikes Back* their favorite of the saga, which is proven through numerous polls on fan sites such as TheForce.net and in publications such as Topps' *The Best of Star Wars* magazine. In the Topps publication, which preceded the release of *The Phantom Menace*, 44% of more than 200,000 fans polled believed that *Episode V* of the saga is the best *Star Wars* movie. *The Empire Strikes Back's* 1997 re-release made evident the drastic change in critical sentiment that had occurred in the seventeen years since the movie's initial release. Many critics now consider *The Empire Strikes Back* the greatest sequel of all-time.

Return of the Jedi received more negative reviews than either of its predecessors. The movie drew criticism from the majority of the nation's critics, who felt it contained too much action, too shallow of a plot, and too many Ewoks. The movie succeeded with fans, but critics despised the ending to the popular saga. *Return of the Jedi* received four Academy Award nominations, but won only one.

The change in sentiment towards *Return of the Jedi* was never as evident as when Lucasfilm re-released it on March 14, 1997. Originally lambasted, *Return of the Jedi: Special Edition* drew praise from the vast majority of critics, who felt that it ended the saga appropriately and provided excellent entertainment along with a great message. Most critics still feel it lags behind the first two movies in the saga, although they recognize its merits and appreciate it for the entertainment value it provides. Most fans understand that the final chapter of the *Star Wars Saga* is much more than just entertainment, but filmmaking at its finest and a masterful end to the greatest saga ever created.

Understanding the critical reaction to the first three *Star Wars* movies produced is essential to understanding the critical reaction to *The Phantom Menace*. The build-up of hype and anticipation for the prequel hurt its chances of being fairly and objectively reviewed, if such a feat is possible at all. Years of expectations about the film's plot, characters, and visual style heavily influenced the opinions of moviegoers and critics alike when they finally viewed the finished film.

On Tuesday, May 4, 1999, Fox showed *The Phantom Menace* to critics in Los Angeles, New York, Boston, San Francisco, Dallas, Chicago, Washington, D.C., and Toronto. Industry executives, theater owners, and other VIPs attended the event, although several Internet spies also managed to secure places in the audience. Many people loved the movie, but others expressed disappointment. Nonetheless, most people agreed the movie would be popular with audiences.

Variety reported tepid applause after the movie, but such reports are more a matter of opinion than fact. They quoted an industry insider, who said, "There was polite applause, kind of tepid—not the sort of whooping and cheering you'd expect." Finding an adequate definition for tepid applause is difficult; other media organizations reported better reactions to the film. *The Los Angeles Times* claimed that people who attended the event loved *The Phantom Menace.*

Traditionally, newspapers nationwide publish their movie reviews the day of the film's release, which is usually a Friday. A longstanding agreement exists between movie studios and press organizations that reviews are not to be released before the movie arrives in theaters. Although, nothing about the release of *The Phantom Menace* resembled a normal movie's opening, so several newspapers broke their deal with Twentieth Century Fox and Lucasfilm.

Three major papers reviewed the movie after seeing a sneak preview Saturday night, May 8. The papers published their reviews more than ten days in advance of the movie's release, which is unprecedented for newspapers. Magazines typically release early reviews because of their publication schedules, which generally lead to weekly publications for organizations such as *Time* and *Newsweek.* The review embargo does not apply to magazines, but only to newspapers.

Tom Sherak, chairman of Twentieth Century Fox's Domestic Film Group said, "It's really disappointing that the publications that did [release early reviews] didn't have high enough standards to uphold the agreement with the studio." Fox considered barring journalists from the offending publications from future screenings, but said that any retribution would be temporary. Sherak said, "I don't know what we're going to do. If we can't trust them, we'll have to do something."

The *Los Angeles Daily News* released its positive review of *The Phantom Menace* in their Sunday edition. The paper chose to print a report about a mob of Chinese protesters that attacked and burned a United States consulate in China at the bottom of the page and printed the review of the prequel at the top. The paper reasoned that the movie had become news, not just entertainment, therefore the review warranted placement on the top of the front page. Sherak strongly disagreed, saying, "The bottom line is that this isn't news; it's a movie." *The Phantom Menace* had already become more than just a movie, however.

The *Toronto Star* also released an early review of the movie, as did the *New York Daily News*, which touted its review as the first. Unlike the *Los Angeles Daily News*, the *Toronto Star* gave *The Phantom Menace* a modest two-and-a-half star rating. John Ferri of the *Toronto Star* said the early review represented "a rare and extraordinary circumstance," but the publication unfairly broke their agreement, regardless of his comments in defense of their decision. The Toronto area is heavily competitive for newspapers, so Ferri felt that the review would give his publication an edge. "The combination of high public interest and self defense is what prompted our move," he stated. Fox retaliated against the paper by politely informing another *Toronto Star* journalist that he was not welcome at Lucas's press conference.

Cynics suggested that Fox only cared about the early reviews because they believed several of them tarnished the reputation of the *Star Wars Saga*. Sherak denied the rumor and said, "It has nothing to do with whether it's a good or bad review." His statement is believable considering the *Los Angeles Daily News* critic gave *The Phantom Menace* a glowing three-and-a-half star rating. Sherak then commented of the papers, "They're being devious. There are rules and they decided they didn't want to follow the rules."

The negative reviews did not phase Lucas, who said at a press conference in New York the day after the private screening, "Remember, most of the *Star Wars* movies opened to generally bad reviews, so I expect for the movie not to do well critically." He said the early mixed reviews did not bother him whatsoever.

As the reviews continued to amass, the pre-release excitement began to dampen slightly, although most fans realized that the critics' opinions do not matter in the greater scheme of *Star Wars* history. Fans hoped that critics would finally understand a *Star Wars* movie on its first release, but once again most reviewers demonstrated their inability to comprehend the *Star Wars Saga* and its intricacies.

On a basic level, many critics still did not understand what character represented "The Phantom Menace" from the movie's title, even after watching the movie. The phantom menace is Darth Sidious, who is the character behind the blockade of Naboo and the master of Darth Maul. He menaces the Galactic Republic by breaking laws and killing innocent people, but he is a phantom because nobody knows his true identity, let alone the reasoning behind the havoc he causes. In the original *Star Wars Trilogy*, the villain is always apparent and revealed, but an unseen villain is much more dangerous and disturbing. A critic who cannot even determine the main villain in *The Phantom Menace* has no place reviewing movies, let alone reviewing the most anticipated film of 1999. Six-year old kids understood the plot better than many critics who reviewed the prequel. Without identifying the main villain in the movie, comprehending the plot is nearly impossible.

Debates raged on the Internet concerning the relationship between Darth Sidious and Senator Palpatine. Most fans believed the two characters are actually the same person with logic seeming to support their conclusion. Senator Palpatine eventually becomes the emperor of the galaxy through deceit and treachery in the following two prequels, so *The Phantom Menace* only begins his rise to power. Darth Sidious's manipulation of the Trade Federation allows Senator Palpatine to become the Supreme Chancellor of the Galactic Senate, so Darth Sidious is likely the same person, only disguised, fans reasoned. Rick McCallum, producer of *The Phantom Menace*, confirmed that Ian McDiarmid acted as both Darth Sidious and Senator Palpatine, but suspiciously Darth Sidious does not appear in the credits.

Many critics said the opening crawl explaining the events immediately prior to the movie reads too much like a history book and fails to interest moviegoers like the crawls from the original *Star Wars Trilogy*. The opening text scroll is more trivial than the previous three movies, but its effect is intentional. The galaxy is enjoying a long period of peace and prosperity as *The Phantom Menace* begins, which makes financial concerns seem overly important.

Moviegoers learn that the Galactic Republic is quickly deteriorating from its own corruption, through slight foreshadowing such as in the final space battle, when a female Naboo pilot says, "It's blowing up from the inside!" Not only does her line refer to the immediate destruction of the Trade Federation Droid Control Ship, but the ship is also a symbol of the Republic, which is deteriorating from within because of corruption and treachery in the ranks of the senate. No serious wars occupy the galaxy at the time of *The Phantom Menace* and no major villain openly threatens democracy and freedom, but an evil force is growing that threatens to crush the government and send the galaxy into turmoil. *The Phantom Menace* only begins to explain the deterioration of the Galactic Republic while the two additional prequels continue to show the galaxy's plunge to dictatorial leadership.

Many critics complained that the movie is packed with action and effects, but contains very little plot development. Again, if the critics actually watched the movie and first understood the original *Star Wars Trilogy*, they would find that *The Phantom Menace* is much more developed than they thought. Understanding the significance of *The Phantom Menace* is impossible unless one has a firm grasp of the events in the other *Star Wars* movies.

The Phantom Menace accomplishes several important goals. The primary purpose of the movie is introducing young Anakin Skywalker, who is the main character of the entire saga. He is portrayed as an enthusiastic and kind boy, which makes his eventual fall from grace even more shocking. The movie also shows Obi-Wan Kenobi's rise to Jedi Knight and informs moviegoers of how Anakin

Skywalker came to be his apprentice. Most importantly, the movie displays the events that lead to Palpatine's rise to power. Palpatine is a central character in the saga, but especially in the prequel trilogy. Because of Palpatine's lust for power, the galaxy is thrust under the rule of a corrupt empire, as the original *Star Wars Trilogy* shows.

A segment of critics and fans insist that major plot mistakes exist in the movie, although they are almost always mistaken. Obi-Wan Kenobi tells Luke in *The Empire Strikes Back* that Yoda instructed him, so many fans think since Qui-Gon Jinn appeared to be Kenobi's main mentor, Yoda could not also have taught him. Once again, when moviegoers actively watch *The Phantom Menace*, they will notice that Kenobi makes reference to Yoda's teachings. One can fairly conclude that Yoda also instructed Obi-Wan, but Qui-Gon Jinn is his primary mentor. *Star Wars: Episode II—Attack of the Clones*, with a scene showing Yoda instructing young Jedi trainees, confirms such an explanation.

Perhaps the most widely voiced criticism of the movie is the advanced technology visible throughout the film. Many people believe that the technology in *The Phantom Menace* is more advanced than in the original *Star Wars Trilogy*, which would not make sense because the events in the prequel occur roughly 32 years before Luke Skywalker destroyed the Death Star in the first *Star Wars* movie. The complaint is valid, although easily explainable. The galaxy is in turmoil throughout the original *Star Wars Trilogy* and in the midst of what is known as The Galactic Civil War. Both sides, the Rebel Alliance and the Galactic Empire, are more concerned with the functionality of their craft than making them aesthetically pleasing.

In *The Phantom Menace*, the galaxy is enjoying a period of relative peace, so the opposite is true. The Naboo society is more concerned with art than with war, which is embodied in Queen Amidala's elaborate dresses, of which there are many, and the lack of a standing army. Aesthetics are paramount for the Naboo people. They believe their society should look superior and developed, but need not prepare for war because diplomatic negotiations are a preferable means of conflict resolution. The actual destructive capability of the craft in the original *Star Wars Trilogy* far outstrips that of the vulnerable, yet beautiful, craft in *The Phantom Menace*. For instance, nothing in *The Phantom Menace* even remotely compares to the power of the Death Star and no craft in the prequel is as able and powerful as an Imperial Star Destroyer.

Jar Jar Binks also drew criticism from many people. The first entirely computer generated, live action supporting actor in movie history, Jar Jar Binks serves as the movie's comic center. He is an outcast of his intolerant society because of his clumsiness. Interestingly, many people's reaction to Jar Jar only confirms the message presented, which is that many people cannot accept anyone who is different from them. Internet sites devoted to ridiculing Jar Jar arose after the movie's release, begging George Lucas to kill the character and often showing graphic depictions of his death. The creators of the websites are not good-natured fans of the saga, but instead purveyors of hate and violence.

Many people complain about Jar Jar's voice and his mannerisms. A few people even believe Jar Jar represents a racist stereotype, but they cannot agree exactly what group he stereotypes. A vocal, small group of people insist he is a stereotype of homosexuals, but others say he stereotypes African Americans, and yet others claim he is a Jamaican stereotype.

Lucas deflected such comments with his statements about the nature of the accusers. He told Kirsty Wark of the British Broadcasting Company (BBC), "It really reflects more the racism of the people who are making the comments than it does the movie." He also commented, "Those criticisms are made by people who've obviously never met a Jamaican, because it's definitely not Jamaican and if you were to say those lines in Jamaican they wouldn't be anything like the way Jar Jar Binks says them." If someone believes Jar Jar is a stereotype of homosexuals, their position reveals their own personal prejudices, not the racism of anyone involved with the making of the movie. The mere fact that nobody could agree on what group Jar Jar stereotypes reveals the absurdity of the accusations.

Lucasfilm spokeswoman Lynne Hale said, "Nothing in *Star Wars* was racially motivated." The allegations of racism leveled at *The Phantom Menace* are a fitting example of a society overly concerned with political correctness to the point of absurdity. Racism is a horrible attitude, although searching for it when it simply does not exist is equally unacceptable. Hale also commented, "I really do think to dissect this movie as if it had a direct reference to the world today is absurd." Jar Jar Binks is not the only character who drew accusations of racism; cynics have also singled out Watto and the Neimoidians.

Another group of people accuse Watto of being an Arab stereotype, though other people say he is a stereotype of Jewish people. Once again, different people claim different stereotypes, which further confirms that individual prejudices are at fault, not the characters themselves. The Neimoidians' accent sounds Asian to many of the detractors, so they arrived at the conclusion that the Neimoidians are a stereotype of Asians. The accusers never revealed which Asian society they felt the alien species stereotyped. The mere suggestion that an alien race totally unlike any species on earth is a racial stereotype seems completely absurd and abstract. *The Phantom Menace* actually encourages unity and discourages racism, but some critics and cynical fans never stopped to consider the possibility, even though it is apparent in the movie.

Before the Trade Federation invades the planet Naboo, the Gungan race is notably disturbed by the attitudes of the Naboo people. The Gungan leader, Boss Nass, claims the Naboo act as though their culture is superior to that of the Gungans. Near the end of the movie, Queen Amidala begs the Gungan leader for aid in a dangerous fight against the Trade Federation armies occupying Naboo. Boss Nass is surprised at her humility and recognizes that he has committed an error in judgment by assuming that all of the Naboo people feel they are superior to the Gungans. The Gungans unite in arms with the Naboo in their struggle to free the planet. By the end of the movie, the two cultures are at peace with one another. Jar Jar is also promoted to the status of general for bringing the two cultures together and is accepted back into the Gungan society. Sadly, some people think racist stereotypes exist, yet the movie contains a clear message underscoring the benefits of acceptance, tolerance, and finally integration.

The most revealing fact about the authenticity of the racism accusations came from the people supposedly being stereotyped. The accusers, for the most part, are white Americans. If the racism accusations had any element of truth in them, one would think that the stereotyped individuals would be offended, but they are not. Tamar Gallatzan, a spokeswoman for the Arab-American Anti-Defamation League said her organization feels the accusations of racism are baseless. Furthermore, she says, "It would be a stretch to say [Watto] was a Jewish caricature or an Arab caricature." Few members of the supposedly stereotyped groups even realized such accusations existed, so the film did not offend them.

In addition to accusations of racism, several church officials also accused the movie of promoting an anti-religious message. Specifically, the Church in Mexico advised Christians against seeing the movie because Anakin Skywalker is portrayed as another Jesus in some ways. Many themes from Christianity and other religions are present in all of the *Star Wars* movies, but the saga encourages moviegoers to examine their own spirituality. The Bishop of Oxford, Richard Harries, defended the movie in his comments to the BBC. "I think that if people get reassurance that good will overcome evil through a film, that far from being a threat to religion, it is an echo of what religion, at least the Christian religion, is proclaiming," he said.

On a superficial level, a small number of people frowned upon the film's heavy dependence on computer graphics. Discerning a model from a computer rendered image is nearly impossible most of the time. The complexity of a shot sometimes reveals the technique used to create it, but moviegoers mostly cannot know whether a spacecraft or building is computer generated or built by hand in a model shop. In *The Phantom Menace*, at least one explosion is entirely computer generated, although nobody can objectively discern which explosions computers produced and which ones pyrotechnics experts created. Whenever the option exists, artists at Industrial Light & Magic prefer to avoid using computer graphics. Nevertheless, for many shots nothing else can accomplish the groundbreaking visual effects that help Lucas tell his captivating story. Despite a few critics who expressed distaste for the computer graphics, most of them praised the prequel's visuals and called the movie one of the most visually fantastic movies ever made.

The acting in every *Star Wars* movie is sometimes the subject of ridicule; *The Phantom Menace* is no exception. Most critics enjoyed Liam Neeson's performance as Jedi Master Qui-Gon Jinn, but others felt he was uninterested and detached. Most critics thought Natalie Portman was an impressive Queen Amidala, although several of them expected more emotion from her character. Ewan McGregor's version of Obi-Wan Kenobi also mostly impressed critics, but several of them shunned his performance as well. Jake Lloyd was the most criticized member of the cast, although many people gave him credit for a fine performance as young Anakin. One of the most common problems critics had with the overall acting is the lack of emotion the actors displayed, which emphasizes the critics' lack of understanding more than any failure of the actors.

The Jedi believe that outward expression of one's emotions is dangerous and unhealthy. In perilous and hopeless situations, Jedi are supposed to demonstrate a calm sense of assuredness and confidence, never anger or frustration. The actors portraying the Jedi Knights and the Jedi Masters played their parts perfectly because acting is the ability to accurately portray characters. The acting that critics expected is not consistent with Lucas's vision of the Jedi order. Comments about the stoic nature of Queen Amidala are equally as inept because she is a queen, trained from an early age to act stately and dignified, not distraught and reckless. Portman is excellent as Amidala and displays the dignity and strength of the queen of an advanced, pretentious society.

The most unheralded actor in *The Phantom Menace* is Ian McDiarmid, who played Senator Palpatine. Although Palpatine did not have a large amount of screen time, he is one of the most important characters in the prequel trilogy. McDiarmid was spectacular as Senator Palpatine, the sly and resourceful man hoping to rise through the political ranks and conquer the galaxy.

The space battle at the end of the movie has also drawn some fans' criticism, and that of professional reviewers, who claim the battle is too short and inferior to the space battles seen in *A New Hope* and *Return of the Jedi*. In fact, the space battle is not as long as either of the main space battles in the other films, and it is not as impressive either, but it is not the centerpiece of the action in *The Phantom Menace*. The lightsaber duel between the two Jedi and the Sith Lord is the primary conflict and is the main focus of the film's climactic ending. The space battle is still impressive and entertaining, but the story did not require a massive space engagement above Naboo, only a relatively minor skirmish. *The Empire Strikes Back* focused on an impressive ground battle at the start of the movie between Rebel Alliance forces on Hoth and invading Imperial forces under the command of Darth Vader. *The Phantom Menace* also mainly focuses on an engaging ground battle and a riveting lightsaber duel that is widely considered the best in the saga.

Another criticism stems from Anakin Skywalker's supposed "lucky" shot that destroys the Trade Federation Droid Control Ship. As previously mentioned, most supposed flaws in the movie stem from a lack of understanding by the viewer, not a lack of quality in the movie. Earlier in *The Phantom Menace*, Jedi Master Qui-Gon Jinn asserts that nothing happens by accident. While many people might question the validity of the statement, it is true and valid in the *Star Wars* universe because of the existence of the Force. When Anakin Skywalker destroys the Droid Control Ship, the Force is subconsciously guiding his actions, so he does not realize the power he is harnessing. The Force gave Anakin the ability to race pods, although for years he never knew what enabled him to have such quick reflexes when other humans could not accomplish such a feat.

The success of *The Phantom Menace* never depended on its critical reviews, only on the audiences' response. The reality that their reviews did not matter whatsoever annoyed many critics because it stripped them of their usual power to influence audiences. Nevertheless, an increasing number of moviegoers are ignoring critics and considering each movie based on their own knowledge because critics are sometimes jaded and cynical.

Overall, critics enjoyed *The Phantom Menace*, giving it average to slightly positive reviews. Few critics gave the movie under a two star rating, but few gave it more than three stars either. Several critics praised the movie and awarded it high marks, such as Roger Ebert, who gave the movie three-and-a-half stars, and Shawn Levy of *The Oregonian*, who gave the movie an A-minus.

Most critics attempted to spoil the excitement of anxious *Star Wars* fans and dampen the pre-release atmosphere, but most fans never worried about the movie's quality. Instead, enthusiasts worldwide trusted that Lucas and his talented cast and crew would deliver another masterpiece in the ongoing *Star*

Wars Saga. The mixed reviews did not deter the fans who lined up outside of Mann's Chinese Theatre to see the movie on its first showing at the historic location. Audience response to the movie far surpassed the critics' timid reviews, making the film one of the most successful in box office history.

Marathon Lineup

When *Star Wars* opened in 1977, lines greeted moviegoers at every theater at which the movie played. It only opened in 32 theaters on May 25, 1977, but almost every one of them reported new house records for attendance. Although moviegoers sometimes lined up for many hours, the movie had very little advance word of mouth compared to its sequels and prequels. Fans coordinated lineups that began several days in advance of *The Empire Strikes Back's* theatrical release. Three years later, some fans waited more than one week outside of theaters for *Return of the Jedi*. Despite the fanaticism of fans during the late 1970s and early 1980s, sixteen years of anticipation for *The Phantom Menace* led to the longest and best coordinated wait outside of theaters for a movie in the history of the world.

Lincoln Gasking, Webmaster of the *Star Wars* Countingdown.com site, helped organize more than 60 lineups around the world. The most famous, and the longest, began outside of Mann's Chinese Theatre in Los Angeles, California. Most of the lines were scattered around North America, ranging from Omaha, Nebraska to New York City and numerous locations in California. In addition to North American lines, Gasking coordinated lineups in his own country, Australia, along with New Zealand, England, Germany, and France.

Lincoln Gasking, Tim Doyle, Kolby Kirk, and Phillip Nakov helped plan the primary lineup. The idea arose roughly a year before the lineup began, during which time the Countingdown crew worked diligently to plan the lines and clear the necessary permits and permissions. Kirk suggested that the lineup should take place outside of the famous Mann's Chinese Theatre, which has hosted numerous major film premieres, beginning May 18, 1927 and continuing through the present. Mann's Chinese Theatre is the flagship of its parent company, Mann Theatres.

Outside of the theater, the Forecourt of the Stars has more 150 different stars' shoeprints and handprints. The tradition began by accident when the theater was under construction in 1927. Sid Grauman took Mary Pickford, Douglas Fairbanks, Sr., and Norma Talmadge to witness the construction of the theater, but Miss Talmadge accidentally stepped in the wet cement. Seeing the imprint that her shoe created, Grauman asked his visitors to make hand and shoe imprints and a tradition was born. On August 3, 1977, *Star Wars* had become the biggest box office sensation of all-time, leading to 8,000 fans arriving to watch Darth Vader, R2-D2, and C-3PO immortalized in concrete in the Forecourt of the Stars. The *Star Wars* characters have one of the closest spots to the street while George Lucas's handprints are cemented immediately behind their square. Harrison Ford also gained a spot in a ceremony on June 4, 1992.

In December 1998, Gasking asked Kirk to help him plan the lineup, so Kirk began working formally on it almost immediately. Kirk said, "Once Lincoln said 'go for it' with organizing the lineup, I was at first excited, and then at a loss...How can you organize something that's never been done before?" He started by "thinking of it as an event and not a line. And, in fact, it really *was* an event and not a line." Kirk and Gasking began thinking of ideas for activities in which fans lining up could participate, including karaoke, trivial pursuit, costume contests, and other ideas, not all of which became reality. "One thing I learned was that only about 30% of your expectations for this type of event actually come true," Kirk said.

Kirk contacted many restaurants in the area attempting to work out occasional food arrangements, which would give the restaurant publicity and the fans free food, although few places were interested enough to participate. They always claimed to be entertained by the idea, Kirk said, but never followed through on any serious discussions. He said, "It got to the point where I figured they really weren't interested at all."

While many of the plans did not materialize, several companies were very helpful in providing assistance to the fans. For instance, DVDExpress.com, which was one of the largest DVD stores on the Internet, provided fans in the lineup with ten to fifteen movies, all for free. The fans watched the movies on Gasking's Dell laptop and a DVD projector. Hollywood Souvenirs, located on the West side of Orange Street next to Mann's Chinese Theatre, provided power and phone lines for the lineup. Scour.net dealt with the financial details of the Internet access and provided equipment to the lineup, such as Webcams, for the first three weeks. Also, Dell donated a laptop to the lineup that Gasking used to conduct his real estate business while in line. Besides organizing sponsorships, Countingdown had to explain their plans to the city of Los Angeles and the theater itself.

Phillip Nakov, who lived in Hollywood at the time, dealt with negotiations between Countingdown, the city, and the Los Angeles Police Department, which Kirk said was the most difficult part of the planning stage. After the discussions,

Countingdown obtained permission to lineup, though the city specified that no more than 250 people could be part of their group. After contacting the city, the organizers received an "Information Card" that stated their purpose for being in line. The LAPD had no problems with their lineup plans, although they wanted the group to behave appropriately and not become rowdy, which was not a problem for the *Star Wars* fans in line.

Police cars routinely patrolled the lineup and even arrested a group of delinquents for egging the line while the fans were camped out for tickets. Mann's Chinese Theatre also was enthusiastic about the lineup, which brought the theater a wealth of publicity in the months leading up to the release of *The Phantom Menace*. Lincoln's planning also included a hefty insurance policy from the Acord Insurance Association in the event of any mishaps in line. By the end of January 1999, the lineup outside of Mann's Chinese Theatre had more members committed to it than similarly impressive lines outside of the Mann's Westwood Village Theatre in Los Angeles, the United Artists Coronet Theatre in San Francisco, and the Clearview Ziegfeld Theater in New York City. After securing permission to lineup, more details remained before the plans became reality.

The fans were happy to lineup for *The Phantom Menace*, but also wanted to benefit charity in the process. Countingdown spoke with the Starlight Children's Foundation concurrently with other negotiations and came to an arrangement that raised tens of thousands of dollars for the charity. Every fan who joined the line had to raise at least $75 for the charity, but almost everyone raised more than the minimum. While many people contributed a lump sum of money that they collected from others, or paid themselves, other fans convinced friends and family members to pledge specific amounts of money for each hour they waited. For instance, fans could ask that their friends donate $1 for every hour they waited in line. After the lineup ended, the friends made their contributions.

Countingdown chose Starlight because it is Mark Hamill's favorite charity. The lineup augmented many other charity events relating to *The Phantom Menace*. The Starlight Children's Foundation is dedicated to brightening the lives of seriously ill children through wish granting and state-of-the-art in-hospital entertainment. Starlight's worldwide presence in hospitals is significant and continues to grow steadily. At the time of Countingdown's announcement of partnership with the company in late January, the organization helped more than 57,000 children each month.

Fans who lined up at Mann's Chinese Theatre had to agree to a number of rules that Kirk wrote on behalf of the Countingdown crew, to which all of the organizers agreed. The first rule, created for insurance purposes, stated that no one under the age of eighteen could participate in the lineup, unless accompanied by a parent or guardian. Second, nobody could sell their tickets to anyone else, regardless of the price. Fans also had to refrain from selling anything else while in line.

The lineup, which was publicly stated to last one month, actually began on April 7 outside of the historic Mann's Chinese Theatre. In an interesting twist to the lineup story, seventeen-year-old Daniel Alter began lining up outside of the Mann's Westwood Village Theatre on the same day, only a few hours earlier than the Countingdown crew. He chose the theater because of its supposedly superior sound quality. Alter said, "The Chinese may be more famous, but this has the best sound system in the world."

Alter took credit from many media outlets for "forcing" Gasking and his crew to begin lining up on the same day, but it was actually part of their plan already. Kirk said, "It was our plan all along to line up for six weeks rather than just a month. Lincoln was worried that someone might want to jump in line a day or so before we lined up on April 19, so we had planned from the beginning to start lining up six weeks in advance." He added, "It was a simple coincidence that he lined up the morning that we planned on lining up at the Chinese." Nevertheless, it created somewhat of a frenzy.

Gasking heard about Alter standing in line and became slightly panicked, fearing that other fans would soon converge upon the Chinese Theatre. Kirk said, "For some reason, Lincoln thought that, because Danny lined up at the Westwood Theatre a few hours before we planned on lining up in Hollywood, people would start heading over to the Chinese and ultimately be in front of our group." Jim Corbin, one of the first fans to begin standing outside of Mann's Chinese Theatre as a member of Counting's crew said, "He'd called Scott [McAfee] from the street and said to 'e-mail everyone and tell them the line has started and to get down here!' So Scott wrote a quick e-mail, sent it to everyone he had on a list (about 50 or 60 people), and then he came by my house and we went down there."

Although Alter began lining up a few hours earlier, Corbin observed, "It seemed like Lincoln had the better deal from the beginning because Daniel was always getting harassed by the police while we never had any problems." On Thursday, the day after he began lining up, the police told him that he could not camp out on the sidewalk, although the manager of the Westwood Village Theatre allowed him to stay on their property for the duration of the wait. When the media asked Gasking if Alter beat him in lining up, he conceded that he had, but said, "It's not a competition. We're here for the movie and for the Starlight Foundation."

The line began at roughly 7:00 p.m. on April 7 with only five people that night outside of the Chinese Theatre, but by the time the media arrived early the next morning, there were seven or eight, Corbin said. During its first week, the lineup received numerous media mentions, not only from local papers such as the *Los Angeles Times* and the *Los Angeles Daily News*, but also from the *Associated Press*, *Wired*, *Variety*, *USA Today*, and many other national media groups.

The media attention continued throughout the lineup, much to the dismay of some fans. Kirk said, "If I learned just one thing while in line, it was never to trust the media. They usually mold the facts into a story of their own." Linda Gomez, another fan who lined up about three weeks early said of the media, "They were there every day either in person or calling on the phone constantly." A pay phone next to the line gave fans the opportunity to call and offer their support of the lineup, but it also provided journalists the opportunity to call and seek commentary. While in line, Gomez wrote, "The pay phone rings off the hook as people from across the country and around the world call to give us their best wishes and to say they wish they could be there with us." Even radio show hosts phoned the lineup, which became the source of worldwide media attention, though not always positive. Gomez commented, "Most of the media tried to portray us in a bad light."

Not only did the media often inaccurately write about the lineup, but they bothered the fans almost constantly. Kirk said, "The media bugged us everyday from 2:00 a.m. to midnight." He explained, "Starting at 2:00 a.m., radio stations from around the world would call us and ask the questions we all became experts at answering. At about 10:00 a.m. through noon, the different news crews would come down from stations such as *Telemundo*, *CNN*, *E! Entertainment*, *Access Hollywood*, and *Entertainment Tonight*." Having already added to the intense frenzy surrounding the movie, news crews were eager to find new stories about the film. The Countingdown lineup provided an unusual news story that was especially attractive because of its connection to *The Phantom Menace*. "We became the center of the entertainment world for a while. It was an interesting experience to say the least," Kirk said.

Despite the media's generally negative commentary about the lineup, and especially the fans taking part in it, most of the members who lined up are no slouches. In her journal, Gomez wrote, "The people in line are all very intelligent and talented individuals. Many of them are artists and writers, or involved in the movie or television business [in another way], or are interested in getting into it one day." Despite the media's notions, most of the fans are not obsessed worshipers of Lucas, but just devoted individuals who lined up hoping to enjoy a fun and memorable experience. Gomez commented, "I truly felt, for the first time in my life, that I was not alone."

In addition to the media attention, the tourists visiting Los Angeles also enjoyed watching the lineup. Gomez wrote at the time, "As we are standing in line the tour buses unload at the curb and we are the first stop in their Hollywood tours. They just point at us and stare and talk about us as if we weren't even there." She added, "Now I know how animals in the zoo probably feel." Most people in line had no idea that they would become the focus of worldwide press coverage and attention from fans everywhere, but the hype surrounding *The Phantom Menace* created a frenzy of stories about the lineup. "I never knew this would be such a big deal when I signed up to do it six months ago," Gomez wrote.

Lucasfilm also noticed the lineup. Rick McCallum, producer of *The Phantom Menace*, loved it. "It is insane, and I just love it," he said. McCallum even planned to visit the line, although his schedule never permitted it. He said, "I think the real reason behind it is that kids can have that experience at a rock concert, but they've never had that experience at a movie. I really do think that it is part of the phenomenon—it's a collective fun thing to do."

Steve Cote, a member of the lineup outside of Mann's Chinese Theatre, even had the opportunity to speak with Lucas by phone while in line for the movie. *Access Hollywood* covered the lineup almost every day, so "one day, the producer who was working with us, Mary Jaras, told me she would be in New York in a few days to cover the press junket for *Episode I*," Cote said. Jaras offered Cote the opportunity to ask Lucas one question; he gladly accepted. After conferring with the fans in line, he later asked Lucas if he had any projects planned for after his work on the *Star Wars* movies. Lucas told him that he had many ideas, although he could not focus on them until after completing the prequel trilogy.

During May, international fans began to join the lineup from countries such as Australia, the United Kingdom, and many other European nations. *Variety* even featured an article titled, "'Star' tourists trek to 'Menace'." According to the article, not only was the film destined to boost ticket sales worldwide, but it also appeared likely to benefit the United States tourism industry.

One company called Sports Mondial, which usually helps fans travel to sporting events, offered a special air-hotel package for *Star Wars* fans traveling from the United Kingdom to New York to see the first prequel. The package cost 649, or roughly $950, and included a flight to the United States, a two-night stay in a three star hotel, and a ticket to the movie. Howard Gough of London's STA travel agency told *Variety*, "We've had people coming in specifying that going to see *Star Wars* is the reason they're booking flights." Many people who flew to the United States chose to line up outside of Mann's Chinese Theatre with the Countingdown group.

Helen Winterbottom, a fan from the United Kingdom, flew from LHR airport on May 16 to join the line at Mann's Chinese Theatre along with several other fans from the country who she met through the Internet. Two British news crews even followed the group and spent time interviewing the die-hard fans. On opening day, she woke up at 5:00 a.m. and "spent the whole day being interviewed for TV, radio, newspapers, and even someone's college project!" Of the movie experience itself, Winterbottom said, "Seeing the *Star Wars* logo come up on a cinema screen again was magic." After she saw the movie in the United States, she also lined up with fellow fans to see the premiere of the film at the Leicester Square Theater in London before traveling to Paris for opening night in fall 1999.

Clare Whipps, another European fan who lined up outside of Mann's Chinese Theatre, also departed for the United States several days before the opening of the film and arranged for one week off from work, which for Whipps involves radio. She said, "I'd been working on the UK 'invasion' for about six months, and had been in touch with Lincoln for about nine months." Like Winterbottom, Whipps also lined up in London and Paris for the two foreign premieres. She said, "I've seen a lot of cool stuff in my time with my job, but nothing will compare to the atmosphere in that cinema [on] opening night."

Star Wars is a worldwide phenomenon that prompted fans from around the world to converge on the United States to attend the *Star Wars* Celebration in late April and early May and also to see the movie in its first country of release. Gomez wrote, "People from all over the United States and the world started arriving in Los Angeles for the sole purpose of seeing *Episode I* at the best theatre in the world to see it—The Mann's Chinese Theatre in Hollywood."

The fans who lined up for weeks outside of the theater received a variety of reactions from people passing the line, ranging from amused and interested to negative and concerned. Gomez stated, "We had a little of every type of reaction. Many people thought it was great what we were doing for charity," though she admitted, "Others thought we were crazy." Kirk said, "Most of the people who passed us were friendly. Some even seemed a bit jealous and wished they could stay in line with us." Recalling one incident while in line, he said, "I remember one young boy and his mother stayed with us for an hour or two because he was such a huge *Star Wars* fan. He thought it was more fun than going to Disney-land."

On May 12, tickets to *The Phantom Menace* went on sale at Mann's Chinese Theatre and other box offices across the United States. Many fans in line described the event as more frenzied and historic than even the night before the movie finally premiered. Countingdown arranged for one mass purchase of tick-ets from the theater after asking fans in line how many tickets they planned to purchase, although Lucasfilm set a strict limit of twelve per person. Peter Gen-ovese was closely involved with the ticket purchase and his brief story describes the event:

> I was awoken at about 7:35 a.m. at my house by a phone call from Amy Cote asking me if I could drop by her work to pick up $1,000 cash on my way to the line, because they were short some for the tickets. So I got ready, went to her work, and before I knew it, I was on the freeway with $1,000 cash sitting next to me in an envelope. When I got to the line, I hooked up with Steve and then we went into the tent where I gave him the money, and we added it together with $3,000 that he had in there already. We counted it out together and tallied everything to get exact amounts. Next stop was the bank to get a cashier's check for the Chinese Theatre. Scott [McAfee] drove Steve [Cote] and I to the bank where we guarded the money closely.

The group of ticket buyers finished their transaction at the Bank of America and left by 10:30 a.m. They then talked to the manager and "discussed how we were going to do the tickets, and they gave us vouchers for the first 63 people in line to receive twelve tickets each," Genovese said. Gasking and Tim Doyle were the first to receive their tickets, but "I actually got to go third because I was going to be standing there the whole time collecting everyone's tickets," Genovese said. They collected everyone's tickets without any incidents and placed them in a safety deposit box at their hotel room.

On May 14, Ray Park, who played Darth Maul in the first prequel, visited the lineup, pleasantly surprising everyone outside of the theater at the time. The stuntman-turned-actor was on his way to see *The Matrix*, but fans hounded him before he could reach the ticket window. Gomez wrote in her journal, "We were filming the whole time he was there. He signed Darth Maul figures and plastic toy lightsabers that we had on hand." She added, "He also gave a demonstration with one of the lightsabers of moves that he did in the movie. He even posed for pictures with a few people in our group but soon had to get going if he wanted to see the movie." Jake Lloyd, who played Anakin Skywalker in *The Phantom Menace*, also visited the lineup on April 14 to talk with the fans.

Everyone who waited in line had a specific place depending on the number of hours they waited, which were carefully logged. The system was fairly complicated, although it was meant to reward the most dedicated fans with the most points, which would in turn determine their position in line. Each hour gave fans a certain number of points, with the number decreasing as the days until the film's release dwindled. In other words, fans who lined up six weeks in advance received significantly more credit for each of their first hours than fans who began lining up in May. Fans earned points through shifts of four hours each, beginning at midnight each day and ending with the sixth shift 24 hours later. Although many people waited in line for most of the time, nobody was there every day for 24 hours. Everyone left at least a few times, sometimes just to shower or sleep somewhere more comfortable, and other times to work or go to school.

International fans who flew in to the United States to see the movie were automatically awarded extra points, which is logical because of the level of commitment required to fly thousands of miles just for lining up to see a movie. For traveling between 500 and 599 miles to reach the lineup, fans received 20 points automatically. The number increased up to 200 points for fans traveling more than 7,000 miles. International fans also had to notify either Gasking or Kolby Kirk when they planned to arrive at the line and they had to show identification and plane tickets proving their country of origin. While in the states, international fans, who often arrived only days in advance of the release, had to spend at least 80% of their time in line.

At the conclusion of the lineup, everyone was assigned a new place in line based on their total number of accumulated points. Also, fans in line could transfer any number of points to their friends and fellow fans, although everyone had to have at least 200 points total. In addition to the point requirement, everyone who planned on attending the movie had to be present for the final 72 hours of the wait, which was by midnight on May 16.

Throughout the final three weeks of the lineup, a company called Play based in San Francisco provided the lineup outside of Mann's Chinese Theatre with a prototype Trinity unit, which is an advanced video setup that allowed for the live transmission of video footage to Internet users. The unit was the first and only one of its kind at the time and continued the theme of advanced technology used with *The Phantom Menace* and related events. Countingdown created a special Website at Countingdowntv.com to provide fans worldwide with an inside look at the line; fans even performed special shows to entertain worldwide audiences. Play also provided Countingdown with four staff members to help with the Trinity, which was running 24 hours a day, seven days each week for three weeks straight leading up to the release of the film.

Trinity is a powerful video setup that "redefines the economics of video production, combining all the tools of a network television broadcast studio into a single, simple product," according to Play's Website. The Website states, "We want everyone to be able to communicate powerful stories and ideas, and not be limited by budget or technical expertise." The Trinity worked very well for Countingdown and the lineup, giving everyone a chance to feel as though they were part of the event in at least a limited way. "From primetime network television producers to middle school students, from corporate video departments to live event producers, stories are being told in rich, compelling ways never before possible. Trinity is here, and the world of video will never be the same again," the site boasts.

In addition to the camera, Countingdown set up an Internet Relay Chat (IRC) channel that served as a place for fans to talk with people in line and complemented the live video footage well. The site also offered photo galleries for people to see some of the more exciting events that occurred during the lineup. While some of the fans were camera shy, most of them wanted as much time in front of it as possible, fortunately for fans watching on the Internet.

As the release date neared, the fans in line prepared to witness the return of *Star Wars*. Gomez said, "Everyone thought it would be a great idea to watch the trilogy the night before we saw *Episode I*." She explained, "Someone had set up a large screen TV on the back of a pickup truck and arranged chairs for us at the back of the truck. They showed the wide-screen versions of *Star Wars*, *The Empire Strikes Back*, and *Return of the Jedi* back-to-back on the TV." Mann's Chinese Theatre even supplied the group with free popcorn that night, which was May 17, the night before fans would pour into the theater to watch *The Phantom Menace*.

The next day was the final one in line before the movie arrived in theaters and it was a memorable day for fans nationwide, but especially for the people lined up outside of Mann's Chinese Theatre, where some fans had spent time in line off and on for 42 days. Gomez said, "At 2:00 p.m. we were all at the theater to see the *Star Wars* sign go up on the Chinese Theatre for the first time in sixteen years. We all had our video cameras and were filming and cheering as they changed the signs." The day became more exciting as the night drew closer, though.

On opening night, "It seemed like everyone in Los Angeles was there to see the movie." Even local papers reported that May 18 seemed like a holiday in the city as thousands of people skipped work to line up the day before to see the midnight screenings in theaters around the city. Mann's Chinese Theatre began to usher fans into the auditorium two and a half hours in advance of the beginning of the first screening. Gomez said, "We were separated from the press by a chest high barricade. As we walked to the theater the sound of cameras going off was so loud that it sounded like helicopters and the flash bulbs were blinding."

The packed theater provided a positive atmosphere for fans to enjoy the movie with a group of equally enthusiastic moviegoers. Gomez commented, "There was a lot of energy in the theatre that night." News crews waited outside to hear from fans, who anxiously awaited the beginning of the movie for which they had waited sixteen years, and up to 42 days in line. "It was like the Force surrounded us that night; there was a certain electricity in the air," Gomez said. Finally, after the longest wait outside of theaters in the history of the world, the fans watched the newest *Star Wars* movie in the world's most famous theater.

Hundreds of fans became part of history through the lineup, but most importantly they contributed to the impressive total that the line raised for the Starlight Children's Foundation. After the lineup ended, the total amount of money raised stood at $30,000. Although Countingdown created a media frenzy over the line that often portrayed *Star Wars* fans as obsessed freaks, the people who lined up are intelligent and successful individuals who teamed together to raise tens of thousands of dollars for charity in a period of only six weeks. People who criticized the fans' passion for the films and the lineup likely did nothing as generous during the entire year. While in line, Lincoln eloquently stated, "It's not about the tickets. It's about the anticipation."

Menacing Expectations

The first three *Star Wars* movies were phenomenally successful at the box office, which created great expectations for *The Phantom Menace*. In North America, *Star Wars: Episode IV—A New Hope* grossed $461 million after six theatrical releases while the two sequels also amassed huge box office totals. *The Empire Strikes Back* grossed $290.3 million after four releases and *Return of the Jedi* collected $309.2 million after three. *The Empire Strikes Back* was the highest grossing first sequel in history at the time. In North America, *A New Hope* has sold 169 million tickets, *The Empire Strikes Back* 97 million, and *Return of the Jedi* 93 million.

After the first *Star Wars* reclaimed its top ranking in North American box office receipts during the 1997 theatrical release for its twentieth anniversary, the *Star Wars* franchise had regained its glory. The victory celebration did not last long, however, as a new rival quickly appeared, usurping the box office throne. On March 14, 1998, after more than ten weeks at the top of the weekend box office charts, James Cameron's *Titanic* defeated *A New Hope* to claim the title of highest-grossing movie. The event displeased *Star Wars* fans nationwide who desired *A New Hope* to remain number one for years into the future, but instead it ceded its throne to *Titanic* after just more than one year.

The feud between *Titanic* fans and *Star Wars* fans reached a climax quickly, although the movies' creators did not share the rivalry. George Lucas placed a full-page ad in several Hollywood trade papers congratulating Cameron for his monumental success. Regarding what many fans saw as a competition between *The Phantom Menace* and *Titanic*, Lucas said, "This is not a contest. Our society makes everything adversarial." Perhaps unfortunately, it became a contest for the fans. He added, "Everyone has to be a winner or a loser. It's a movie." Lucas predicted that *The Phantom Menace* would finish its box office run ahead of *Jurassic Park* (1993), but below *E.T.: The Extra Terrestrial* (1982). He said he would be disappointed if it failed to become one of the top ten highest grossing movies of all-time, but few people doubted that it would succeed at such a relatively modest goal.

The dethroning of *Star Wars* led to a showdown between the first prequel and *Titanic* for box office supremacy, at least in the minds of the fans. Box office ranking is a matter of pride for *Star Wars* fans, who have enjoyed seeing their favorite movies at the top of the charts since the saga's beginning.

As early as a year prior to the opening of the movie, debates raged among fans and moviegoers concerning which movie would ultimately prevail as number one. In the May 1, 1998 issue of *Entertainment Weekly* an article titled, "Will the Next *Star Wars* Sink *Titanic*?" formally started the box office showdown. The Internet served as the primary battlefield between devoted fans. *Star Wars* enthusiasts insisted the new movie would crush *Titanic* because they believed the disaster epic could never withstand the anticipation and excitement of *The Phantom Menace*. Nonetheless, the $600.8 million that *Titanic* grossed at the North American box office alone looked insurmountable. Even more impressively, *Titanic* grossed $1.835 billion worldwide.

According to a poll of Internet users on the popular Yahoo! search engine prior to the movie's release, 84% of the voters believed *The Phantom Menace* would crush *Titanic*. Also revealing, 61% of people polled believed it would top $800 million while 32% of the moviegoers believed it would top $1 billion in North America alone. Die-hard fans were not the only ones hoping for *The Phantom Menace* to annihilate *Titanic*. Kate Winslet, the leading actress in the romantic epic, told reporters that she hoped "*Star Wars* sinks that ship."

In the years since *Star Wars* made its first impression on North American audiences, watching the box office results has become a pastime, much like tracking stock prices or box scores. When a movie bombs at the box office, both the film and its director quickly become the subject of jokes at dinner tables nationwide, and even on national television. In 1995, Kevin Costner's *Waterworld* became the subject of national ridicule because of its high budget and failure to draw audiences to box offices. In 1998, people scoffed at the relatively unimpressive box office gross for *Godzilla*. Other examples abound. Unfortunately, people often judge a movie only by its box office success and not by the quality of the movie itself. Even so, there is some justification for assuming that box office performance is linked to quality, despite the negative effects of a society overly concerned with the raw numbers.

When a movie opens to large crowds, but ticket sales plummet on the following weekend, negative word-of-mouth has often taken hold. Popular movies can continue their momentum throughout their entire box office runs, but some movies lack the proper advertising budget or star power to gain recognition, therefore failing to attract audiences. Other great films appeal only to a specific group of people, so they fail to achieve widespread commercial success. Nevertheless, when a movie's weekend gross plummets after the opening Friday through Sunday period, the sharp drop typically indicates that audiences disliked the movie. Conversely, when a movie displays resilience, the success indicates excellent word-of-mouth approval.

Most box office analysts did not believe that *The Phantom Menace* would outsell *Titanic*, although nearly everyone expected that it would set a new opening weekend record. On Memorial Day weekend in 1997, *The Lost World: Jurassic Park* grossed $72.1 million in just three days and $92.73 million over the four-day holiday weekend, both of which were records. Many analysts expected *Godzilla* to crush the record in 1998, but audiences did not flock to the monster movie as studio executives had wished. Although *Godzilla* fell short, *The Phantom Menace* seemed a sure bet to topple the records that *The Lost World* set.

One online gambling organization gave moviegoers the option to bet on the outcome of the opening weekend box office battle. On April 17, 1999, Intertops.com announced that fans and interested moviegoers could bet money on the outcome of the showdown between the dinosaur sequel and the *Star Wars* prequel. Intertops.com listed *The Phantom Menace* at 1:20 odds and *The Lost World* at 17:1 odds. Only the first four days of each movie's respective box office gross counted towards the bet. Simon Noble, executive director and co-founder of Intertops.com said, "The release of *The Phantom Menace* has conjured unparalleled expectations for a feature film. Our site opens another avenue for fans to participate in the film's intensely anticipated opening weekend." Customers had to place their bets on or before the film's release date of May 19.

Intertops.com is the Internet's first and foremost sports betting site and also features a large range of casino games. The site gives customers a chance to bet on the Oscars, among other entertainment events. Intertops.com features the Internet's lowest deposit and minimum bet requirements and has paid out more than $200 million since its inception in 1995.

Lucasfilm's strict requirements for sound and visual quality ensured audiences a superior presentation of the movie, although they also made predicting the movie's opening weekend box office significantly more complicated. For most major blockbusters, the studio secures as many theaters and screens as possible to ensure a massive opening weekend box office gross. Analysts initially believed *The Phantom Menace* might only open on about 2,200 theaters; however, as the release date neared, the number ballooned to nearly 3,000. Other considerations complicated the prediction process as well, such as the number of theaters that offered midnight showings of the movie and the small number of theaters that played the movie 24 hours a day. The numerous uncertainties about the opening of *The Phantom Menace* made an accurate prediction of its opening weekend box office total nearly impossible.

Aside from fans expecting *The Phantom Menace* to be the movie equivalent of the Second Coming, theaters relied on its success at the box office to boost overall ticket sales. United Artists, a theater chain that operated 2,148 screens in 316 theaters as of May 1999, announced on May 14 that their revenues declined 18% in the first quarter of the year to $134.9 million. United Artists CEO Kurt Hall stated, "The success of individual films such as *Titanic* last year had a significant impact on our comparative quarterly operating results." Recently completed theaters "have positioned us very well for the scheduled release of the *Star Wars* prequel and several other highly anticipated films," Hall said. Overall losses for United Artists tripled compared to the same quarter of the previous year, but most other exhibitors faced similar problems, in some cases resulting in even worse losses.

AMC, owner and operator of 2,645 screens in 217 theaters in May 1999, reported losses of $19.1 million for their first quarter, which represented a five-fold increase in net losses during the three months leading to April 1. *Variety* reported AMC's losses just two days after reporting United Artists' financial situation. AMC enjoyed a 7% revenue increase, but blamed the industry-wide slump for their losses, citing the 6% fall in revenues across the industry as a whole. AMC co-chairman Peter Brown, although disappointed with the results said, "We are extremely excited about the upcoming film product, particularly *Star Wars: Episode 1—[The] Phantom Menace*."

Carmike Cinemas reported a 16% decline in revenues to $97.7 million. Analysts expected the decline, which reflected the general industry downturn. Movies released during the winter season rarely boost attendance as much as *Titanic*, which artificially inflated the first quarter's results and made future comparisons unfair. Carmike CEO Michael Patrick said, "Management continues to work on cost-cutting measures and controls while preparing and looking forward to our summer season," adding that he expected *The Phantom Menace* to increase attendance dramatically.

Compounding the expectations, the box office in North America lagged behind the record levels established in 1998, in part because of the success of *Titanic* during the usually calm winter season. Beginning with the early second quarter debut of *The Matrix*, the gap began to close week by week as *Entrapment* and *The Mummy* amassed impressive totals at the box office. When *The Phantom*

Menace opened on May 19, the discrepancy had narrowed considerably, but a sizeable rift still remained.

Most movies are released to relatively minimal hype, few expectations, and no fanfare. *Star Wars* movies are always a major event, but *The Phantom Menace* had more expectations heaped upon it than nearly any other movie in history. Box office failure would have tarnished the *Star Wars* name and destroyed the success that has long been a tradition of the saga. Conversely, success would benefit theater chains nationwide and instill life into a sagging industry, propelling 1999 to new record highs at the box office.

Rival studios scheduled their event movies well after the release of *The Phantom Menace*, hoping to avoid the deafening hype and direct competition with the most anticipated movie of all-time. At ShoWest, the annual convention of theater exhibitors, analyst Dan Marks of ACNielsen EDI said, "It's going to be difficult to compete because *Star Wars* is clearly going to appeal across all demographics." Some analysts insisted that surrendering May to *Star Wars* would be a big mistake and suggested that studios counter-program by releasing movies aimed at the female audience. Several studios agreed, choosing to compete directly with the *Star Wars* juggernaut. "If you don't take the risk, holding back can become a self-fulfilling prophecy," said Tom Borys, president of ACNielsen EDI. Nevertheless, most studios avoided direct confrontation with *The Phantom Menace* and scheduled their releases a safe distance away from the movie's opening.

The Mummy, which opened May 7, had ample time to draw moviegoers into theaters in advance of *The Phantom Menace's* May 19 opening. Studios also estimated that the high demand for *The Phantom Menace*, coupled with the relatively low theater count for an event movie, would lead to a spillover effect. In other words, studios hoped moviegoers who could not see *The Phantom Menace* because of sold-out showings would chose to see other movies already in theaters. "What everyone is hoping for is that there will be a spillover effect," affirmed John King Jr., manager of Pacific's Winnetka All-Stadium 20 in suburban Los Angeles.

Several industry executives feared that *The Phantom Menace* would monopolize audiences and leave little room for other movies, but many observers believed it would stir interest and increase theater visits. "The new *Star Wars* is not a menace—it is the greatest catalyst for moviegoing ever," Disney marketing executive Chuck Viane commented at ShoWest. He added, "Once you start it rolling, people are going to be drawn to the movies. If you have a trailer placed before *Star*

Wars, you're going to reap huge benefits." In retrospect, Viane's assessment seems almost prophetic.

New Line scheduled *Austin Powers 2: The Spy Who Shagged Me* for release on June 11, which fell on *The Phantom Menace's* fourth weekend, so the film avoided immediate, direct competition. Paramount initially scheduled *The General's Daughter* to open on the same weekend as the *Austin Powers* sequel, but eventually moved the release back one week to avoid competition.

Universal scheduled Julia Roberts' *Notting Hill* for release on June 18, but on Monday, April 5 the studio decided to move the release date directly into the path of *The Phantom Menace*, choosing May 28 as the new opening day. Universal's distribution head Nikki Rocco said, "Hopefully there's two audiences: kids who want to see *Star Wars* and mom and dad who'll be in the mood for a little romance." Universal's strategy demonstrated a perfect example of counter-programming. In hopes of luring the females who are uninterested in *Star Wars* to multiplexes, Universal figured *Notting Hill* would provide an appealing alternative. "You can counter-program," insisted Borys, adding, "You can't just give up the whole summer to *Star Wars*." Borys noted, "Five studios have already given a wide berth to *Star Wars*."

Most studios left sizeable holes in their release schedules to accommodate the opening of *The Phantom Menace*. Warner Brothers opened David Spade's *Lost and Found* on April 23, but opened nothing else until Will Smith's *Wild Wild West* on July 2. Similarly, Paramount released *Election* on April 23 and waited until June 18 to release *The General's Daughter*. Disney had nothing competing with *The Phantom Menace* when it opened, instead releasing *Ten Things I Hate About You* on March 31. The studio waited until June 4 to release *Instinct* in competition with *The Phantom Menace* on its third weekend and the animated feature *Tarzan* just two weeks later. Fox left its May and June schedule entirely devoid of competing movies.

DreamWorks, the studio partially owned by Lucas's best friend, Steven Spielberg, chose a more direct approach. Hoping to lure female audiences, *The Love Letter*, starring Spielberg's wife, Kate Capshaw, opened just two days after *The Phantom Menace*. Distribution chief James Tharp said, "Our thinking is that the primary demographic will be women on what will be a huge weekend." He added, "We think *The Love Letter* will do well enough for us to expand it in the following weeks." Sony attempted a similar strategy, opening sci-fi thriller *The Thirteenth Floor* on Memorial Day weekend, which analysts expected *The Phantom Menace* to dominate.

Studios made numerous last-minute changes to their release schedules to avoid competing with *The Phantom Menace*. Paramount moved *South Park* from June 18 to June 30 and MGM moved the remake of *The Thomas Crown Affair* from June 4 to August 6. In addition, Sony shifted *Arlington Road* from May 14 to July 9 while Universal moved *American Pie* from May 28 to July 9. In May and June 1999, only fourteen movies opened in more than 800 theaters nation-wide compared to twenty the previous year during the same period. In turn, the July and August months saw an increase to 29 movies in wide release compared to 25 in 1998.

Despite the initial appearance of a soft slate, *The Phantom Menace* faced surprisingly stiff competition. Major blockbusters and a number of sleeper hits made the summer of 1999 one of the most competitive in movie history. Fortunately, the prequel enjoyed three weekends with relatively no serious competition, making its voyage into the record books slightly easier. Despite heavy competition, tens of millions of people showed up for what Carlos Petrick, marketing director for Marcus Theatres Corporation, said is "the film event of the decade, if not the millennium."

The Phantom Menace quickly became an event, not just a movie, prompting millions of employees to skip work on May 19. One Wall Street stock trader insisted, "I'm going to see it opening day. I have to!" Many people planned to call in sick, then begin to line up at a local theater. They reasoned that being among the first to see *The Phantom Menace* outweighed any risks associated with lying to their employers. Initially, few people considered the consequences of the absenteeism that *The Phantom Menace* might cause, although reports began to spread warning employers and employees alike.

Employment consultant John Challenger told the *New York Post*, "This has the potential of being the largest day of work absenteeism in the history of the United States." He added, "A lot of companies might as well close the doors that day because they're not going to have enough work force to operate up to normal." Some companies actually heeded the advice, giving the entire day off so their employees could see the film. "We're declaring May 19 a cultural holiday. Everybody in our office gets it off," said Steve Hartford, vice president of Play, Inc. The company employed 250 people at the time.

Based on information from the Federal Bureau of Labor Statistics, the Challenger, Gray & Christmas firm estimated that 2.2 million people would skip work on May 19 to see *The Phantom Menace*. The firm based their estimate on the number of people who work each day, the number of those people who skip work each day, and the 4.7 million people who saw *The Lost World: Jurassic Park* on its opening Friday. While *Star Wars* fans eagerly anticipated *The Phantom Menace*, employers had reason to worry. According to estimates, the absenteeism cost businesses more than $300 million in lost wages.

The statistics startled The Society for Human Resource Management, which urged employees not to skip work when the movie opened. The society represents the interests of nearly 70,000 professional and student members worldwide. Sue Meisinger, vice-president of the society said, "Don't start a war with your employer over a movie," although for most fans *Star Wars* is not just a movie. She advised employees to inform their employers of the absence and take the day off as vacation time. Meisinger humorously added, "Otherwise, you may be seeing the empire strike back, in addition to *The Phantom Menace*."

Fox did not waste much money on advertising *The Phantom Menace*, instead relying on free media coverage to promote the movie. In the *Los Angeles Times* on Sunday, May 16, a small three-column ad on page nineteen trumpeted the release of the movie. The ad only named six key theaters and included the common phrase "and a theater near you." Tom Sherak, Chairman of the Twentieth Century Fox Domestic Film Group said, "People who are going to see it Wednesday already know where they're going to see it."

The small size of the ad that Fox placed in the *Los Angeles Times* shocked some observers, but absolutely no ads appeared in the Sunday edition of the *New York Times*. Typically, studios position ads in the *New York Times* even for relatively low budget movies because of the paper's wide readership. Sherak questioned, "When you have awareness of 100%, what do you need newspaper ads for?" Lucasfilm president Gordon Radley commented, "It wasn't like you needed to do advertising to make people aware of this movie."

The unprecedented media coverage accomplished what advertising usually would by letting moviegoers know of the movie's presence. Furthermore, magazines and newspapers already gave moviegoers a mostly positive impression of the prequel. Harold Vogel, a veteran entertainment industry analyst based in New York said, "In this case, you don't spend something to whip it into a frenzy when it's already in a frenzy. It's a huge picture." A researcher with Competitive Media Reporting (CMR), a New York firm that tracks advertising spending said, "It looks like they're not spending any money on this at all." Lucasfilm wisely used the media to its advantage in promoting the movie, although the plan somewhat backfired immediately before *The Phantom Menace's* release because of the growing negative publicity.

After the media wrote countless stories about *The Phantom Menace*, they began criticizing the hype and the ubiquitous nature of the movie and its tie-ins.

Regardless of journalists stating otherwise, the media created the hype, not Lucasfilm. "In a lot of ways the media ran with it because of their own needs. [They] created the hype, and then they're sitting around passing judgment on it," Radley said. The media ran far too many stories about *The Phantom Menace*, although the attention made marketing the movie relatively easy, at least in the United States.

Promotional deals with Pepsi, TriCon, Hasbro, and Lego increased advertising spots for *The Phantom Menace* on television without further expenditures by Lucasfilm or Fox. Despite the licensees' advertising, Lucasfilm designed five unique television spots focusing on the movie's characters. The commercials, called *tone poems*, provided viewers with an insight into the primary characters. The commercials emphasized one value for each character: One Truth for Darth Maul, One Will for Queen Amidala, One Dream for Anakin Skywalker, One Destiny for Qui-Gon Jinn, and One Love for Shmi Skywalker.

Prior to the more elaborate ads, Lucasfilm barely advertised the movie on television at all. Between January and April, CMR reported Lucasfilm ran only five television ads, which is "almost nonexistent," a CMR researcher said. Veteran entertainment analyst Harold Vogel said, "If you can get one minute of air time on every television station in the country for free, why pay?"

Fox never disclosed their advertising budget for *The Phantom Menace*, but it likely came in below $20 million, which is significantly less than the industry average. According to *Advertising Age*, a major industry publication, Fox spends between $20 and $30 million advertising most of their movies. Major event movies usually cost much more to market, which was true of *Godzilla*; Sony spent upwards of $40 million promoting the monster movie. Concern for moderation also influenced Fox's low advertising budget. "They're concerned there's going to be a backlash," said Marty Brochstein, executive editor of *The Licensing Letter*, based in New York. He added that Fox and Lucasfilm feared that "people will become so sick of it, they won't go to see the film."

After years of buildup and expectations, the movie's release date rapidly approached. Fans hoped the movie would meet their high expectations and return them to the galaxy far, far away. Exhibitors needed the film to boost theater attendance and instill life into a sagging industry. Toy and other merchandising companies waited anxiously to see whether or not they invested their money wisely, or whether the first prequel would become another *Godzilla*. With the greatest burden of expectations in movie history, the countdown to the film's launch reached zero.

North American Box Office

After intense speculation about its box office potential, years of expectations from eager fans, and the financial future of entire industries riding on its success, *The Phantom Menace* finally opened to enthusiastic crowds on Wednesday, May 19, 1999. The movie played in 2,010 theaters at 12:01 a.m., but 960 additional theaters began playing it during regular hours, bringing the opening day total to 2,970 in North America.

At the beginning of planning the movie's theatrical release, Fox and Lucasfilm did not expect *The Phantom Menace* to open in nearly 3,000 theaters, but the number increased considerably just weeks before the movie's release. The theater count, while considerable, came nowhere near the number that movies such as *The Lost World: Jurassic Park* (1997), *Godzilla* (1998), *X-Men* (2000), and *Scream 3* (2000) occupied. Fox did not reveal the exact number of screens on which the movie played, but industry analysts estimated the number at around 5,500, well below the 6,000 held by *The Lost World* and the 7,000 or more occupied by *Godzilla*.

Nearly 120 theaters played the movie 24 hours the first day, and many of them continued their constant screenings for the entire five-day opening period. Several notable theaters playing the movie twenty-four hours daily included the Ziegfeld and Union Square theaters in New York, the Village and Chinese theaters in Los Angeles, and the Mercado in Santa Clara, among others.

The Lost World grossed $26.1 million on its opening Sunday, which fell on May 25, 1997, setting the record for the highest grossing Sunday and highest grossing single day in history. Based on reported pre-dawn grosses from roughly 600 theaters that played *The Phantom Menace* at 12:01 a.m., Fox estimated that the movie grossed $7.5 million in its first six hours of release, an astronomical amount of money for movie showings in the early morning hours. Tom Sherak cautioned that the gross estimate could vary by as much as 20% because Fox extrapolated the figure from a limited sampling of theaters. *Independence Day* holds the record for the highest gross from advance screenings, collecting $11.1 million on July 2, 1996, the day before its official release, though unlike *The*

Phantom Menace, exhibitors had the option of showing *Independence Day* starting at 6:00 p.m.

Analysts already estimated that *The Phantom Menace* would easily break all single day records, but on May 20 the official figures confirmed their predictions. *The Phantom Menace* grossed $28,542,349 in its first day of release, a non-holiday Wednesday with a holiday atmosphere. The opening day total shattered all previous records and set a new single day record, eclipsing *Independence Day's* Wednesday gross of $17.4 million on July 3. Logically, the massive total also surpassed all opening day grosses, including *The Lost World: Jurassic Park's* $21.6 million opening day gross on Friday, May 23, 1997. On its opening day of December 19, 1997, *Titanic* grossed $8,61 million, but it showed remarkable durability at the box office over the months following its release.

The Phantom Menace's opening day gross yielded an average of $9,610 per theater, which is considered excellent for most movies during an entire weekend. Put in perspective, *The Phantom Menace* grossed in one work day only $100,000 less than *Titanic* grossed over its entire opening weekend (Friday—Sunday). Tickets sold for the *Star Wars* prequel represented 88% of total ticket sales for the entire day, eclipsing the past record that both *The Lost World: Jurassic Park* and *Mission: Impossible* set at 67% of overall ticket sales on their opening days. Despite the impressive gross, many rivals expected *The Phantom Menace* to gross between $30 and $45 million, which was an unrealistic expectation for one day at the box office in a limited number of theaters, regardless of the movie's popularity. The mixed reaction to the opening day gross set the tone for the first week of the movie's box office run.

On its second day, *The Phantom Menace* grossed $12.3 million, an all-time record at the time for a non-holiday Thursday. The Thursday gross dipped considerably from Wednesday's monstrous take, but industry analysts expected the decline. While many people skipped work on Wednesday to see the movie, few fans could afford to skip work again the following day. Adding to the drop, most theaters did not offer early morning screenings of the movie. The $12.3 million gross is still impressive for a weekday, and an amount that most movies never achieve during a single day of their entire box office runs.

Regardless of the facts, journalists who do not understand the specifics of the box office wrote about the "downer" Thursday. Daniel Frankel of *E! Online* felt that Fox officials seemed unnaturally upbeat about the weekend after Tom Sherak said, "Show me the kids!" Fox anticipated a massive opening weekend gross largely because many kids did not have the opportunity to see the movie until Saturday or Sunday. Only the industry trade paper *Variety* offered insightful observations about the movie's box office prospects. Many media organizations speculated without proper knowledge, confusing readers and twisting the facts.

By Sunday night, Fox released estimates for *The Phantom Menace's* opening weekend. The daily gross for the film increased predictably from Thursday's lower total to $18.4 million Friday, the highest non-holiday Friday gross ever. Initial estimates placed Saturday's gross at $24.2 million, although the movie actually grossed $24.4 million according to final figures. The gross set an all-time record for a Saturday not falling on a holiday weekend. Following the record setting Friday and Saturday grosses, Sunday also set a non-holiday record. The Sunday estimate of $19.3 million, however, was considerably less than the actual gross, which Fox reported on Monday. The overall estimate for the movie's opening weekend was $61.8 million and $102.7 million for the opening five-day period.

Daily box office totals are posted at Showbizdata.com, but weekend data is not always entirely accurate because studios estimate the figures based on partial information. Furthermore, Sunday box office grosses are estimated based on empirical data and a number of other factors, not on actual Sunday grosses. The studios then estimate the movie's opening weekend gross from two days of partial data and one day's estimated box office total. When making their estimates, studios occasionally compensate for a major sporting event that might decrease movie attendance, like the Super Bowl, or a holiday that traditionally cuts into the daily box office totals.

Sunday box office numbers are almost always lower than Saturday's, primarily because most people have to return to work on Monday, so the evening showings are less full. When kids are out of school during the summer months, Sunday grosses increase slightly in relation to Saturday. Studios typically overestimate the weekend box office gross by several hundred thousand dollars because they overestimate the Sunday total, although there are exceptions. Nearly every major entertainment publication reports the weekend estimates and they appear in newspapers everywhere on Monday morning, so studios believe that slightly exaggerating the figures is beneficial, but not dishonest. There is no advantage in underestimating a movie's weekend box office revenue.

In rare instances, a movie actually earns more than the studio estimated, which almost always indicates that a movie's future prospects are encouraging. Fox significantly underestimated *The Phantom Menace's* sales, specifically the Sunday box office gross. When studio executives tallied the Sunday figures, *The Phantom Menace* actually grossed $21.9 million, a drop of only 10% from the massive Saturday gross. A decline of between 25-40% from Saturday to Sunday is fairly typical for most movies. The strong hold indicated the prequel appealed to families, who typically attend Sunday showings in larger numbers than other days of the week.

In Canada, *The Phantom Menace* grossed more on Sunday in many locations than on Saturday because Victoria Day, a legal holiday, fell on Monday. The final numbers gave *The Phantom Menace* $105.7 million after five days and $64.8 million for the three-day weekend, both of which were records. The actual first weekend gross exceeded estimates by about $3 million, though *The Phantom Menace* continued to beat studio predictions on many future weekends.

The Phantom Menace's $21,822 per theater average over the three-day weekend ranked among the all-time best for a movie in wide release. Typically, only small art house films achieve such high per theater averages while playing in a few of the nation's higher capacity theaters. While *The Lost World* grossed considerably more during its first three-day weekend than *The Phantom Menace*, the prequel's per theater average almost equaled that of the more widely released dinosaur sequel, which took in an average of $21,985. Most hugely successful movies average roughly $10,000 per theater on opening weekend. An average of $15,000 is rare, let alone more than $20,000. *The Phantom Menace* filled theaters all over North America, just as fans and analysts expected.

Several theaters enjoyed especially high grosses for *The Phantom Menace*, notably prestigious theaters in large city areas. For instance, the movie grossed about $473,000 at the United Artists Union Square 14 and $343,000 at the Clearview Ziegfeld, both in New York. Moviegoers spent $309,000 seeing the movie at the historic Mann's Chinese Theatre in Los Angeles, where fans waited outside for more than a month to see the first episode in Lucas's timeless saga.

The massive three-day gross represented the best non-holiday weekend in history, placing second only to *The Lost World* overall. Despite the three-day gross lagging behind *The Lost World's* torrid pace, *The Phantom Menace* handily defeated its five-day record of $95.8 million, becoming the quickest movie in history to pass the $100 million mark. Regardless of the record-shattering debut, media organizations and analysts around the country downplayed the results.

E! Online wrote, "*The Phantom Menace* is big at the box office, but is it big enough? Depends on how you crunch the numbers." *The Phantom Menace* set numerous all-time opening records regardless of how anyone chose to crunch the numbers, so the statement was absurd and inaccurate. A record can never be anything short of impressive. *Mr. Show Biz* headlined, "Phantom Huge, But Not Biggest Ever." Instead of focusing on the numerous records the movie set, most media publications chose to emphasize the single record that it did not topple.

A company called National Research Group (NRG) provides market research for the studios and predicts each movie's opening weekend gross based on the general interest among moviegoers. Many times, the estimates are significantly higher than the actual performance of the movie. By late October 1999, a few studios began blocking NRG's estimates for their releases, partially as a result of their overestimation of *The Phantom Menace's* opening weekend box office and similar occurrences with many other movies, such as *Fight Club*.

The box office is surprisingly influential in the minds of many moviegoers. If a movie performs below expectations, perhaps it is not worth seeing, some people believe. When NRG predicts a movie will open with $15 million, but instead it makes $12 million during the weekend, the public perceives the film as a failure. Sherak told *The Wall Street Journal*, "All week, you wind up fighting off the question, 'How did you feel not meeting the expectations'?" Unfortunately, the media often gains access to the reports. Even successful movies sometimes suffer from inaccurate estimates.

NRG estimated that *The Phantom Menace* would gross an unrealistically high $150 million for its first five days, so many media outlets perceived its record $105.7 million as a relative disappointment. Basing success or failure on an estimated figure is unreliable and inaccurate, so Fox and Disney told NRG to stop distributing box office estimates for their movies.

A few analysts made foolish comments about *The Phantom Menace's* box office potential after only the first weekend of release. When speaking of the film, one industry insider reportedly told *Mr. Show Biz* writer Jeffrey Wells, "It's this year's *Godzilla*." The *Mr. Show Biz* article called the movie's Friday and Saturday grosses "disappointing" and further criticized the record Thursday box office gross. "If I had to pick a number for all it will do before it starts to drop off, it's around $200 or $210 million," the supposed insider opined. Despite drawing massive crowds and shattering numerous records, the media had finally turned on *The Phantom Menace*. After months of intense interest and enthusiasm, the film never again enjoyed the benefits of objective reporting from most media outlets. The supposed industry insider naïvely told *Mr. Show Biz*:

> Friday should've doubled what they had on Thursday if this picture was working. Thursday was disappointing. But they should have at least come close to doubling that Thursday number on Friday. This picture has no heat—it's over.

Entertainment Weekly quickly became one of the most ardent detractors of the movie and never missed a chance to deride Jar Jar or the film's box office gross. In the June 4, 1999 issue of the magazine, their subtitle read, "*Phantom* is off to a great start. But should it have been greater?" They quoted an unnamed marketing executive at a rival studio who said of the movie, "It won't even beat *Jurassic Park* [$357 million]. It will only get repeat business from young kids and geeks." His bias against *Star Wars* quickly made him look like a fool, so one must lament the fact that he lacked the conviction to leave his name.

Despite negative comments from many industry insiders and entertainment commentators, *The Phantom Menace's* box office voyage had just begun. Exhibitor Relations president Paul Dergarabedian, an independent observer, told the *New York Times*, "Despite expectations that [cited] hugely inflated numbers, the numbers that came in are quite amazing." Sherak firmly stated that the results "absolutely, positively, unequivocally" did not disappoint the studio. He noted, "If we had wanted to set the record we could have released the picture next week," referring to the more lucrative Memorial Day Weekend frame. He added, "This wasn't about records. This picture would have set any early record it wanted to set." The prequel succeeded in annihilating the competition on opening weekend.

The Phantom Menace left little space in the marketplace for other movies during its massive first weekend as it accounted for 58% of total ticket sales. DreamWorks' effort at counter-programming with *The Love Letter* proved entirely futile. The movie grossed just $2.7 million over the three-day weekend, placing fifth at the box office. *The Mummy*, which led the box office the previous weekend, fell 45% to second place with $13.8 million. *The Matrix* dropped 37% to $2.9 million and fourth place in the wake of *The Phantom Menace*, which was the largest drop for the movie since it opened in March and compared unfavorably with the dip of just 23% the prior weekend. Despite appealing to a different core audience, *Never Been Kissed* dropped 30% compared to 17% the week before, earning $1.7 million. Overall, *The Phantom Menace* had a hugely beneficial effect on the box office, boosting ticket sales 50% from the previous weekend and up 54% from the same weekend a year earlier.

After sixteen years of waiting, moviegoers finally could see the first chapter of the *Star Wars Saga*; most people loved it. *Variety* reported that 94% of moviegoers surveyed rated the movie "excellent" or "very good," while 84% said they would definitely recommend the movie to others. Confirming the approval of audiences in North America, online readers of *Entertainment Weekly* gave the movie an A-, which was well above the average critical review. More importantly,

72% of readers said they would most likely see the movie again and 74% said they would recommend it to others. Despite mixed critical reviews, *The Phantom Menace* drew praise from moviegoers everywhere. Positive word of mouth is vital to the success of any movie, so early feedback indicated box office longevity for the first *Star Wars* prequel.

Other audience statistics revealed the demographic breakdown for *The Phantom Menace*. Predictably, males constituted 59% of audiences, which is roughly identical with past *Star Wars* movies. Typically, mothers are more likely to bring children to the movies than fathers, but for *The Phantom Menace*, the reverse proved true (52% versus 48%). The core audience for *Star Wars* movies has always been predominantly male, but the series appeals to all ages and genders.

One organization did not benefit from the results of *The Phantom Menace's* opening weekend, namely online betting site Intertops.com. After four days, *The Lost World* had grossed $92.7 million, while *The Phantom Menace* reached $83.7 million. The company issued no official statements regarding their losses, but a spokesperson for the company said they lost in the six digit numbers. Customers cautious enough to avoid being seduced by the movie's hype won sizeable payoffs for what once seemed like an impossible scenario.

Despite some declarations of a disappointing opening, valid reasons exist for *The Phantom Menace's* inability to top *The Lost World's* opening three-day weekend gross. *The Lost World* played in a considerably larger number of theaters on opening weekend and consequently held more screens. In addition to the larger theater count for *The Lost World*, *The Phantom Menace's* Wednesday opening gave eager moviegoers two days to see the movie before the weekend even started, slightly diluting opening weekend attendance. *The Lost World* opened over the Memorial Day Weekend frame, whereas Fox released *The Phantom Menace* during a non-holiday weekend. Also favoring customers who bet on *The Lost World*, the prequel's first four days included three workdays and only one weekend day. *The Lost World's* first four days included the extended three-day weekend and only one workday, further favoring the dinosaur sequel.

In addition to the differing opening weekend conditions, *The Phantom Menace* actually suffered somewhat from the engulfing media coverage. Stories about thousands of fans waiting in line days before the movie opened appeared in newspapers all around North America, so many families and other moviegoers feared the long lines and sold out showings and decided to avoid theaters on opening weekend. In reality, the media exaggerated the situation in many instances; most theaters could still accommodate moviegoers who arrived at least thirty minutes early. Perhaps most importantly, kids occupied more seats for the PG-rated prequel than the PG-13 rated dinosaur sequel. Because nearly all theaters offer a discount for younger children, *The Phantom Menace* suffered from a greater number of discount admissions. Nevertheless, the inflation in ticket prices between 1997 and 1999 might have offset the slight disadvantage.

Despite a sudden backlash against the movie from major media groups and the absurd reaction to the movie's opening weekend box office, *The Phantom Menace* forced the media and several industry analysts to retract their previous statements. Beginning immediately after opening weekend, *The Phantom Menace* began to convert doubters and impress analysts who once questioned the movie's long-term prospects. While *The Lost World* won the opening weekend battle, *The Phantom Menace* quickly outperformed the dinosaur sequel.

Industry executives focused on $400 million as the benchmark that separates a major blockbuster from a true phenomenon. While *Star Wars, E.T., Jurassic Park, Forrest Gump, The Lion King, Independence Day*, and *Return of the Jedi* had all crossed $300 million at the time, only *Titanic* had grossed more than $400 million at the end of one single release in North American theaters. *The Phantom Menace* quickly rose to challenge the all-time box office titans, defying ardent detractors of Lucas's space saga.

Monday's box office results further proved *The Phantom Menace* would not fade quickly. *Variety's* Thursday headline declared, "B.O. turns 'Menace'-ing." The $10.9 million Monday gross for *The Phantom Menace* was a non-holiday record for the weekday. The massive total nearly doubled *The Lost World's* first weekday gross of $5.7 million, which fell on a Tuesday because of Memorial Day. The Monday gross for *The Phantom Menace* fell only 50% from Sunday, whereas *The Lost World's* Tuesday box office fell 69% from its $18 million holiday Monday. The strong hold for *The Phantom Menace* supported the theory that many moviegoers chose to avoid seeing it on opening weekend because of the long lines.

On Tuesday, *The Phantom Menace* added another $8.2 million to its total. While the gross fell slightly from Monday, the results in many cities where summer vacation had just begun encouraged Fox executives. For instance, the Cinemark Tinseltown in Plano, Texas outside of Dallas sold $18,541 worth of tickets, compared to $10,947 on Monday. The United Artists' Continental in Denver grossed about $16,900 Monday and increased to roughly $18,400 on Tuesday. On Wednesday and Thursday, *The Phantom Menace* added another $7.8 and $7.5 million. After the stunning week at the box office, *Mr. Show Biz* observed, "Midweek box office totals appear to indicate that reports of *The Phantom Menace's* box office demise have been greatly exaggerated."

Box office analysts can often predict a movie's future prospects from its daily grosses and how they relate to each other. For instance, when a movie barely increases its gross from Friday to Saturday, the small increase is interpreted as a sign of minimal long-term prospects. Analysts are often wrong, though, because many movies geared primarily towards a teenage audience experience a minimal increase from Friday to Saturday, yet still perform well for weeks after their release. When a movie experiences more than a 40% decline from Saturday to Sunday, the movie usually is the subject of negative word of mouth and consequently experiences rough declines in subsequent weeks. The conclusions at which analysts arrive from the Saturday to Sunday drop depend largely on the movie and its rating. R-rated, adult movies usually suffer steeper declines than PG-rated, family movies, especially during the summer months when kids are on vacation. For many movies, Sunday is the worst day of the weekend at box offices while Saturday is the best, but the pattern for *The Phantom Menace* differed from the average movie.

The Phantom Menace always enjoyed higher grosses on Sunday than Friday and the movie increased significantly each Saturday from the earlier day. From the small Sunday decline to the massive weekday grosses, analysts had reason to predict a massive holiday weekend for the *Star Wars* prequel. Despite indications of success, few analysts expected such a strong second weekend for the year's most highly anticipated movie. In 1997, *The Lost World* tumbled 53% after its opening weekend and disappeared quickly from theaters. Similarly, 1998's *Godzilla* dropped 59% on its way to a disappointing $136.3 million gross in North America. Many highly anticipated movies draw massive crowds on opening weekend, only to lose their audience as a result of poor word of mouth, but *The Phantom Menace* provided an exception to recent trends.

Entering the weekend with an already impressive gross of $140 million, *The Phantom Menace* grossed an estimated $64.8 million from 3,022 theaters over the four-day holiday weekend. Once again, however, the actual total exceeded the estimates by a significant margin. The final tally revealed a gross of $66.9 million for *The Phantom Menace* during the entire four-day holiday weekend, $51.4 million for the three-day period from Friday through Sunday. The three-day weekend gross represented the largest second weekend in box office history at the time, annihilating the previous record of $38.5 million that the first *Jurassic Park* set in 1993. The surprisingly strong second weekend erased most people's doubts about *The Phantom Menace's* long-term prospects.

The Lost World and *Godzilla* suffered from audience disapproval, but *The Phantom Menace* benefited from excellent word of mouth, which led to a miniscule decline from opening weekend. Paul Dergarabedian said, "Often, you'll see films drop off 40 percent or more [in ticket sales] in their second week, but when we looked at the first three-day weekend of *Phantom* and this past weekend's three days, the drop-off was only about 21 percent." The holiday weekend helped the comparison also because Sunday's box office numbers seemed more like those for a Saturday as a result of the Memorial Day holiday. *The Lost World's* opening weekend exceeded *The Phantom Menace's* by roughly 10%, but the prequel's second weekend gross bested *The Lost World's* by a whopping 51%.

The Phantom Menace averaged $17,009 per theater for the three-day portion of the weekend, which is an unusually high average for a second weekend, indicating many sold out showings. The four-day gross ranked as the second largest Memorial Day Weekend total in history, trailing only *The Lost World*, which is remarkable because the prequel achieved that mark on its second weekend of release. Final numbers gave the movie $13.5 million Friday, $19.3 million Saturday, $18.5 Sunday, and $15.5 Monday, which was the second highest Monday gross behind only *The Lost World*. The impressive second weekend gross pushed *The Phantom Menace* over $200 million in only thirteen days, setting another record. *Independence Day* held the record at 21 days before the *Star Wars* prequel destroyed its mark by an impressive eight-day margin. Previously, *The Phantom Menace* also broke the record of fastest movie to gross $150 million, taking only ten days to eclipse the mark.

Universal's bid to counter-program with Julia Roberts' *Notting Hill* succeeded, unlike DreamWorks' pathetic effort with *The Love Letter*. *Notting Hill* collected $27.7 million, $22.2 million for the weekend's first three days, which was an all-time opening weekend record for a romantic comedy. Sony's *The Thirteenth Floor* did not have the power to compete with the *Star Wars* prequel and opened to a disappointing $4.3 million. For the second consecutive weekend, despite respectable competition from *Notting Hill*, *The Phantom Menace* grossed more than every other movie in the top ten combined. *Star Wars* helped the box office to an 8% increase over the previous Memorial Day Weekend, but still not to 1997's record highs when *The Lost World* reigned supreme.

After two weekends in release, *The Phantom Menace* had amassed $207.1 million. The rapidly increasing box office total made the prequel the highest grossing movie in the month of May. Overall box office revenue for May increased nearly 25% from the same month in 1998, largely on the strength of *The Phantom Menace*, but *The Mummy* aided considerably as well.

During the winter months of the year, the weekend box office accounts for nearly all of weekly ticket sales. Most smaller theaters even reduce the number of daily weekday showings because attendance usually drops during the workweek. As summer approaches, however, the weekend to week ratio decreases, meaning that the workweek compares more favorably to the weekend, which includes Friday for box office purposes. Despite the narrower gap in the summer months, Monday through Thursday grosses are still well below the Friday through Sunday totals.

PG-rated movies have an edge over PG-13 and R-rated films, largely because they have a higher grossing potential during the week, regardless of the season. Because schools are not in session during the summer, PG-rated movies such as *The Phantom Menace* enjoy a considerable advantage over movies that adults predominantly attend. After Memorial Day Weekend, the prequel began to earn an increasingly higher percentage of its weekly total from the Monday through Thursday period of each week.

Following the successful Memorial Day weekend gross, *The Phantom Menace* collected $5.5 million on Tuesday, $5.3 million Wednesday, and $5 million Thursday before its third straight weekend at the top of the box office charts. The prequel grossed another $32.9 million on its third weekend, although estimates once again proved incorrect and the weekend total exceeded the predicted $32.2 million. The movie grossed $8.3 million Friday, $13.9 million Saturday, and $10.6 million Sunday to bring its cumulative gross to $255.8 million after less than three full weeks in theaters. For the weekend, *The Phantom Menace* averaged $10,877 per location.

On Sunday, June 6, *The Phantom Menace* eclipsed $250 million on its 19th day of release, the fastest ever ascent to that mark. The *Star Wars* prequel annihilated the previous record of 36 days, which *Titanic* set in 1998, taking nearly double as long. *The Phantom Menace* achieved a massive gross in only a few days, but it also maintained momentum, which allowed it to crush summer blockbusters from the preceding decade.

Titanic lost one record, but held onto another, if only barely. *The Phantom Menace* missed *Titanic's* record third weekend gross by only about $400,000, but still had to settle with second place. The prequel experienced a rather steep decline from its record highs one week earlier, but the weekend following Memorial Day is typically slow at the box office.

The 36% decline did not startle industry observers, who realized the box office always falls slightly after what is usually one of the highest grossing weekends of the year. Nevertheless, *Entertainment Weekly's* headline questioned, "Dwindling Force?" A gross above $30 million is laudable for almost any movie on opening weekend, but *The Phantom Menace* grossed $32.9 million on its third weekend of release, nearly breaking a record. For a movie that cast aside numerous box office records during only a few weeks in theaters, *The Phantom Menace* received an unacceptable level of negative press about its performance. Regardless of the slightly larger percentage decline, *The Phantom Menace* never again experienced a decline greater than the third weekend drop of 36% while in the weekly box office top ten.

No film provided serious competition for *The Phantom Menace* during its third weekend. *Instinct*, starring Cuba Gooding Jr. and Anthony Hopkins, grossed a rather disappointing $10.4 million in third place, but no other new movie cracked the top ten at the box office. *Notting Hill* remained in second place with $15 million. A sizeable number of onlookers reasoned that because *The Phantom Menace* fell sharply while enjoying relatively minor competition, it would suffer greatly the following weekend when *Austin Powers 2: The Spy Who Shagged Me* entered theaters. Their predictions never materialized, however, and a headline from *E! Online* adequately summarized the situation: "'Phantom Menace' Unstoppable."

In less than three weeks of release, *The Phantom Menace* boosted its distributor above its competitors as Fox seized the market share lead for the first time since 1991. Through Sunday, June 6, movies released under the Fox banner had grossed $457.9 million, nearly $45 million more than the nearest competing studio, Warner Brothers. At the time, Fox movies claimed 17% of total ticket sales for the year. The studio last enjoyed the market share lead in February 1991 because of holiday hits such as *Home Alone* and *Edward Scissorhands*. The summer 1999 triumph occurred almost entirely as a result of *The Phantom Menace's* success, which accounted for almost 56% of Fox's total box office gross. The studio last claimed the annual market share crown in 1983, when *Return of the Jedi* dominated box offices in North America. *The Phantom Menace* also helped the box office cut into 1998's lead over 1999. Through the weekend ending June 6, the 1999 box office lagged only about one percent behind the record pace set in 1998, but the following weeks entirely erased the deficit as the summer box office gross soared to new record highs.

The films that premiered during the first three weeks of *The Phantom Menace's* release provided no serious threat, although the competition during the rest of the summer was some of the most formidable in history. *Austin Powers 2* opened in 3,312 theaters, a record at the time, and set numerous box office gross records, easily snatching first place from *The Phantom Menace*. *Austin Powers 2* grossed an astonishing $54.9 million over its opening weekend, which is more than the first *Austin Powers* (1997) made in its entire release. The debut ranked third all-time, just behind *The Phantom Menace*, which allowed the Mike Meyers sequel to claim the highest grossing opening weekend for a comedy and the highest grossing weekend ever recorded in June at the time.

Despite the force that *Austin Powers 2* displayed in its debut, *The Phantom Menace* held up well amidst the competition, dropping only 22.1% to $25.6 million for an average of $8,476 per theater. The strong hold surprised most box office analysts, who never expected *Austin Powers 2* to open with more than $50 million, but figured *The Phantom Menace* would lose a significant portion of its audience because of the competition. Dergarabedian said, "It's been holding its own really well, but July is going to be a very crowded month." *Austin Powers 2* only began the onslaught of movies that dominated the summer movie marketplace.

The impressive fourth weekend catapulted *The Phantom Menace* into the top ten highest grossing movies of all-time. During the weekend, *The Phantom Menace* became the ninth highest grossing movie in North American box office history, pushing *Home Alone* to eleventh place and passing one of its predecessors, *The Empire Strikes Back*. The *Star Wars* prequel entered the top ten in record pace. At the time, *Star Wars* movies accounted for four of the top ten highest grossing movies of all-time at the North American box office. After four weekends, *The Phantom Menace's* total reached $297 million.

On Tuesday, June 15, its 28th day in theaters, *The Phantom Menace* crossed the $300 million mark. The prequel became only the ninth blockbuster ever to gross $300 million, accomplishing the feat far faster than any movie in history. In a lopsided victory, *The Phantom Menace* shattered the previous speed record of 44 days that *Titanic* set just more than a year earlier.

The Phantom Menace's fifth weekend fell on one of the most competitive of the year, when *Tarzan* debuted in first place with $34.2 million, which was the second highest opening weekend gross ever for an animated film. *Austin Powers 2* fell 43% to second place with $31.4 million. The two impressive grosses set a box office record. Never in history had two movies grossed more than $30 million during the same non-holiday weekend. In addition to *Tarzan's* impressive debut, John Travolta's *The General's Daughter* opened with $22.3 million, helping to set two more records: 1) No movie in third place had ever grossed as much, and 2) The weekend saw three movies collect in excess of $20 million during the same three-day period for the first time in history.

Despite direct competition from *Tarzan* for young audiences, and from *Austin Powers 2* for teenage audiences, *The Phantom Menace* displayed remarkable stamina. In fourth place, the prequel grossed $18.9 million, which Fox initially underestimated by $1.1 million. The prequel averaged $6,247 per theater for the weekend and its final gross represented a decline of only 26.4%, which is excellent for any weekend, but especially noteworthy because of the heavy competition. "It has lived up to expectations and hasn't let us down," Sherak said. Showbizdata.com commented, "*Star Wars: Episode 1: The Phantom Menace* continued to amaze experts over the past weekend as it continued to show strength at the box office." The movie's total had soared to $328 million, with $400 million still within reach. At the time, the prequel's total stood 39% above *Titanic's* at the same point in its release.

On Friday, June 18, the 1999 box office surpassed the record pace set in 1998. After the massive weekend led by *Tarzan*, the 1999 box office total reached $3.05 billion, 1.2% greater than the comparable total one year earlier. Blockbuster hits such as *The Matrix*, *The Mummy*, *The Phantom Menace*, and *Austin Powers 2* positioned the 1999 box office to set a new all-time record gross. While the start of the summer was a lucrative several weeks at the box office, a string of surprise hits and star vehicles continued to push the year ahead of 1998's record pace.

Adam Sandler's comedy, *Big Daddy*, easily defeated *Tarzan* on the weekend beginning June 25. The movie grossed a mammoth $41.5 million, which was the second largest opening weekend for a comedy, just behind *Austin Powers 2*. *Tarzan* displayed impressive staying power and grossed $24 million in its second weekend, down less than 30% from its opening weekend total. *Austin Powers 2* fell 41.6% to $18.3 million, bringing its total to $150.6 million. *The Generals Daughter* held up well, despite receiving unfavorable reviews, dropping to $15.2 million for its second weekend.

After six weekends, *The Phantom Menace* remained in the top five highest grossing movies at the weekend box office, taking in another $14.1 million, an average of $4,514 from 3,126 theaters, which is the highest number of locations in which the movie played during its entire theatrical release. The prequel dropped only 25.2% from the previous weekend, bringing its total to $351.6 million. The total gross moved it into fifth place on the all-time box office chart, ahead of *Forrest Gump* at $329 million and just behind *Jurassic Park* at $357 million. Even jaded analysts had to concede that *The Phantom Menace* would end with a gross upwards of $400 million.

On Sunday, its 40th day of release, *The Phantom Menace* passed $350 million, setting another speed record. *Titanic* held the previous mark, achieving the same gross in 58 days. The *Star Wars* prequel set a speed record for every $50 million increment from $100 million to $350 million, six separate records. Nevertheless, the next $50 million required considerably more time, so *Titanic* finally began to catch *The Phantom Menace's* record pace.

At the June box office, *The Phantom Menace* ranked second, barely behind *Austin Powers 2*, which claimed the top spot for the month. The prequel grossed $150.7 million during the month, $357.8 million total, but *Austin Powers 2* collected $157.8 million in twenty days of release. Nevertheless, the prequel outperformed the comedy in every succeeding month in which both movies played every day, despite opening more than three weeks earlier than *Austin Powers 2*.

During the week preceding the July Fourth holiday weekend, *The Phantom Menace* displayed signs of phenomenal staying power. For instance, on Monday, June 28, the movie grossed $2.11 million, down only 11% from the $2.37 million it recorded exactly one week earlier. On Tuesday, June 29, the $2.24 million gross represented a decline of only 7% from the prior Tuesday gross of $2.42 million. The low mid-week declines seemed to indicate that the weekend drop would be the best ever, but an unfortunate loss of theaters ruined the movie's momentum.

On Friday, July 2, *The Phantom Menace* ceased playing in 495 theaters, which was nearly 16% of its previous total, bringing the weekend theater count to 2,631. Throughout the movie's box office release up until July Fourth Weekend, the Friday gross typically increased more than 50% from Thursday's figures. The loss of theaters immediately impacted ticket sales, resulting in only a 37% increase from Thursday to Friday at the box office.

For the three-day portion of the weekend, *The Phantom Menace* collected $9.5 million and $13.3 million for all four days of the holiday weekend. The movie fell 33% during the three-day weekend for an average of $3,615 per theater. As a movie begins to lose theaters, gauging its percentage decline per theater is useful in determining its staying power, as well as finding the overall decline. On its seventh weekend, *The Phantom Menace's* average gross per theater dropped only 20%. The prequel ranked sixth for the weekend and raised its total to $373.2 million, 21% above *Titanic*, which had amassed $308.1 million at the same point in its release.

Playing in 3,342 theaters, *Wild Wild West* grossed $36.4 million during the four-day weekend. The debut for Will Smith's critically panned movie did not impress any analysts, but it collected enough to claim first place for the weekend. *Big Daddy* dropped considerably to $26.8 million, but *Tarzan* remained popular and grossed an additional $19.3 million. *South Park* opened in fourth place with $14.8 million, barely ahead of *The General's Daughter* with $14.2 million.

The weekend was especially competitive as seven movies grossed more than $10 million from Friday through Monday. After only four weekends, *Austin Powers 2* fell behind *The Phantom Menace*. Despite grossing more than double as much as the prequel on its first weekend, excellent staying power for *The Phantom Menace* allowed it to easily outlast the high grossing comedy. *Austin Powers 2* even enjoyed a larger theater count of 3,091, but still only grossed $12.1 for the four-day period.

On its eighth weekend in release, *The Phantom Menace* ranked seventh, but dropped only 22% for $7.5 million, an average of $3,061 per theater. The small depreciation came despite the loss of another 184 theaters. *Titanic* gained further ground on the prequel, which now ran only 14% ahead of the disaster movie. The box office atypically provided somewhat weak competition for the weekend beginning Friday, July 9.

American Pie debuted in first place with $18.7 million, which meant no movie grossed more than $20 million, a rarity for the 1999 summer box office. *Wild Wild West* fell sharply in its second weekend compared to the other movies in the top ten, although its $16.8 million ranked second. *Big Daddy* showed impressive strength in third place, dropping only 20% to $16 million. *Tarzan* continued its successful run, adding another $10.8 million, as did *The General's Daughter*, collecting $7.9 million during its fourth weekend. *Arlington Road* grossed $7.5 million for its opening weekend, placing it sixth. *South Park* opened above *The Phantom Menace* just one week earlier, although it fell below the prequel into eighth place.

Stanley Kubrick's *Eyes Wide Shut* dominated theaters for the weekend beginning July 16, grossing $21.7 million. *American Pie* held second place with $13.6 million. *Lake Placid*, a competing Fox release, grossed $11 million during its opening frame, while *Big Daddy* added another $10.4 million. *Wild Wild West* continued its downward spiral, grossing only $10.1 million. *The Wood* grossed $8.5 million in its opening weekend and *Tarzan* placed seventh with $7.5 million, just ahead of *The Phantom Menace*.

After nine weekends in release, *The Phantom Menace* ranked eighth with $5.6 million, down 24.6%, which was impressive considering that 593 additional theaters chose to stop playing the box office titan. The movie's per theater average of $3,053 fell less than 1% from the previous weekend's average of $3,061. The negligible decline in average theater attendance indicates the movie might have grossed considerably more if it had played in the same number of theaters as the previous weekend, but heavy competition forced theaters to clear space for new releases. Even though three new movies debuted above *The Phantom Menace* on the box office chart, the prequel managed to pass both *The General's Daughter* and *Arlington Road*, which helped it lose only one position on the weekend rankings. Many analysts expected the prequel to drop from the top ten during its tenth weekend, but they once again underestimated the power of the Force.

After grossing $395.2 million, *The Phantom Menace* had established a string of 61 consecutive days grossing at least $1 million per day. Typically, the movie ranked higher during the weekdays than on weekend days. Because many younger viewers attended *The Phantom Menace*, mid-week numbers consistently placed the movie higher on the top ten charts than it had ranked during the weekend. *The Phantom Menace* typically performed weakest on Fridays compared to competing movies.

On the weekend beginning July 23, *The Haunting*, starring Liam Neeson, grossed $33.4 million in first place and *Inspector Gadget* opened strong with $21.9 million in second place. *American Pie* grossed another $10.1 million, but *Eyes Wide Shut* dropped drastically to slightly less than $10.1 million in fourth place. *Big Daddy* collected $6 million, which represented a moderate decline from the previous weekend. *Lake Placid* tumbled to $5.6 million and *Wild Wild West* fell significantly to $5.3 million. *Tarzan* grossed $4.9 million and *The Wood* finished just ahead of *The Phantom Menace* with $4.8 million.

The prequel remained in the top ten on its tenth weekend, adding $4.2 million in 1,614 theaters, down 236 from the prior week. The movie's weekend gross declined 25.7%, but the film enjoyed a drop of less than 15% in attendance per theater. The weekend gross pushed *The Phantom Menace* past the final major benchmark that separates blockbuster from phenomenon.

On Saturday, July 24, after 67 days of release, *The Phantom Menace* eclipsed $400 million at the North American box office. Unfortunately, *The Phantom Menace* failed to steal the record from *Titanic*, which broke the mark in 66 days. Nevertheless, the prequel became the third movie in history to cross the $400 million barrier, and only the second film to do so in one single theatrical release; the original *Star Wars* took six releases spread over twenty years.

The gigantic box office total vaulted *The Phantom Menace* past *E.T.'s* $399.8 million total and made the first prequel the all-time highest grossing summer movie after one release, as well as the third highest grossing movie of all-time in North America. Dergarabedian said, "At first people thought it would [only] start out big…but the film has continued to do well and has continued to play." He added, "It's just one of those perfect summer movies. There's always a place for it in the plans of a lot of moviegoers."

The Phantom Menace required only five days to earn its first $100 million, eight days for the next $100 million, then fifteen more days to reach $300 million. Its voyage from $300 million to $400 million took 39 days, which is still impressive considering the movie had already played in theaters for more than a month.

The all-time third place ranking for the prequel also kept an important *Star Wars* box office tradition alive because every previous movie in the saga had entered the top three highest grossing movies of all-time in North America on its first release to theaters. The first movie, *A New Hope*, became the top grosser, while *The Empire Strikes Back* reached second place three years later, just behind its predecessor. Finally, *Return of the Jedi* ranked third all-time behind *E.T.* and *A New Hope* after its release to theaters in 1983.

Variety headlined, "'Menace' cume boffo" in an article praising the movie's box office success. Sherak said, "This has been an incredible ride for all of us here at Fox." He added, "We have been privileged to be a part of the continuing *Star Wars* phenomenon." Despite the fitting opportunity to marvel at *The Phantom Menace's* box office run, the movie still enjoyed many more months in theaters.

On its eleventh weekend, *The Phantom Menace* gained a rank by moving up to ninth place, taking in an additional $3.4 million, which represented a decline of only 18.5% after actually increasing its theater count by 14 to 1,628. The decline was the lowest of its entire release, which allowed *The Phantom Menace* to pass four movies, all of which opened above it on the box office charts just weeks earlier. The prequel passed *Tarzan*, *The Wood*, *Lake Placid*, and *Wild Wild West* on the same weekend.

Despite overtaking four movies, heavy competition from three new releases prevented the prequel from gaining more than one spot on its final weekend in the top ten. *Runaway Bride*, the second movie starring Julia Roberts to compete with *The Phantom Menace*, opened strong with $35.1 million. The most unbelievable success story of the weekend, however, belonged to *The Blair Witch Project*. Produced for less than $100,000, it grossed $29.2 million in only 1,101 theaters for an amazing average of $26,528 per venue. *Deep Blue Sea*, starring Samuel L. Jackson, grossed $19.1 million and placed third. The competition destroyed *The Haunting* as it fell 54% to $15.3 million. *Inspector Gadget* declined moderately to $14.1 million, as did *American Pie*, which added another $6.8 million.

Audiences shunned *Eyes Wide Shut*, which fell 57% to $4.3 million. The massive declines each weekend for the Kubrick film assured *The Phantom Menace* an opportunity to pass the movie in daily box office receipts within only a few weeks of its release. *Big Daddy*, while enjoying a successful run at the box office, only barely defeated the prequel with $3.6 million. The gap between the two movies had narrowed considerably since *Big Daddy* opened in June.

During July 1999, moviegoers spent $917.3 million at the box office, an all-time record and a 13% increase from the same month in 1998. Overall ticket sales totaled 182.7 million, which was an increase of about 1% from 1994's record. For the month, *The Phantom Menace* grossed $49.8 million and ranked seventh behind *Wild Wild West* at number one, followed by *Big Daddy*, *American Pie*, *Tarzan*, *The Haunting*, and *Eyes Wide Shut*.

The weekend beginning on Friday, August 8 introduced too many new movies into the marketplace for *The Phantom Menace* to remain in the top ten. In addition to falling from the top ten, the movie lost another 429 theaters, but its average gross barely dropped. The trend continued throughout August as the movie began to lose most of its theaters, but continued to draw roughly the same number of patrons per theater. *The Phantom Menace* played in only 497 theaters by the end of August, but added another $12.1 million for the final summer month, bringing its total to $419.6 million.

A new movie occupied the number one spot nearly every week during the summer of 1999, which helps explain the competitiveness of the season. Although only 45 movies opened, compared to 49 the previous year, they grossed much more on average than films from the previous year, propelling the summer box office to a new record. During the season, moviegoers spent a total of almost $3 billion on films in theatrical release, which amounted to roughly 610 million admissions. Although the box office in 1999 ran somewhat behind the previous year before the beginning of summer, numerous blockbusters quickly erased the deficit.

During the summer, eleven movies crossed the $100 million mark, setting a new record. The box office gross eclipsed the previous record by nearly 20% and admissions also increased in the double-digit numbers from the previous year. *The Phantom Menace* received credit for bringing moviegoers to theaters and convincing them to return each week. Chuck Viane, President of Distribution for Buena Vista said, "Trailers in front of *Star Wars* at the beginning of the summer really encouraged movie fans to come back over and over again once they saw the exciting lineup of films making their way to theaters." Dergarabedian agreed, "You had a lot of people seeing trailers and posters and getting revved up for the summer."

The success of *The Phantom Menace* nearly made Twentieth Century Fox the top distributor during the summer season, although Buena Vista barely took the edge on the last weekend of the month. Besides the prequel, Fox movies failed to generate much attention at the box office, making the *Star Wars* film the only real hit for the studio. *The Phantom Menace* easily took the crown as the summer's top grossing movie.

Ticket prices also increased markedly before the summer season, presumably in anticipation of *The Phantom Menace*, which theaters expected to become one of the top box office performers of all-time. Box office tracking firm Exhibitor Relations (ER) reported that the national average ticket price increased to $5.08 for 1999 compared to $4.75 for the year earlier. The average ticket price can be somewhat misleading, however, because PG-rated movies will inevitably have more discounted children's admissions than R-rated films. ER estimates total ticket sales for each movie based on its gross and the average ticket price during the year of its release. Their formula means that PG-rated movies might have higher ticket sales than estimated, while R-rated movies might have fewer. Although *The Phantom Menace* led the record summer and earned most of its money during the season, it continued to play in theaters throughout the fall.

September is typically a poor month for box office revenue, so successful late summer movies continue to play in major theaters. *The Phantom Menace* began a new phase of release in discount theaters nationwide, while simultaneously playing in many of the larger first-run theaters. By the end of September, it had increased from 497 theaters to 766 and added another $5 million, bringing its total to $424.7 million. The decline in grosses from August to September was the smallest percentage monthly decline in its entire run, which is understandable because the movie gained theaters and began experiencing smaller weekly declines.

Discount theaters are often referred to as either "second-run theaters" or "dollar theaters," although many of them charge significantly more than a dollar per ticket. The discount theaters allow people to see a movie that has already played in most major theaters. Because the discount theaters often have poor sound systems and inadequate facilities in general, admission prices are usually much cheaper than those at a first-run theater. They also allowed many fans to see the movie again and again for several additional months.

During both August and September, *The Phantom Menace* remained among the top twenty highest grossing movies every weekend. It also enjoyed two more weekends on the chart during the month of October, before finally exiting after spending 22 consecutive weekends in the top twenty, which is a rare accomplishment. The prequel spent exactly double as many weekends in the top twenty as it did in the more publicized top ten. For the month of October, the movie grossed another $2.7 million, showing another low decline from the previous month. The theater count during October fell to 331 by the end of the month as the movie's first theatrical release was nearing an end.

On November 4, 1999, *The Phantom Menace* completed its first release in North American theaters, having grossed an astonishing $427.7 million in 170 days of release, or nearly one half of a year in theaters. Several non-discount theaters nearly played the movie for every single week of its release. After only six months in theaters, *The Phantom Menace* sold just more than 84 million tickets, which is only 15% less than *A New Hope's* 99.2 million tickets in 1977. No summer movie had sold as many tickets as *The Phantom Menace* since *E.T.* became the highest grossing movie of all-time in 1982.

The Phantom Menace set several additional noteworthy records. First, no sequel or prequel in history has ever sold as many tickets in only one theatrical release, so the prequel is also the highest grossing fourth part in a movie series, more than doubling the nearest rivals, none of which are among the top 50 highest grossing movies of all-time. *The Phantom Menace* finished its release as the third highest grossing movie ever, but many people believe inflation is the primary reason for the movie's triumph over the two *Star Wars* sequels, *The Empire Strikes Back* and *Return of the Jedi*. Their assumptions are incorrect, however, as *The Phantom Menace* significantly outsold both of the sequels when comparing just the ticket sales during the first release for each movie.

In addition to outperforming the previous *Star Wars* sequels, *The Phantom Menace* displayed better staying power than almost every summer movie. Although many movies opened above it during the summer and fall, *The Phantom Menace* eventually passed most of the less durable titles in much the same way as it defeated *Austin Powers 2* in July.

Movies that opened above the *Star Wars* prequel, but eventually fell below it in daily grosses, include:

American Pie	*Lake Placid*
Arlington Road	*Mickey Blue Eyes*
Austin Powers 2: The Spy Who Shagged Me	*Mystery Men*
Big Daddy	*Runaway Bride*
The Blair Witch Project	*South Park*
Bowfinger	*Tarzan*
Brokedown Palace	*Teaching Mrs. Tingle*
Deep Blue Sea	*The Thirteenth Warrior*
Eyes Wide Shut	*The Thomas Crown Affair* (remake)
The General's Daughter	*Universal Soldier II: The Return*
The Haunting	*Wild Wild West*
Iron Giant	*The Wood*

Several methods exist to measure a movie's staying power. The easiest, rough assessment just looks at how many weeks it remains in theaters, but the simplicity of counting weeks in theaters fails to portray a movie's staying power as accurately and quantifiably as other methods. Weekly decline percentage is an effective indicator of staying power while a movie is still in theaters, but an even more reliable system exists for determining the staying power of movies that have concluded their theatrical releases. By dividing a movie's gross during the first three days of its first weekend by its entire cumulative box office total, analysts can determine exactly how well each movie withstood its competition.

As a general rule, an average movie makes 25% of its total money on the Friday through Sunday portion of just its opening weekend. For instance, analysts can expect a movie that opened with $25 million to gross at least $100 million if it displays average staying power. A movie that makes only 20% of its total gross on its first weekend is one that held up well in the weeks following its release, which indicates mostly positive word of mouth. A movie that does not gross more than three times its opening weekend box office sum likely faded quickly from theaters and failed to appeal to audiences, or at least failed to attract them. A small percentage of movies gross well more than five times their opening weekend total, which indicates very favorable word of mouth.

A movie that amasses roughly 85% of its total outside of its first weekend is one that displayed remarkable staying power. Box office analysts and researchers must draw comparisons between movies regarding staying power only when the movies experienced relatively similar openings. For instance, a movie that grosses only $1 million on opening weekend at least has some chance of making 100 times its first weekend gross, but a movie opening at even $15 million has absolutely no chance of accomplishing the same feat. In other words, the more people who see a movie during its opening weekend, the fewer people who will be available to see it in subsequent weeks. Therefore, comparing *The Phantom Menace* to other blockbusters that opened similarly is appropriate and helps underscore its remarkable staying power.

The Phantom Menace earned about 15.15% of its total gross on its first weekend, which fell on May 21 through May 23. The statistic is impressive when compared to many past blockbusters with similarly large openings because most of them displayed average to below average staying power. Movies opening to impressive crowds or displaying great staying power are fairly common at the box office, but films that open to large crowds *and* display excellent staying power, such as *The Phantom Menace*, are extremely rare.

The Lost World earned more than 31% of its entire gross from just the first three days of its release, which demonstrates the importance of strong staying power. Although the movie outperformed *The Phantom Menace* on its first weekend, it grossed barely more than half of what the *Star Wars* prequel made over the course of its entire release. *Mission: Impossible 2* (2000) grossed $57.85 million on opening weekend, which was roughly 27% of its total gross, while *Austin Powers 2* opened with a similar $57.44 million that represents nearly 28% of its entire gross. *Toy Story 2* (1999) earned more than 23% of its box office total from its massive $57.38 million opening weekend. *Mission: Impossible* (1996) earned $45.4 million for its opening weekend, which was more than 25% of its overall gross while *Godzilla* collected $44.05 million during its opening weekend, an appalling 32% of its cumulative gross.

In the staying power competition, *The Phantom Menace* annihilated almost every other major blockbuster that had a similarly large opening weekend gross, although several movies had performed just as well or better. For instance, *Independence Day* grossed $50.23 million during its opening weekend, which accounted for just more than 16% of its total. *Batman* grossed $42.71 million during its first weekend, which was almost exactly 17% of its total at the box office. *Jurassic Park* slightly bested *The Phantom Menace*, having grossed $50.16 million opening weekend, representing only 14% of its cumulative box office total.

A small number of displeased moviegoers continue to argue that *The Phantom Menace* achieved its box office gross because of hype and the *Star Wars* name alone, but their argument is completely invalid. *Batman* is a hugely popular franchise, but its favor with audiences did not prevent negative word of mouth from ruining *Batman and Robin's* potential at the box office. *Godzilla* enjoyed far more marketing and studio hype than the *Star Wars* prequel, but negative word of mouth similarly destroyed its longevity. *The Lost World* had the benefit of being the sequel to the highest grossing movie in worldwide box office history at the time of its release, but its predecessor's status did not prevent the movie from eroding quickly at the box office. If *The Phantom Menace* had displeased a significant percentage of audiences, it could never have climbed the ranks of the box office elite.

There are many reasons why *The Phantom Menace* did not beat *Titanic* and become the highest grossing movie of all-time. Hurting the prequel's chances, summer 1999 was one of the most competitive seasons in history. Beginning with *Austin Powers 2*, a new movie ruled the box office every week for nine consecutive weeks. Each film usually opened strong in thousands of theaters nationwide. The competing movies provided far too much competition for *The Phantom Menace* to overcome. Multiplexes could not accommodate the wealth of movies in the marketplace.

Titanic enjoyed nearly no competition during its entire reign at number one. During its first fifteen weeks at the box office, another movie grossed over $20 million on only two weekends. During the first weekend in which *Titanic* played, *Tomorrow Never Dies* opened with $25.1 million and it also made $20.5 million on its second weekend. *Lost in Space*, an April release, became the next movie to gross more than $20 million for a weekend, which consequently ended *Titanic's* fifteen week reign as America's most popular movie. The competition up until *Titanic's* supremacy ended proved incredibly weak; many times no movie made even $10 million against *Titanic* in the same weekend, let alone $20 million.

The Phantom Menace faced exponentially greater competition. During its first fifteen weeks at the box office, one movie recorded over a $50 million gross at the weekend box office, another one collected greater than $40 million, and four movies managed to gross more than $30 million during several summer weekends. The box office witnessed an astounding twenty occurrences of a movie grossing at least $20 million during the first fifteen weeks of *The Phantom Menace's* release. The number of $20 million weekend grosses within fifteen weeks of *The Phantom Menace's* release exceeded *Titanic's* by tenfold. James Cameron's disaster epic sailed through a weak three months at the box office with relative ease, allowing it to claim the title of highest grossing movie ever.

The heavy competition for *The Phantom Menace*, combined with weak competition for *Titanic*, meant that most theaters played the romance epic far longer than they played the prequel. After six weekends, *The Phantom Menace* had not suffered any loss of theaters, but after ten weekends, it played in just more than half the theaters it once occupied. *Titanic*, however, increased its theater count weekly until it played in more than 3,000 theaters. It only began to lose theaters in mid-April, after nearly four months in release. The movie enjoyed 25 weeks playing in at least 1,000 locations, compared to twelve weeks for *The Phantom Menace*.

For a movie to continue to enjoy impressive grosses every week, it must occupy a large number of theaters. On the weekend of April 10-12, 1997, *Titanic* averaged $2,621 from 3,265 theaters. On *The Phantom Menace's* tenth weekend, it averaged $2,600, but played in only 1,614 theaters, less than half the number *Titanic* occupied while drawing roughly the same number of people per showing. The less competitive winter season allowed *Titanic* to play in more than three thousand theaters even when its average gross per theater had fallen considerably. When *The Phantom Menace's* per theater average fell, its theater count also dropped significantly and the prequel experienced early elimination from many screens. Theaters held *Titanic* even while it declined because few other movies provided competition for space in their auditoriums.

Theater chains benefited from *Titanic's* success, although its strong weekly grosses could not make up for a weak movie slate. Most major exhibitors reported a decline in earnings or flat earnings during the first quarter of 1998, despite *Titanic's* presence. For instance, the biggest exhibitor at the time, Carmike Cinemas, reported a 15% decline in earnings from the same quarter in 1997. Major theater chain AMC reported nearly no profits for the quarter. Alison Sachs, an analyst from Lehman Brothers, blamed the declines on the quality of the movies, which "aside from *Titanic* has been weak and attendance per screen will likely be lower than last year." Doug Stone, AMC's senior vice president for national film settlements, verified that movies did not perform as well as the same quarter in 1997 for the theater chain.

The *Star Wars* movies possess a massive audience because they potentially appeal to all ages and both genders. Nevertheless, because *The Phantom Menace* was the fourth *Star Wars* movie released, moviegoers who did not enjoy the other movies in the saga already had a bias against it, regardless of whether they knew much about the film. Contrarily, millions of fans awaited its release and supported the movie throughout its box office run, helping to propel it into the box office elite.

The rivalry between Cameron's romance epic and Lucas's prequel is somewhat absurd. Comparing *Titanic* to the first *Star Wars* movie is more logical. *Star Wars: Episode IV—A New Hope* has sold far more tickets than the disaster epic, ranking as the second most viewed movie in theaters, behind only *Gone With the Wind*. *The Phantom Menace* had the ability to compete with *Titanic*, which is impressive given that no sequel or prequel has ever become the highest grossing movie.

Every movie in the *Star Wars* series has performed very well at the box office, which is a remarkable achievement given the first film's phenomenal success and the usual declining returns of sequels. *The Phantom Menace* met analysts' realistic expectations at the box office and even performed better than two of its predecessors. Not only did every movie in the saga become an instant blockbuster, but each episode became an individual phenomenon. After 1999 ended, *The Phantom Menace* remained the year's highest grossing movie, easily defeating the nearest movie, *The Sixth Sense*, which grossed $293.5 million over the course of its entire release. Each of the first three *Star Wars* movies also claimed first place at the box office during their respective years of release.

Fox could not convert the prequel's success into a market share win for the year. The studio released sixteen movies in 1999, including *The Phantom Menace*, but the prequel grossed more than the other fifteen movies combined. Fox only received a modest distribution fee for the movie, therefore industry observers viewed the studio's year as disappointing. In 1983, *Return of the Jedi* helped the studio rank first for the year, but not even the power of a new *Star Wars* movie could compensate for a weak slate of movies. Fox ranked fifth for the year, behind Buena Vista in first place, followed by Warner Brothers, Universal, and Paramount.

The box office's total gross for 1999 rose to $7.448 billion, an increase of 7.2% from the previous year. Although the gross represented a new record, it occurred only as a result of inflated ticket prices; actual admissions decreased 1% to 1.465 billion. *The Phantom Menace* accounted for just less than 6% of the ticket sales during the entire year, which is impressive for a single movie in a crowded marketplace.

Overcoming mixed reviews, a late backlash, and unprecedented box office competition, *The Phantom Menace* continued the financial success of the *Star Wars Saga*. Despite the pessimistic predictions of many analysts, *The Phantom Menace* proved its doubters wrong and smashed countless box office records on its voyage to becoming one of the most popular movies of all-time. The success also transferred into most other facets of the movie's release, including the international box offices.

The highly anticipated prequel drew tens of millions of moviegoers to theaters in North America, but it also performed well in countries around the world. Despite the impressive gross for the film in the United States and Canada, it made even more from theaters in foreign countries. The box office triumph for

The Phantom Menace began in North America, but the domestic release only represented the start of a long and successful performance around the world.

International Box Office

The Phantom Menace enjoyed a successful theatrical release in North America, but it also performed similarly well in many countries around the world. In countries such as Japan, the United Kingdom, and Australia, audiences enjoyed the movie just as much as fans in the United States and Canada. Nevertheless, in countries where *Star Wars* is not a cultural phenomenon, *The Phantom Menace* performed similar to other major blockbusters, but did not achieve phenomenal grosses. Overall, the prequel was the highest grossing movie of the year in many countries and set new opening weekend records in almost every territory around the world, despite not setting the record in North America.

Worldwide, *A New Hope* has grossed $783.6 million, *The Empire Strikes Back* $533.8 million, and *Return of the Jedi* $470.2 million. Worldwide ticket sales are impossible to determine because not all countries track their yearly average ticket prices or direct sales. International audiences mostly embraced *A New Hope* on its release decades ago, although it never sparked as much interest in many countries as it did in North America.

When *A New Hope* opened worldwide in 1977, it performed well in many countries, but other territories failed to understand its appeal. Almost 63% of its total box office gross came from North America. Theater chains have continued expanding in countries all over the world, which means movies commonly gross as much as two-thirds of their worldwide total from outside of North America. Although *A New Hope* performed well worldwide, *The Phantom Menace* provided a financial boost to troubled markets and theaters everywhere.

While theaters in the United States and Canada needed *The Phantom Menace's* success to boost the 1999 box office revenue, international theater chains and film industries also relied on the prequel's success. Similar to North American theaters, box offices worldwide suffered from the lack of any major movie such as *Titanic*, which powered ticket sales in the first half of 1998.

In the United Kingdom, ticket sales declined 2.7% in 1998 from the previous year, despite the *Titanic* boost and an increase in multiplexes. Industry observers expected *The Phantom Menace* and other high profile movies to bolster ticket sales in 1999. Despite the hopes of exhibitors in England, ticket sales continued their slump through the first half of 1999 through June, when *The Phantom Menace* opened. Odeon, a theater chain based in the United Kingdom, reported a 1.5% decline in ticket sales for the first half of the year, though the chain noted that when *The Phantom Menace* opened, the figures already began to improve.

Australian-based exhibitor Hoyts reported flat results for the year ended December 31, 1998. At the time, Hoyts controlled 1,662 screens in Australia, New Zealand, Mexico, Argentina, Chile, Uruguay, Germany, Austria, and the Northeast region of the United States. For twelve years, Hoyts posted solid growth in Australia, but a weaker slate of movies led to a 16% decline in profits for the year. Hoyts CEO Peter Ivany said he expected *The Phantom Menace* and other blockbusters to lift the theater chain out of the brief slump.

On June 21, 1999, the eighth annual Cinema Exposition International opened in Amsterdam. The exposition is a gathering of European exhibitors, but the lackluster box office results affected the general mood at the exposition in 1999. Exhibitors hoped and expected that *The Phantom Menace* would boost admissions and save the industry from a dismal year, which they made clear at the exposition. Karsten-Peter Grummitt of Dodona Research, moderator of the first seminar said, "The industry has spent much of the last twelve months caught in a kind of limbo between one big hit, *Titanic*, and what everyone thinks will be another, *Star Wars: Episode I—The Phantom Menace.*"

United Kingdom exhibitors also discussed the sagging box office grosses in their country. Most countries experienced adverse effects as a result of comparisons between quarters that benefited from *Titanic* and the same quarters a year later, but the United Kingdom suffered more than any other European territory. Exhibitors could not determine the reasons behind the slump. Steve Knibbs of United Cinemas International said, "We're not really sure why that was," but the theater chains expected *Star Wars* to help the country's struggling box office.

Titanic amassed more than $1.2 billion in international box office receipts. When combined with its domestic gross, it made more than $1.835 billion, nearly doubling the second highest grossing movie ever made, *Jurassic Park*, which collected $919.8 in 1993. In every country in which *Titanic* opened, it eventually became the all-time highest grossing movie. *The Phantom Menace* could not outperform the romantic epic, although it enjoyed remarkable success worldwide.

The Phantom Menace debuted in Puerto Rico on May 27, grossing $977,000 on 59 screens and eclipsing the previous record that *Independence Day* held by 10%. Although Puerto Rico received the prequel before any other country, it is a territory of the United States, so the first official worldwide debuts occurred the following week.

The Phantom Menace's first major international debut took place in Australia on Thursday, June 3. In its first 24 hours of release, the movie grossed $1.5 million from 372 film prints at 184 theaters. The gross set a new record for the territory, surpassing *Independence Day* by 41%. The movie collected $640,000 from midnight screenings on 324 prints. After the first day, Australian exhibitors predicted that *The Phantom Menace* would set a new opening weekend record and could rank among the top grossing movies of all-time.

Despite the impressive first-day gross in Australia, several problems occurred in theaters projecting the movie. Audiences at a cinema in Penrith, Australia did not enjoy a pleasant first showing of the highly anticipated movie. The film projector broke once near the very beginning of the movie, then again at the end of it. Ross Schwartzkoff, 19, told *The Daily Telegraph*, "It totally ruined the movie, and I had waited so long to see it." At the same theater, a print of the movie caught fire twenty minutes after starting. As a result of the malfunctions, nearly 700 people had to wait for a repeat screening at 3:00 a.m.

In addition to the debut in Australia on June 3, the movie also opened in Singapore and Malaysia, although heavy pirating of the movie occurred prior to its official release. *The Phantom Menace* collected $932,000 in its first six days from 42 locations in Singapore and $553,000 in five days from 41 locations in Malaysia. The two debuts did not impress many analysts, but the numbers represented solid opening frames, although not record breaking. In Australia, however, the opening amazed analysts and exhibitors alike.

During its opening week, *The Phantom Menace* grossed $7.6 million in Australia, beating *Independence Day*, the prior record holder, by 19%. Most exhibitors expected the movie to crush the previous record, but the margin of victory especially impressed box office onlookers.

The following weekend, *The Phantom Menace* debuted in New Zealand, collecting $877,000 from 33 locations, which easily topped *Independence Day* and set a new record. The prequel also debuted in Colombia with $368,000 from 58 venues. In its second weekend in Australia, it fell only 27%. After fourteen days, the prequel had crossed the $13 million mark faster than any other movie. *Independence Day* took 24 days to accomplish the same feat. The prequel suffered steep declines in both Malaysia and Singapore, however, which are both typically fast-burn markets, meaning movies typically erode quickly at the box office. In Malaysia, it fell 47%, bringing its total to $971,000, and in Singapore it fell 52%, totaling $1.4 million. The prequel grossed $7.2 million for the period, bringing its international total to $16.5 million.

As *The Phantom Menace* opened in more and more countries, the gross continued to increase, but slowly and consistently. Twentieth Century Fox spread out the movie's worldwide release dates considerably, so it enjoyed more than six months as one of the top grossing movies in international release every week. Records tumbled weekly in territories around the world as *The Phantom Menace* continued its worldwide rollout.

On its third weekend of international release, the prequel opened in Thailand on 168 prints, grossing $1.4 million, which topped all previous openings. It also posted a non-holiday record in Bolivia with $82,755 from five film prints. *The Phantom Menace* continued its success in Australia during its third weekend, but fell behind *Austin Powers 2*. The new openings and continued success in other countries pushed the prequel's cumulative international gross to $22.8 million.

The Phantom Menace grossed $8.5 million from 1,388 screens in thirteen countries during its next week of international release, bringing its cumulative gross to $31.6 million. The prequel set new opening records in Brazil, South Korea, Chile, and South Africa. In Brazil, the prequel grossed $2.3 million from 371 locations; in South Korea, it collected $1.5 million from 95 theaters; in Chile, it added $634,000 from 45 venues; and in South Africa it made $465,000 from 88 locations. The movie earned $744,000 in Taiwan from 52 locations, although the strong opening set no new records. In addition, *The Phantom Menace* grossed $2.3 million from previews in 280 theaters in Japan. Through four weekends in Australia, it had collected an impressive $17.3 million, which ranked it tenth on the all-time box office list.

Continuing its domination of new box office markets every week, *The Phantom Menace* earned $3.4 million from 320 screens in Mexico, soaring past *Godzilla*'s record opening by 31% and besting *Titanic* by 64%. The prequel opened in Hong Kong with $358,000 on its first day, collecting $1.44 million from its first full week in the country. In the Philippines, it grossed $1.2 million from 89 screens. Giving *The Phantom Menace* a further head start in Japan, the movie grossed another $2.1 million from previews in 264 locations, bringing its total to $4.4 million before its national premiere.

In Australia, the prequel continued to perform extremely well, reaching the $30 million mark in Australian dollars in just 32 days, compared to a full 51 days for *Titanic*. In its fifth weekend of release in the country, the movie dropped only 13% and brought its total to $20.2 million, making it the seventh highest grossing movie in Australian history.

George Lucas greatly appreciates Japanese cinema and its influence on the *Star Wars* movies is apparent and important. Lucas drew inspiration from many of director Akira Kurosawa's movies, such as *The Seven Samurai* (1954) and *The Hidden Fortress* (1958), in addition to tens of classic myths and cultural texts. The director greeted Japanese journalists in Japan on June 2 to answer questions about the movie during a press conference. Twentieth Century Fox as well as box office analysts expected *The Phantom Menace* to earn more from Japan than from any other country outside of the United States. Possibly in anticipation of the huge gross, Fox decided to release their own movies in Japan just a half of a year earlier. Previously, the studio had worked in association with Toho-Towa, which is a subsidiary of the Toho Corporation, a major film giant in Japan.

Before its release in the land of the rising sun, *The Phantom Menace* enjoyed nearly 100% recognition while roughly 85% of moviegoers had a positive impression of the film. Like the United States, print publications of all genres featured stories on the movie and its stars. Unlike in North America, however, the ad budget in Japan rivaled that of *Titanic*. Fox's Japan office estimated the prequel would collect roughly $84.2 million in film rentals. Toshio Furusawa, national marketing director for the Far East division of Twentieth Century Fox said, "*Star Wars: Episode I* is the must-see film of the summer and there are three generations of fans out there."

Analysts in the territory and trade papers in the United States observed that the movie would face stiff competition from films such as *Pocket Monsters Revelation Lugia* and *My Neighbors the Yamadas*. Nevertheless, Furusawa insisted, "The two animated films will have no impact on our results," noting that the movies target only kids, while *The Phantom Menace* has much broader appeal.

On Saturday, July 10, *The Phantom Menace* opened in Japan and records fell. The movie grossed $12.2 million in only two days from a record 403 theaters on sales of 913,392 tickets. The gross annihilated *The Lost World's* first two days by 20% and tripled *Titanic's* opening. Including the two weekends of previews, the prequel had already amassed $16.7 million in Japan.

For the entire week, *The Phantom Menace* grossed $25.6 million from 2,343 screens in 22 countries, which brought its cumulative total to $85 million. In addition to the Japanese opening, the movie premiered in Argentina with $1.5 million from 115 locations, a record for Fox and the second best opening of all-time behind *Titanic*. In Australia, *The Phantom Menace* continued to perform well in its sixth week of release.

After the record-shattering debut in Japan, another major country received the movie the following week. In the United Kingdom, theaters intended to show the prequel nonstop for 24 hours, although several weeks prior to its release Twentieth Century Fox thwarted their plans. Several theater chains such as Warner Village Cinemas, Virgin Cinemas, and Odeon Cinemas had already made arrangements with local authorities to screen the movie constantly. Nevertheless, insiders said Lucasfilm and Fox felt the screenings would not sell out and therefore forced theaters to begin playing it at 9:00 a.m.

Analysts expected *The Phantom Menace* to gross $15 million in the United Kingdom for its first four days, beginning with its opening on Thursday, July 15. A spokeswoman for Warner Village Cinemas said, "We had 60,000 people through the doors on the first day." She added, "Evening showings have been sold out across the country."

Advance ticket sales in the United Kingdom for *The Phantom Menace* destroyed all previous records, much like in North America. Odeon Cinemas reported record sales, Warner Village Cinemas said the movie sold 150,000 tickets in advance, and Virgin Cinemas said the prequel sold seven times as many advance tickets as any previous offering. Early success indicated a record debut in the United Kingdom.

During the four-day weekend, *The Phantom Menace* slightly exceeded expectations, grossing $15.1 million from 460 screens. The prequel surpassed the previous record holder, *Men in Black* (1997), by 33% and accounted for 76% of the business during its opening weekend. In Peru, *The Phantom Menace* grossed $295,000 in five days from 38 locations, which topped *Titanic*, the previous record-holder, by a stunning 66%.

In its second weekend in Japan, *The Phantom Menace* fell 55% to $5.5 million. The large decline occurred partly because of the two animated movies entering the market, which provided significant competition for the prequel. Nevertheless, the large decline presented a false alarm because the movie displayed excellent staying power for many months in Japan. *The Phantom Menace* ranked fourth during its seventh weekend in Australia. Overall, the movie grossed $26.7 million on 2,649 screens in 24 countries, bringing its cumulative international gross to $116.4 million. The movie became the seventh of the year to cross $100 million in international grosses.

Despite the decline in Japan, the movie set a record for its first full week in release, taking in $21.24 million during its first seven days, easily topping the previous record that *The Lost World* set in 1997. The dinosaur sequel grossed $16.95 million during its first week and *Independence Day* grossed $14.59 million, which was the third highest one-week total.

After six days in the United Kingdom, *The Phantom Menace* had collected $22.4 million. A *Variety* report on July 26 indicated the movie had grossed $43 million in the week prior, bringing its rapidly growing total to $132.7 million. *The Phantom Menace* set opening records in seventeen of the 28 countries in which it had premiered. In Japan, the movie had grossed $32.8 million through its twelfth day of release.

Setting another speed record, *The Phantom Menace* accumulated $36 million in Japan through its first two weeks on 2.65 million admissions, easily defeating *The Lost World's* previous record of $29.2 million. The movie set opening day attendance records in addition to the one week and two week speed records. Industry analysts already predicted the movie would gross $100 million in Japan before the end of its theatrical release.

During its eighth week in international release, *The Phantom Menace* grossed $30.3 million from roughly 2,400 screens in 24 territories. In the United Kingdom, the prequel dropped 39%, bringing its total to $37.9 million in only thirteen days. In Japan, however, it dropped only 18% in its third weekend, bringing its cumulative gross to $42.9 million after nineteen days. The movie kept pace with *Independence Day* in Taiwan and South Korea, but failed to match the 1996 blockbuster in Malaysia and Singapore; *Star Wars* does not enjoy a strong following in either of the two countries. Through another successful week, *The Phantom Menace's* total rose to $168.1 million, rapidly ascending the foreign box office charts.

The Phantom Menace drew intense audience applause after its debut at the 21st International Film Fest in Moscow. The warm reception only foreshadowed further success in the country. In Moscow, the movie shattered house records in its opening at the Pushkinsky Theater, earning $217,000 in its first week and expanding to 34 prints over the next weekend.

For the week, *The Phantom Menace* soared to $193.7 million after grossing $21 million on 2,475 screens in 25 countries. In the United Kingdom, *The Phantom Menace* had to cede its throne to *Austin Powers 2*, although it held up well against the comedy sequel. In Japan, the prequel remained on top of the box office for its fourth consecutive week, bringing its cumulative gross to $53 million and dropping only 4% from the previous weekend. Fox International reported that *The Phantom Menace's* total in Brazil hit $9.5 million after six weekends, the second highest gross in history for the country behind only *Titanic*. On August 9, *The Phantom Menace* became the first movie of the year to cross the $200 million mark at the international box office.

In Finland during the following weekend, *The Phantom Menace* grossed $544,689 from 55 prints, equating to 73,900 admissions. The debut did not topple *Independence Day*, however, and its 89,200 admissions remained a record. In Finland, the opening of the prequel signified the closure of summer as students returned to school after the weekend. For the full week, the prequel collected $854,146.

By the end of its tenth weekend in international release, *The Phantom Menace* climbed to $210.6 million after adding $10.9 million from 26 countries. A successful weekend in Russia led to more than $603,000 total, including $313,000 from the prior week. In the United Kingdom, the movie's total stood at $54.6 million and in Japan it had collected $58.8 million, still in first place at the weekly box office. Through the week, *The Phantom Menace* had ascended to $218.8 million.

During the following weekend, *The Phantom Menace* reclaimed pole position in the United Kingdom, beating newcomer *Wild Wild West* and passing previous champ *Austin Powers 2*. In its fifth weekend of release in the territory, it ranked first at the box office and brought its total to $62.3 million. In Japan, the prequel rose 28% in its sixth weekend because of the Obon vacation, catapulting its cumulative gross to $71.1 million and still the number one choice for Japanese moviegoers.

In Iceland, *The Phantom Menace* grossed $134,000 from just six cinemas, which topped the prior record holder, *Independence Day*, by 40%. For the weekend, the prequel grossed $10 million from 26 countries, bringing its total to $233.7 million. The next weekend witnessed several major openings that helped add revenue to the movie's international release. One foreign country was surprisingly receptive to the Lucas epic.

When the first *Star Wars* movie opened in Russia, media organizations and cultural critics called it a blatant attempt to turn the rest of the world "anti-Soviet." Many people in the country viewed it as capitalist propaganda and the movie proved entirely unsuccessful in the territory. *The Phantom Menace* performed far better in Russia than its predecessors, however.

The Russian media did not inundate the public with stories about the prequel, so it received almost no hype and little advance word. Gemini Films, however, pitched the prequel bigger than any previous movie with which they had worked, including *Titanic*, which won them the local award for best distributor of 1998. In addition to relatively little hype or familiarity with the past *Star Wars* movies, financial woes in the country led to local economic downturn.

Regardless of the factors working against it, *The Phantom Menace* enjoyed its only victory against *Titanic* in Russia, becoming the best-attended movie of the entire decade with 422,687 admissions and $1.2 million through Wednesday, August 18. The surprising success in Russia nullifies any arguments that *The Phantom Menace* succeeded based on its hype alone because it passed *Titanic* in one of the few countries where hardly anyone anticipated its release. In fact, one could argue that the lack of hype in the territory made it a greater relative success; only surprises are able to claim the title of highest grossing movie of all time in a country, which is why sequels virtually never rank first.

Many European exhibitors complained about the lack of quality film product during the summer of 1999, and also various other factors such as extreme heat, that negatively impacted the box offices in many European nations. Nevertheless, *The Phantom Menace* fulfilled its role as box office savior by setting opening records in five countries in mid-August.

In Germany, *The Phantom Menace* opened on 1,001 screens, which was an all-time record, and grossed $12.4 million in its first four days. The gross narrowly surpassed the previous record holder, *Men in Black*. The prequel accounted for a shocking 90% of all ticket sales on its opening Thursday and 70% of ticket sales during the Friday through Sunday portion of its four-day opening frame.

In Spain, *The Phantom Menace* grossed $4.3 million in three days from 352 prints, beating *Independence Day* by 46%. Passing *Lethal Weapon 4's* opening by 36%, the prequel collected $1.6 million from 100 prints in Sweden during its first four days of release. Similarly, in Austria it grossed $1.3 million from 110 screens in four days, passing *Independence Day* by 36%. *The Phantom Menace* smashed industry records in Denmark with $932,000 from 66 screens in four days, accounting for 64% of box office receipts for the weekend. In Norway, the movie grossed $890,000 from 73 screens in three days, but the total ranked second behind *Independence Day* and was the only debut of the week not to set a new record.

Recording its seventh consecutive weekend at number one in Japan, *The Phantom Menace* rose to $79.8 million. In the United Kingdom, the prequel retained its number one ranking on its sixth weekend, bringing its cumulative box office gross to $67.9 million. The movie valiantly resisted the competition and managed to spend four non-consecutive weekends at number one in a competitive marketplace. Through its twelfth weekend internationally, *The Phantom Menace* had amassed $271.1 million.

Despite a record opening in Germany, exhibitors in the territory complained because Twentieth Century Fox limited advance ticket sales to 50% of capacity at each auditorium, which theaters claimed hurt the movie. Theater owners also complained about the high rental costs for the prequel, which collected $17.1 million through six days. By August 25, the movie played on 3,300 screens in 27 countries and totaled $285.2 million. It crossed $300 million by the end of August.

After six days in Spain, the movie reached $7.3 million, which was 43% ahead of *Independence Day*. On its opening weekend, it sold more than one million tickets, which no movie had accomplished before *The Phantom Menace*. It made $2.1 million in six days in Sweden and $1.8 million in Austria, which was 25% ahead of *Jurassic Park*. In Denmark, the movie grossed $1.2 million in six days while in Norway it reached $1.1 million in the same number of days. The total for Japan rose to $81.9 million.

Over the following weekend, *The Phantom Menace* added $18.4 million from 3,347 screens in 27 countries, bringing its total to $307.4 million and also making it the eleventh most successful movie of all-time internationally. In Germany, the movie declined 39% to $7.5 million, bringing its total to $24.7 million. In Spain, it added $2.7 million, which was off 37% from the massive first weekend gross, but its total ascended to $10.9 million. In Sweden, the movie fell only 20%, adding $893,000 for a total of $3.1 million. The prequel debuted with a strong $1.1 million in Switzerland on 92 screens, but the opening ranked as only the fourth highest ever and was 18% less than first-ranked *Independence Day*. The movie still held first place in Japan after eight weeks.

By September 2, *The Phantom Menace* had reached $317.9 million after adding $29 million during the previous week. It totaled $1.4 million in Switzerland, which helped it become the tenth highest grossing movie ever outside of North America. The prequel passed *Ghost* with $300 million, *E.T.: The Extra Terrestrial* with $305 million, and *Terminator 2: Judgment Day* with $312 million.

On Thursday, September 9, *The Phantom Menace* became only the fourth movie in Japanese box office history to cross the $100 million mark with 7.2 million admissions. Japan also became the first and only country outside of the United States where the prequel grossed more than $100 million. *Titanic* ranked first in Japan, ahead of *Princess Mononoke* (1997) and *Armageddon* (1998), but animation director Hayao Miyazaki's internationally acclaimed *Spirited Away* (2001) easily annihilated the boat epic several years after *The Phantom Menace* failed to do so. Despite competition from *Pocket Monsters Revelation Lugia*, which grossed $52.2 million through the same date, the prequel held pole position in Japan during the entire summer after its opening on July 10.

Through its fourteenth week in international release, *The Phantom Menace* eclipsed the lifetime international gross of *A New Hope*. The prequel reached $339.1 million, passing the $337 million that the first *Star Wars* movie amassed. *Variety's* September 13 headline read, "'Phantom' Fantastic." For the weekend, the prequel's $13.6 million gross was the highest in a weak frame. It earned $19 million during the entire week.

The Phantom Menace ranked first in Japan for the ninth consecutive weekend, dropping only 27% to $2 million. In most major territories around the world, the prequel remained in the top-five for the week. In Germany, it totaled $35 million from 4.9 million admissions in just eighteen days. In Spain, the cumulative gross reached $16.7 million while in the United Kingdom it ascended to $75 million. In Europe, the movie had grossed $148 million total.

The Phantom Menace collected $9.4 million during the following weekend from 2,788 screens in 24 countries, bringing its total to $352.1 million. The prequel passed *Forrest Gump's* $350 million to claim seventh place on the all-time list of international winners. In the United Kingdom, the movie became the third highest grossing of all-time behind *Titanic* in first and *The Full Monty* (1997) in second, both of which Fox released.

Through the week, *The Phantom Menace* grossed $12 million and raised its total to $354.6 million, passing *Armageddon's* $353 million to become the sixth highest grossing movie of all-time at the international box office. The prequel brought its total to $76.2 million in the United Kingdom.

On its sixteenth weekend abroad, *The Phantom Menace* grossed $13.2 million from 31 countries, raising its total to $369 million. The movie opened in Italy with $3.8 million in three days from 605 screens, which was the third best opening ever for Fox. The first *Star Wars* grossed $9.6 million in Italy during its first release, but only made $3.3 million on its re-release in 1997. *The Phantom Menace* collected $979,000 from 80 screens in Poland, marking the second highest debut in the country, behind the local movie *Fire and Sword*. It also smashed industry records in six other Eastern European territories, led by $441,000 from 39 screens in Hungary. The prequel slipped to second place in Germany on its fifth weekend.

In Italy, the prequel boosted its total to $5.1 million after six days and in Poland it reached $1.2 million in five days. In Hungary, it climbed to $560,000 after six days. For the week, the prequel made $17.3 million, pushing its cumulative gross to $373.1 million while rapidly soaring to the $400 million mark internationally and $800 million worldwide.

Entering October, *The Phantom Menace* ranked second in Germany during its sixth weekend, but only dropped 25% from the previous weekend. It enjoyed four weeks in first place before finally falling to second for several weeks. The prequel ranked first again in Italy and ascended to $387.6 million internationally.

The following weekend, the prequel enjoyed excellent business in Holland, Portugal, and Turkey. In Holland, the movie made $1 million, which was the second biggest debut ever behind *Jurassic Park*. It added $465,000 on 69 screens in Turkey, which was also the second best opening ever, behind only *The Matrix*. The prequel also set a new industry record in Portugal with $421,000 on 79 screens. For the weekend, its total rose to $397.2 million after adding an additional $8.4 million. During the week, *The Phantom Menace* became only the fifth movie to gross $400 million outside of North America, adding $12.2 million in its eighteenth full week of release and bringing its cumulative gross to $401 million.

During its nineteenth weekend of international release, *The Phantom Menace* earned a relatively puny $5.3 million from holdovers in many countries. Its total climbed to $407.7 million, which included $104.3 million from Japan, $79.1 million from the United Kingdom, $49.9 million from Germany, and $23.5 million from Spain. One final wave of releases awaited the prequel, which helped push it higher in the all-time worldwide and international box office charts.

The Phantom Menace finally debuted in France on Wednesday, October 13, setting a new opening day record with $2.5 million from 793 screens. For the week, it grossed $10.8 million in 27 countries as its total increased to $413.2 million through October 14. The theater business in France was somewhat slow before the prequel's massive opening, but *Star Wars* helped remedy the lackluster sales. European countries already accounted for nearly $200 million of the prequel's foreign box office gross, while the total in Japan reached $105.7 million.

During the weekend, *The Phantom Menace* grossed an impressive $11.02 million from 793 screens in France, which ranked as the best opening ever for a movie from the United States, although it placed third overall. In Belgium, the prequel set a new record for an opening Wednesday and achieved the fifth biggest five-day gross, collecting $1.07 million from 102 screens. In Greece, it recorded the third best opening for a Fox movie while in a limited two-city release in India it grossed $40,134 from 20 screens. In Egypt, it debuted impressively with $50,127 from five screens.

Five of *The Phantom Menace's* final international rollouts occurred during the next weekend. Its $16.5 million gross from 2,924 screens in 31 countries pushed its cumulative gross to $428 million, which was higher than its domestic gross of

$426.8 million, though it was still playing in North American theaters. One final release awaited the prequel, but most of its remaining box office gross flowed from countries where the movie had already opened, specifically France. In one week, the movie collected $13.8 million in the country from 2.2 million admissions. It performed well in France, although several exhibitors still complained that it should have opened even more impressively.

The Phantom Menace declined 33% in its second weekend in France, grossing another $7.4 million in first place. The prequel earned $11.6 million for the weekend from all remaining territories in which it played, bringing its total to $444.7 million. For the entire week, the prequel ascended to $450.4 million. One week later, it became the fourth highest grossing movie outside of North America, climbing to $463.5 million and passing *The Lion King* (1994) at $455 million.

The Phantom Menace earned $6.7 million from 25 countries in its 22nd week of international release, bringing its total to $470.3 million. It grossed $152,000 from previews in China, which was the last country where the movie had yet to premiere nationally. Relatively few movies are allowed to open in China at all, so the country provided an appropriate final destination for the first chapter of the *Star Wars* prequels.

The Phantom Menace continued to decline in its international release and its successful worldwide tour was nearly complete. Nonetheless, it grossed $4.3 million during the next weekend to bring its total to $478 million by the middle of November. The total box office gross for the prequel in France reached $37.2 million and the cumulative international gross increased to $481 million from a strong fifth weekend in France and $2 million in China through two weeks.

After another several weeks, *The Phantom Menace* played in only three countries and had no new openings, but still grossed $1 million over the final November weekend, bringing its total to $485 million. The few remaining holdovers could not push the movie past $500 million, meaning the prequel ended its release as the fourth most successful movie of all-time outside of North America.

By the end of its international box office run, which lasted into the year 2000, *The Phantom Menace* reached $491.4 million overseas, ranking fourth behind *Independence Day* at $505.3 million, *Jurassic Park* at $563.0 million, and *Titanic* in first place with more than $1.2 billion. The prequel shattered box office records in almost every country and performed exceptionally well in many of the larger markets. Nevertheless, it could not top either *Jurassic Park* or *Independence Day* overseas, both of which it easily defeated in North America.

In Japan, *The Phantom Menace* enjoyed phenomenal success, spending nine weekends in first place and reigning as the fourth highest grossing movie of all-time and the third highest grossing movie from the United States. In the United Kingdom, the prequel ranked first for the year and third all-time, helping to save the struggling 1999 box office, which exceeded admission levels from 1998 by roughly 5%. For July, the month of release for *The Phantom Menace* in the United Kingdom, overall theater attendance reached 14.6 million, the highest total for the month since 1971 and an increase of 48% over the previous year. The prequel accounted for $42.5 million during the busy month. In Australia, *The Phantom Menace* grossed more than $24.5 million, exceeding the expectations of many analysts by becoming the third highest grossing movie of all-time, behind *Titanic* in first place and *Crocodile Dundee* (1986) in second.

In Australia, Brazil, Japan, Russia, and the United Kingdom, *The Phantom Menace* achieved phenomenal relative grosses with a level of success comparable to North America. The first prequel received a very favorable response from audiences in Japan, where *Star Wars* has always enjoyed popularity. Lucasfilm filmed each of the first four *Star Wars* movies at studios in England and also employed actors from the country, so British moviegoers have always enjoyed the saga and watched its success, partially because the movies have a strong British influence.

In Germany, *The Phantom Menace* ended its release with $52 million and ranked first at the box office for the year. In Finland, the prequel sold roughly 435,500 tickets and reigned as the year's top grossing movie. In France, Italy, and Spain it fared well, although it did not stand out as one of the highest grossing movies of all-time, only a very large blockbuster. In many of the European countries, sizeable *Star Wars* fan bases have arisen, although the saga is not a cultural phenomenon as it is in the United States and several other countries.

The Phantom Menace was the most attended movie at the European box office in 1999. The prequel sold just short of 39 million tickets in eleven European Union countries, according to the European Audiovisual Observatory in its annual report. *Notting Hill* placed second with 26 million tickets sold while *Tarzan* came in a close third with 23.6 million admissions. The admission numbers represent an estimated 80% of all ticket sales in European Union countries.

When *The Phantom Menace's* final domestic gross of $431.1 million, after a subsequent charity release, is added to its $491.4 million international total, its worldwide gross amounts to $922.5 million. Although the prequel ranked third in North America and fourth overseas on the all-time box office charts, its combined total gross surprisingly ranked as the second highest of all-time, behind only *Titanic*.

Other than *Titanic*, only *A New Hope* prevented *The Phantom Menace* from taking the top spot in North America, but because the prequel defeated its predecessor by a wide margin internationally, *A New Hope's* worldwide total is lower. Overseas, *Independence Day* barely beat the prequel, but it grossed $124.9 million less than *The Phantom Menace* in North America. Finally, *Jurassic Park* made significantly less than the *Star Wars* epic in the United States and Canada, but beat the prequel handily overseas. Nevertheless, its worldwide total of $919.8 million was several million dollars short of second place.

At the time, only two of the top ten highest grossing movies at the worldwide box office, *A New Hope* and *E.T.: The Extra Terrestrial*, were released before 1990, which demonstrates the constant change of international box offices. Continued theater expansion in countries all over the world gives an increasing number of people the opportunity to see movies such as *The Phantom Menace*. The prequel succeeded at introducing the saga to audiences unfamiliar with the previous *Star Wars* movies, which opened many years ago when fewer countries had a sufficient number of theaters.

The Phantom Menace grossed 53.3% of its total from international box offices, compared to 67.3% for *Titanic*, 62.3% for *Independence Day*, and 61.2% for *Jurassic Park*. The lower margin of international grosses for the prequel indicates the *Star Wars Saga* is still a much bigger phenomenon in North America than it is in many foreign countries. Nevertheless, it reached phenomenal grosses in many overseas countries.

The Phantom Menace broke opening day, opening weekend, opening week, and speed records in a majority of the countries where it played. It maintained its momentum in almost every country and sometimes rose above the status of blockbuster, entering into the realm of phenomenon. Despite returning glory to the *Star Wars Saga*, *The Phantom Menace* suffered from widespread piracy, which significantly impacted its box office gross worldwide.

Piracy

The Phantom Menace became a massive success worldwide, although in several countries the widespread sale of illegal copies of the movie hurt ticket sales considerably. Every country in the world experiences problems with piracy, although it is more widespread in a few Asian countries than in North America. Major movies are especially susceptible to pirating, but *The Phantom Menace* earned the undesirable distinction of being one of the most pirated movies in history.

According to estimates released by the International Intellectual Property Alliance, copyright theft costs businesses between $20 and $22 billion every year. The Motion Picture Association of America (MPAA) estimates that pirated videocassettes cost the industry around $300 million per year in North America alone and between $2.5 and $3 billion worldwide. Before *The Phantom Menace's* release, Rich Taylor, a spokesman for the MPAA said, "We obviously know (the film) is going to be a prize."

Audience members with handheld video cameras create many of the illegal copies of movies, but others are much higher quality and scare studios much more than lousy amateur recordings. Dorothy Sherman, president of anti-piracy consulting firm GrayZone Inc. said, "Unscrupulous people making preview copies will sell copies out the back door." Hollywood is greatly concerned with the possibility of pirates copying the actual film print because they then obtain a perfect copy of the movie from which to mass produce and sell illegal copies on the black market.

Bootlegging is widespread and occurs in every country in the world, but a few organizations attempt to stop it by working with local law enforcement agencies. The MPAA's video piracy unit has assisted in more than 3,000 raids since 1995, which have resulted in the seizure of more than 1.1 million illegal tapes. Along with its many benefits, the Internet is quickly becoming a major source of pirate activity, which adds considerably to the overall damage that the film industry suffers.

A fair number of frequent online users learn of places to download movies for free, such as from postings in newsgroups, where a member can easily send every other member a message indicating how to acquire the movies illegally. College networks, accessible to all students on campus, also provide a hotbed for pirate activity. Typically, a two-hour movie occupies more than one gigabyte of storage space, but with many users connecting to the Internet at increased speeds using cable modems, downloading an entire movie is becoming quicker and easier. Many college campuses even have fiber optic networks allowing for rapid downloads, even of huge files. In the future, an increasing number of Internet users will switch to high speed connections, which will further increase the illegal downloading of movies on the Web.

Lucasfilm sent letters to many Internet service providers warning them in advance of the movie's release that illegal movie clips and pictures would appear with increasing regularity as the release date neared. Nevertheless, the movie appeared on several low profile foreign sites for download in MPEG (Motion Picture Expert Group) format, which is a standard file type used for many video files. Typically, the movie was divided into two parts with the first one using 720 megabytes and the second another 580 megabytes. Together, the two files totaled 1.3 gigabytes. A report on *Wired* magazine's website indicated that individuals in several European nations already had seen the movie on their computers only about one week after its release in North America. The movie did not open in Europe until much later in the year.

Only days after its release, the movie became available in black markets all over the world. One report indicated that illegal Video CDs (VCDs) of *The Phantom Menace* appeared in Macau, a Portuguese protectorate, for just $1.50. At least three different illegal copies of the movie became available in Malaysia by May 22, but the movie also sold on the black market in Indonesia and Singapore. Another report stated that many pirated copies of the movie were available in Hong Kong and plenty also existed in New York City. Videos in New York sold for about $5 each while the *South China Morning Post* reported that copies in Hong Kong sold for between $3.20 and $3.80.

Morally corrupt individuals also placed illegal copies of the movie on eBay.com, the popular online auction site. Lucasfilm requested that the site remove such auctions and eBay readily cooperated. One bootleg auction had reached more than $60 before the site terminated the offering. Lucasfilm spokeswoman Lynne Hale commented, "Given the high level of interest on every aspect of this film, we were certainly expecting [bootlegs] with all the camcorders out there." Nevertheless, bootlegging is costly for filmmakers and studios. Hale said, "It's something we're taking very seriously."

Shortly after the opening of *The Phantom Menace*, a potential disaster occurred. Between late Friday and early Saturday of the film's opening weekend, several thieves stole a print of the prequel from the State Theater in Menomonie, Wisconsin. The manager, Nick LeGros, said to the Associated Press, "In the 23 years I've been doing this, this is the first time I've had a film stolen." The incident particularly worried Fox executives, who feared that the print would be sold for a large sum of money and duplicated, resulting in the illegal production of perfect quality copies of the movie for sale to overeager moviegoers worldwide.

On Wednesday, May 26, two of the thieves turned themselves in to the authorities after consulting with an attorney. The two thieves, who were in their twenties, did not reveal their reason for stealing the print, which would have sold for roughly $60,000 on the black market. A third person who assisted in the theft soon joined his companions. Before the thieves surrendered early Tuesday morning, authorities found roughly five feet of the print not far from the scene of the crime. Menomonie Police Lieutenant Doug Briggs said, "It was pretty crumpled and dirty and looked like it had been rained on." The thieves had the entire print with them upon their surrender, minus the five feet they lost. Briggs said of the print, "We think we got all of it back—at least it sure looks like it." The story did not end with the three young men turning themselves in to police, however.

By the end of June, Judge Rod Smeltzer sentenced the three *Phantom Menace* thieves to five days in jail, roughly $7,400 in restitution to the theater owner because of cancelled screenings, twenty hours of community service each, and two years of probation. Smeltzer said, "It's important you have a taste of being confined." The three thieves, Charles Phillips, 22, and brothers Mark Stearns, 22, and Matthew Stearns, 25, all pleaded guilty to misdemeanor theft. A fourth person involved in the robbery, Zach Snow, 21, had a July 12 court date.

The group had no plans to sell the movie on the black market; they only intended to see the movie in a private screening, but they decided to steal it instead. They unraveled the film print, washed it in the bathtub in an attempt to remove any fingerprints, then sliced it into pieces and shoved the remnants into garbage bags for unrevealed reasons. Phillips said, "What we did was wrong. I can't believe we've done what we've done." The group paid for their crime, but Phillips added, "I never considered myself a bad person. I sincerely apologize."

Initial reports indicated that only two people stole the print from the Wisconsin theater, but the number kept increasing. A fifth person, Luke Katzmark, 18, pleaded innocent to misdemeanor theft. Katzmark worked at the theater and provided a key to the four thieves, but he claimed that he had no knowledge of their plans. The judge set a pretrial conference for October 12. On December 6, Katzmark pleaded guilty to being party to theft for providing the entry key to the theater. The judge ordered him to apologize to the theater owner, perform community service, help pay the restitution, and serve two years probation.

During 1999, *The Phantom Menace* was the most pirated video in the United Kingdom, according to the Federation Against Copyright Theft (FACT). Authorities seized nearly 42,000 pirated video tapes in the country throughout the year, compared to 66,000 in 1998. Although no official reports are available, the prequel likely ranked first in piracy in most countries worldwide.

The widespread pirating of *The Phantom Menace* occurred primarily because of the long wait in many countries for the movie's opening. Fox and Lucasfilm spread the release dates over more than six months, which increased pirate activity in many countries. Although releasing a movie simultaneously worldwide is extremely difficult because of the careful coordination and planning necessary, such a strategy reduces piracy considerably, especially for anticipated movies such as the *Star Wars* films.

Unfortunately, the fight against illegal VCDs went very poorly during 1999 in Asia. MPAA anti-piracy advocates in Asia admitted that they failed to stop the problem. Mike Ellis, regional director of the association that represents the major studios' interests overseas said, "We didn't adapt. We have a lot of catching up to do." During 1997, authorities seized four million VCDs, but the number increased drastically to 48 million in 1998. No additional officers helped stop the flow of illegal merchandise, so the increase in confiscated VCDs occurred despite an equal number of authorities assigned to the task of seizing them. Acknowledging the new threat from Internet downloads, Ellis said, "We have to get up to speed on the Internet, but we still will have to knock down doors."

Not all VCDs are illegal, but the format has a shady reputation because thousands of movies are available on bootleg VCDs. The VCD format became extremely popular in Asia because the discs play on computer CD-ROM drives in addition to most DVD (Digital Video Disc) players. The format is vastly inferior to the DVD and holds roughly 26 times less data, but it is a cheap alternative that Philips, Sony, Matsushita, and JVC created in 1993. Despite its weaknesses, a normal VCD is capable of providing about the same quality as a VHS tape.

VCDs contain MPEG-1 compressed audio and video, which allows the discs' creators to transfer the movie successfully to a standard compact disc. While many VCDs are legal, most of them are intended for sale in specific countries or regions. For instance, the legal VCD of *The Phantom Menace* reads, "Warning: This Video CD is sold on the condition it is not offered for sale or hire outside Malaysia."

Watch groups and Hollywood studios place a strong emphasis on the severe pirating of many movies in foreign nations, but many instances exist of high-profile illegal operations in the United States. For instance, on August 19, 1999, law enforcement authorities raided an illegal production facility in Brooklyn, New York, where the group was readying nearly 35,000 pirated copies of movies for sale on the black market. The lab was the second largest of its kind ever discovered in the United States. The MPAA anti-piracy unit had investigated the ring for more than three months. Law enforcement agents made eleven arrests upon finally crushing the illicit operation. Authorities found many copies of *The Phantom Menace* in addition to other major blockbusters such as *The Sixth Sense, Tarzan,* and *The Blair Witch Project,* among others.

New York is a hotbed for pirate activity in the United States because the densely populated city is the ideal location for bootleggers to earn sizeable profits from selling illegal merchandise. Authorities also discovered the largest piracy lab ever in Brooklyn during November 1997. In addition to bootleg videos, a considerable degree of scalping occurs regularly for major sports events, plays, and other popular events. Scalpers often sold tickets to the premiere of *The Phantom Menace* for inflated prices in The Big Apple.

Illegal copies of *The Phantom Menace* spread throughout the world on VHS tapes, VCDs, and fast Internet connections, costing the movie tens of millions of dollars in lost revenue. In the future, hopefully authorities will be better prepared to combat the onslaught of pirated movies. Meanwhile, a group of *Star Wars* fans in conjunction with the major fan sites on the Internet organized a campaign requesting that Lucasfilm release the last two *Star Wars* prequels simultaneously worldwide.

A worldwide release places great additional strain on filmmakers and studios for several reasons. Perhaps most importantly for many filmmakers like Lucas, the final cut of the movie is not ready for distribution sometimes until just weeks before the release date. Additionally, studios have to find and pay hundreds of voice actors to dub their movies into numerous languages for the international releases. Despite the difficulties involved, Lucasfilm honored fans' requests, making *Star Wars: Episode II—Attack of the Clones* the first movie ever released virtually simultaneously worldwide. Numerous movies followed suit in the years to come, including *Star Wars: Episode III—Revenge of the Sith.*

Merchandise Sales

The Phantom Menace earned Lucasfilm and Fox a large sum of money at the box office, but Hasbro and Lego invested more in the movie than either of the two studios. Expectations ran high among industry insiders and analysts, who thought that *Star Wars* could earn Hasbro at least one billion dollars, which is more than the movie made at the box office worldwide. Expectations and reality are often two different realms, but most products related to *The Phantom Menace* sold well in retail stores.

A report from *Variety* titled "'Menace' masters market" indicated strong results from the movie's licensing program as early as the end of May. David Leibowitz, a Burnham Securities toy analyst said, "Factories are working overtime trying to keep up with demand." He said the high sales are "raising eyebrows, despite very high expectations in the first place." Retailers reported great sales, despite tepid reviews for the movie. Further into the licensing campaign, however, negative articles surfaced.

Media reports from numerous publications indicated that toys for *The Phantom Menace* were selling poorly, but the inaccurate statements merely continued the seemingly endless stream of poor journalism. Most of the false reporting that occurred was a result of inadequate research by busy journalists, but some stemmed from personal biases, especially from writers who disliked the movie and felt they had to downplay its success. Nevertheless, the movie's merchandise appealed to millions of fans and consumers worldwide.

Through the first week in July, Lego reported that sales of their construction toys based on the prequel had exceeded expectations by 15% up until that point. Even the more expensive sets ranging from $50 to $90 sold briskly, according to company president Peter Eio. On July 15, 1999, Hasbro released the most convincing news that *Star Wars* toys had already proven a phenomenal success. The company reported that stronger than expected sales of *Star Wars* products led to record quarterly earnings.

The company's net income of $32.3 million for the quarter easily bested Wall Street's expectations. The analysts' consensus estimate collected by the First Call Corporation of eleven cents per share earnings amounted to five cents lower than the actual profit of sixteen cents per share. Hasbro revenues jumped from $572.1 million during the same quarter of 1998 to $874.6 million for 1999. In 1998, $5.5 million in earnings divided to only three cents per share.

On July 16, the movie industry trade-paper *Variety* headlined, "'Menace' toys boost Hasbro: Company profits out of this world." Hasbro CEO Alan Hassenfeld told the trade-paper, "Our *Star Wars* product line has in many cases exceeded our high expectations." He added, "The international rollouts of *Star Wars* product and the movie continue to be met with great enthusiasm." Unfortunately, the company's performance did not reflect in its stock price, which had fallen 28% since May. On Thursday, July 15, shares closed up $1.44 at $27.63, a 5% gain.

An article in *The Wall Street Journal* on August 13 further explained *The Phantom Menace's* success on store shelves and Hasbro's failure with investors on the stock market. The article emphasized that the declining stock prices came as a result of unfair expectations, not actual sales for *The Phantom Menace* products. Tom Russo, a portfolio manager for Gardner Investments based in Lancaster, Pennsylvania said, "Hasbro's a steal." Several investors said they visited retail stores and observed product sales, which seemed phenomenal. Most analysts and many investors could not comprehend the reason for the stock price's drastic decline since the movie's release.

In July, Hasbro boosted their full-year sales estimates for *The Phantom Menace* from $500 million to $650 million, an indication that sales had exceeded previous expectations. The company said that media reports of weaknesses in the *Star Wars* brand were greatly exaggerated. Hassenfeld said that sales were strong enough to indicate that the yearly figures "may even exceed" the $650 million estimate. Frustrated with the stock's performance, executives at Hasbro began purchasing additional company stock, hoping to take advantage of its lower price. In the United States, during the first three months of the campaign for *The Phantom Menace*, the toy sales actually exceeded internal company estimates.

Toy lightsabers from the movie were an especially hot item, but not just figuratively. Earlier in the summer, Hasbro had to recall 618,000 of the products because of overheating problems, but once the company restocked them, they sold at a torrid pace.

Several supposedly objective reports stated that Hasbro made a profit from the *Star Wars* toys, but the stores did not. Some analysts claimed that the stores overstocked, but Hasbro still made hefty profits. Despite the unconfirmed claims, manufacturers of toys for *The Phantom Menace* reported no cancellations. Shipping ports in California and Washington also said that there were no backups of merchandise.

Some toys inevitably were more popular than others. Any Darth Maul product sold well and the same was true of most products related to the primary cast members. Nevertheless, sales of toys based on lesser characters such as Darth Sidious and Senator Palpatine were somewhat disappointing. "When you have a property this gargantuan, you are going to have hits and misses—and the problem is that they are facing expectations that are far beyond the norm. What would have been a home run for anyone else has become mundane (for the *Star Wars* line)," said Ira Mayer, publisher of *The Licensing Letter*. In addition, an abundance of merchandise caused similarly disappointing sales of T-shirts, baseball hats, and sports jerseys.

On October 14, Hasbro reported record third quarter revenues and earnings per share. The press release indicated that the toy giant would deliver approximately 30% growth in recurring earnings per share in 1999. Worldwide net revenues increased roughly 16% from $945.5 million to $1.098 billion. Hasbro credited higher shipments of *Star Wars* merchandise for some of the gains, in addition to the Pokémon and Furby product lines. Net earnings increased 14% to $85.2 million. Hassenfeld said, "We are very pleased to report another record quarter in all respects." He added, "Our global *Star Wars* product line is tracking to our high expectations for this year. The retail sell-through rate of *Star Wars* action figures, the cornerstone of our line, remains strong and we have a major advertising campaign underway to drive overall sales in the all-important holiday season."

In Hasbro's annual report, Hassenfeld said, "Hasbro had its best year ever in 1999." For the year, net revenues increased 28% to a record $4.2 billion. Despite the successful year, stock prices plummeted from a high of about $37 to around $15 by the end of the year. Hassenfeld said, "While we are disappointed that our efforts have not been reflected in our stock price performance, we firmly believe in our future." During the months preceding the release of *The Phantom Menace*, share prices increased drastically in line with the anticipation and hype. When the movie opened, however, the stock price began a rapid and continued decline, despite the revenue increases.

In 1999, toys based on licensed properties accounted for 46% of overall toy sales, which is up considerably from the 35% in 1996. The Toy Manufacturers of America said that *Star Wars* and Pokémon products primarily led to the increases, but toys based on the Worldwide Wrestling Federation and *Toy Story 2* also accounted for a significant portion of sales. According to the NPD Group, which tracks toy sales, *Star Wars* accounted for about 5.5% of the market share in 1999, which fell just behind Barbie's 6.2%, but well above Pokémon's 2.5% in third place. The toy industry enjoyed a great year in 1999 and posted a 7% increase in retail sales to $22.5 billion. In 1998, products based on *Godzilla* and *Lost in Space* failed to sell as well as expected, leading to a somewhat disappointing year for movie-related merchandise.

Tens of companies had licenses to produce various types of merchandise based on *The Phantom Menace*. Many times, the companies simply produced too many products, forcing consumers to choose between them. Consumers enjoy the benefits when a company produces a large variety of products, although the wealth of merchandise means the company is essentially competing with itself for business. Buying every Hasbro product released in the first three months of merchandise sales alone would cost thousands of dollars, which is a sum of money that very few people are willing to spend on a movie's merchandise. The film's product sales were impressive, especially considering that numerous companies continued to inundate the marketplace with licensed products.

In addition to an abundance of different products, the companies manufactured too many of each item. The hype caused responsible companies to overproduce, which consequently forced stores to slash prices on their products. Several companies should have further evaluated the market to make sure that it could accommodate their merchandise. Instead of designing ten or twenty items, the companies could have concentrated on just five or six. For instance, many *Star Wars* fans already own T-shirts with images from the movies emblazoned on them, so they are not likely to buy ten new ones with designs from *The Phantom Menace*.

British publisher Dorling Kindersley (DK) reported that it printed thirteen million *Star Wars* books, but sold only three million. The massive overprinting seems to be an unintended mistake because thirteen million books is an unbelievably high number. The most popular *Star Wars* books reach sales of approximately one million copies, but DK only had several *Star Wars* books in print. Three million copies sold is an impressive number, which should be viewed as a success, regardless of how many copies the company printed.

An anonymous company insider told the *London Daily Express* that founder and chairman Peter Kindersley had "fallen victim to a terrible error of judgment." The error cost the company its financial independence and also damaged the *Star Wars* name, which a few uninformed media outlets blamed for the losses. Even the best product could be declared a failure if the company massively overproduced it. Regardless of quality, a limit exists to the number of customers for any given item. In the March 10, 2000 issue of *Entertainment Weekly*, Howard Roffman, president of Lucas Licensing said, "DK's sales for *Star Wars* were phenomenal. They made an internal mistake and overprinted beyond what any publisher in their right mind would do."

Amidst the turmoil, DK reported losses of $40 million from the *Star Wars* books and CEO James Middlehurst left the company. Although DK nervously awaited the video release of *The Phantom Menace*, nothing could repair their damages. Instead of filing for bankruptcy, they found another company to acquire them several months after the unfortunate sales announcement.

On Friday, March 31, 2000, the media group Pearson purchased the troubled company for $494.6 million in cash. "Dorling is a nice bolt-on acquisition for Pearson," said Andrew Gordon-Brown, an analyst at Warburg Dillon Read. Kindersley said, "We needed better infrastructure, we needed better warehousing and we also needed ways to develop online—all those things Pearson can help with." Several other media companies also expressed interest, such as Britain's Granada Group, France's Matra-Hachette, and Germany's Bertelsmann.

Despite DK's financial problems, other books associated with the movie sold very well. The novelization of *The Phantom Menace* by Terry Brooks debuted at number one on both the *New York Times* and *Publishers Weekly* hardcover fiction bestseller lists. Eager fans who could not wait for the movie to open in theaters read the novel, which Lucasfilm released on May 3 along with much of the other merchandise. Many fans wanted to wait until the movie's release before reading the book, so it continued to sell well for many weeks. After five weeks in release, the novelization remained first on the *Publishers Weekly* bestseller list. Editor-in-chief Nora Rawlinson said, "It's unusual, but not unique, for a book based on a movie to do this well."

Music critics praised John Williams' score for *The Phantom Menace* while the public made it a commercial success. Sony paid an unprecedented $5 million for the rights to distribute the soundtrack, which far eclipsed any previous deal for a classical soundtrack or for a movie soundtrack. *Godzilla's* soundtrack rights sold for $3 million, but *The Phantom Menace* commanded a far larger sum of money. For 1999, the musical score to the *Star Wars* prequel ranked #99 in sales. The movie score placed first on Billboard's Top Classical Crossover Albums, which is a noteworthy accomplishment. Classical albums are not as popular as those of the boy bands and the top rap artists, but *The Phantom Menace* score was certified platinum, meaning that it sold more than one million copies.

Halloween costumes created to look like characters in *The Phantom Menace* also sold briskly, despite the gap between the movie's opening and Halloween. Joe Marvey, CEO of Spirit Halloween Superstores, a national chain with more than 70 stores, told the *San Francisco Chronicle*, "The talk was that *Star Wars* [sales] wouldn't be good because the movie came out too soon for Halloween, but it's not true." He said all 1,200 Jar Jar costumes sold out in addition to 2,000 Obi-Wan Kenobi costumes and 3,000 of the Queen Amidala version. "The kids rule, and they're buying it," he told the paper. According to a Gallup poll, *Star Wars* costumes were the second most popular behind only Batman, but ahead of Disney characters and witches.

Video game companies such as Nintendo, Sega, and Sony all benefited from games based on *The Phantom Menace*. For instance, *Star Wars Episode I: Racer* debuted on three different platforms including Nintendo's GameBoy and N64 systems and Sega's Dreamcast. Total sales through 2000 reached roughly $20 million. During the 1990s, games based on the *Star Wars Saga* accumulated more than $450 million in sales.

After Pepsi inked a $2 billion deal with Lucasfilm, the company expected *Star Wars* to help sell their beverage and food products. *The Phantom Menace* did not disappoint. After the second quarter in 1999, Pepsi reported that "*Star Wars* promotional activities resonated strongly with consumers." In addition, the company reported that their *Star Wars* promotion significantly cut into Coke's slice of the market share, which Pepsi had anticipated.

Pepsi introduced 24 different designs across their primary brands. Each design featured a different character from the movie and the company staggered the release of the cans over the entire summer. Eight of the characters appeared on Mountain Dew cans, eight more on Pepsi cans, then four characters each appeared on both the Pepsi One and Diet Pepsi brands. Storm bottles also featured the characters. Pepsi worked in collaboration with Lucasfilm's Industrial Light & Magic to produce commercials for their products, which featured a new alien character called Marfalump. The company used the new character for promoting their beverages throughout 1999 and also through the video release of *The Phantom Menace* in 2000.

The multitude of merchandise in almost every retail store in many parts of the world provided fans with a rare opportunity. Walking into a store and seeing *Star Wars* products on display everywhere is a fan's dream, but most companies should have scaled back their product lines. Nevertheless, fans had an opportunity to choose from many types of merchandise and enjoy the release of the newest *Star Wars* movie through toys, T-shirts, and hundreds of other products.

The success of products associated with *The Phantom Menace* negatively impacted second quarter comparisons between 1999 and 2000 for many licensed companies. Hasbro's worldwide net revenues fell 11% to $778.4 million in the second quarter of 2000, primarily because of smaller shipments of *Star Wars* and

Furby toys, the company stated. Grand Toys International also suffered from lesser demand of *Star Wars* products as the company's net sales for the second quarter of 2000 fell to $2.2 million compared to $8.7 million for the comparable period in 1999. Despite the expected overall decline in *Star Wars* toy sales for 2000, the franchise still ranked second among boys toys for the year, behind only *Power Rangers*.

Toys "R" Us experienced a 9.5% decline in second quarter sales from $2.2 billion in 1999 to $2 billion in 2000. The slide occurred because of a lack of phenomenal products in 2000, compared to 1999 when toys for *The Phantom Menace* created a buying frenzy nationwide. The unfavorable quarterly comparisons for many of the larger companies did not surprise most analysts, but the absence of a new *Star Wars* movie had adverse effects on the licensing industry.

Brown Shoe, a footwear company that owns and operates Famous Footwear, reported that their sales totaling $109.58 million for the second quarter of 2000 fell significantly from the $120.35 million in the same quarter of 1999. The decline came largely as a result of strong sales from products related to *The Phantom Menace* during 1999, which boosted earnings and damaged comparisons between the two years. The decline in sales across several industries underscores *The Phantom Menace's* impact in every aspect of its release.

From bath soaps to bed sheets, action figures to posters, candy to fruit snacks, there are *Star Wars* products of all types available. An exact sales figure is not available, but *The Phantom Menace* easily earned licensed companies more than $1 billion and became the all-time most successful movie in product tie-ins within its first year of release. *The Lion King* held the distinction before *Star Wars* returned to glory, but *The Phantom Menace's* wave of merchandise prevailed over the animated Disney movie. The successful sales for *The Phantom Menace* marked the fourth consecutive year that the *Star Wars* franchise ranked first in toy sales for boys, behind Barbie each year overall. The impressive toy sales continued long after the film's release, but *The Phantom Menace* had not completed its success at the box office until Lucasfilm and Fox brought the film to theaters to benefit North American charities once again.

Charity Release

The Phantom Menace's first theatrical release ended on November 4, but it did not stay out of theaters long before making its first triumphant return. Following several unofficial reports in reputable media outlets, Lucasfilm announced on November 22 that the hugely successful prequel to the *Star Wars Saga* would return to theaters across the United States and Canada on December 3, 1999.

The movie played only one week, from December 3 through December 9, but for a worthy cause. For the first time in the history of the motion picture industry, all profits from the movie's box office release accrued to charity. Fox and Lucasfilm worked with theaters in more than 350 cities across North America to benefit more than 180 charities. Lucasfilm President Gordon Radley said, "We are excited to see this grow from an idea to a reality that will benefit so many in need."

The special charity release brought many organizations together in raising money for the benefit of communities nationwide. Radley said:

> We're delighted that so many companies have gotten behind an event that will bring attention and financial support to deserving causes in our communities. The project has gotten the enthusiastic backing of our colleagues at Twentieth Century Fox, theatre owners across the U.S. and Canada, Hasbro Inc. and LEGO Systems Inc., which are helping to advertise the release, local newspapers, which are providing movie listings, and many others whom we also want to thank.

Tom Sherak, chairman of Twentieth Century Fox Domestic Film Group said, "This is truly a unique event in the annals of the film industry, and we and our exhibition partners are thrilled to have this chance to give something back to our communities." *The Phantom Menace* had already raised millions of dollars for charity in May before its national opening, but Lucasfilm recognized the importance of helping the community whenever possible. Few companies concentrate on giving back to society as much as Lucasfilm, which is refreshing in an increasingly cynical world.

Every major theater chain participated in the charity release while newspapers in almost every city donated ad space to promote the one-week event. Participating theaters could decide which charity received the grosses from *The Phantom Menace* at their own discretion. Radley said, "We thought it would be a great opportunity to help local causes, and a wonderful way to end the *Star Wars* theatrical run." Sherak commented that film executives "are always looked at as these cold-hearted money-grabbers," but he said, "Here we have an opportunity to really help out now. Anything we give to these causes is going to make a difference."

Grosses for the movie during the one-week engagement counted towards *The Phantom Menace's* cumulative box office gross, unlike the pre-release charity screenings in May. No new major competition entered theaters during the one-week release, which is typical of the first weekend in December. Radley said of *The Phantom Menace*, "It's a film for all ages. We wanted to take an opportunity to help families spend time together and give local causes a lift." Fox executives declined to comment specifically on how they felt the movie would perform at the box office during the week, but Sherak said, "It's a special thing to give back on this kind of scale."

On Friday, December 3, *The Phantom Menace* returned to theaters, grossing roughly $291,000 in eleventh place. It then grossed roughly $564,000 on Saturday and approximately $437,000 more on Sunday. For the weekend, the movie ranked eleventh at the box office while grossing $1,292,968 playing in 832 theaters, which was considerably more locations than the roughly 750 originally planned. Many theaters decided to become involved in the charity release after its initial announcement, so the planned theater total increased up until the re-release.

During the weekend, the prequel averaged $1,554 per theater, which ranked eighth among the top twenty movies. *The Phantom Menace* barely missed the top ten, falling less than $30,000 behind fellow Twentieth Century Fox release *Anywhere But Here*, starring Natalie Portman. The prequel ranked eighth on Sunday, however, and began to climb its way up the top ten charts during the week.

On Monday, December 6, *The Phantom Menace* grossed $153,211, which positioned it in seventh place. Its average gross per theater of $184 ranked fifth among the top ten. Similarly, it took seventh place with $192,918 on Tuesday, but its $232 per theater average ranked fourth. By Wednesday, the movie moved into sixth place with $234,674, averaging $282 per theater, which was the second best average in the top ten. Fans rushed out to attend the movie on what most people expected would be its final day in theaters for a long time. On Thursday,

The Phantom Menace grossed $287,010 and ranked fifth, still holding the second highest per theater average with $345, compared to $389 for first-ranked *Toy Story 2*.

Although *The Phantom Menace* failed to place in the top ten during the weekend, it moved up six ranks during the week by its final day, refusing to leave theaters without a brief flurry of excitement. If the movie had played in several thousand theaters like the other movies in the top ten, then it would have easily passed many of them. Every weekday, *The Phantom Menace* outperformed *Pokemon: The First Movie*, despite playing in 2,211 fewer theaters. During the week in re-release, *The Phantom Menace* raised $2,160,781 for charity, bringing its cumulative box office total to $429,870,576.

According to Kelly Maloney, a marketing executive for the Harkins theater chain, the Arizona Mills 24 led the Western states in attendance for *The Phantom Menace* during the early days of its one-week re-release. Among published reports of box office earnings, the Grand Forks Herald stated that the charity release raised $1,894.81 for Café Kosmos, an organization keeping kids and teenagers out of trouble.

Sherak said, "To the exhibitors and Lucas and Fox, this was a way to give back. For everyone who was associated with this, we had a feeling this Christmas that I don't think we've had since we were little kids." Although the charity engagement ended on December 9, supposedly ending the box office run for *The Phantom Menace* until presumably many years later, it enjoyed six additional weeks in discount theaters.

Surprising many people, *The Phantom Menace* began playing in discount theaters on December 24 as if it had never exited on November 4. The movie made $114,418 from 368 theaters on its first weekend after the charity release and increased the following weekend to $205,498, despite playing in fourteen fewer theaters. Playing in 296 theaters the next weekend, *The Phantom Menace* grossed $180,997, then $110,254 from 144 theaters the following week, dropping drastically because of the lower theater count. Playing in only 117 locations, the movie made $65,165 on its fifth weekend after returning to theaters, then finished its release the following weekend playing in 103 theaters and grossing $57,510. The movie's final total after playing at least one day each month for nine consecutive months stood at a massive $431,065,444.

Lucasfilm, Fox, Hasbro, Lego, and every participating theater and newspaper performed an admirable deed for charities all around North America. Including the money raised in May, *The Phantom Menace* collected a total of more than $7.4 million for charity organizations in North America. No movie had ever contributed as much to society as *The Phantom Menace*. *Star Wars* fans should be proud to follow a series that not only advocates an optimistic philosophy of the triumph of good in the universe, but whose creator lives in accordance with the values he promotes.

Beyond the Theaters

The release of a blockbuster movie on VHS is not usually a major event, but it is an important one for the studios as video sales account for millions of dollars in additional revenue. *The Phantom Menace's* release to home video quickly became a newsworthy event, as with most surrounding the prequel. If a movie performs poorly at the box office, but sells millions of copies on video or DVD, it might turn into a cult favorite and inspire a successful sequel, as happened with *Austin Powers.* Conversely, when a movie performs well at the box office, but fails to sell many videos or DVDs, the low sales could indicate that moviegoers did not enjoy the film enough to want to see it again or spend any of their money on it. *The Phantom Menace* did not disappoint in the video sales market, once again breaking numerous records and quieting its critics in the process.

On January 5, 2000, Lucasfilm and Twentieth Century Fox announced that *The Phantom Menace* would become the first movie ever released simultaneously on video worldwide. From April 3 through April 8, the prequel became available in every country in the world where videos are sold, except for France and Korea. France received the video release of the movie in fall 2000 because of its late release to theaters the previous year. Major media organizations already learned of the VHS release by late December, although the official announcement explained the specifics of the worldwide campaign.

The simultaneous release for *The Phantom Menace* marked the first time a studio attempted to give fans worldwide the chance to own a movie within one week. Typically, studios spread the release dates for each country over a period of several months, much like the international rollout of the prequel to theaters, which came to some countries months before others. The close proximity of the worldwide release dates also limited video piracy somewhat.

Fox Filmed Entertainment Chairman and CEO Bill Mechanic said, "We're excited to join Lucasfilm in releasing on video the biggest film of the year and, obviously, the most anticipated title for sell-thru." Lucasfilm president Gordon Radley added, "A film such as this is rich with detail and watching it at home provides the opportunity to discover new and different things every time you watch it." *The Prince of Egypt* (1998) previously held the record for the tightest worldwide release, but more than two months passed before it became available in every country worldwide.

In North America, Fox made *The Phantom Menace* available on April 4, but eager fans could begin reserving their copies as early as January 28. In the United Kingdom, the video release occurred on April 3, but the movie did not become available in Brazil or Japan until April 8. Fox released two versions in North America, one pan and scan copy retailing for $24.98 and a special collector's edition for fans. The collector's edition retailed for $39.98 and included the movie in its original widescreen theatrical format. It also included a special documentary feature preceding the movie, a 48-page excerpt version of The Art of *Star Wars: Episode I—The Phantom Menace*, and a unique 35mm filmstrip. Fox strictly limited production of the collector's set to 1.5 million copies. In countries outside of North America, fans could not purchase the collector's edition, but Fox instead produced a special widescreen edition for the more discriminating viewers.

Most hardcore fans in the United States and Canada purchased the collector's edition, mainly because it included the widescreen version of *The Phantom Menace*. A very significant and noticeable difference exists between a movie presented in the pan and scan format and the same movie seen in the widescreen format. Most people who know the difference between the two formats refuse to watch detailed and visually complicated movies such as *The Phantom Menace* in pan and scan because of the significant loss of quality.

People sometimes incorrectly refer to pan and scan as "standard" or "normal," but there is nothing normal about the process of diminishing a movie's impact by cutting off the edges. Televisions have an aspect ratio of 4:3, meaning that for every four inches the set is wide it is three inches tall. Movie screens are vastly different, so most directors chose to film their movies using the standard 2.35:1 ratio, meaning the movie is 2.35 times as wide as it is tall. The pan and scan process cuts the movie so it plays on a standard television, but at the loss of up to half of the movie's viewable surface area for any given picture.

The visual splendor of *Ben-Hur* (1959) is practically ruined after the pan and scan because the filmmakers shot the movie using the 2.66:1 aspect ratio, which means that the pan and scan version actually only contains half of the movie from a visual perspective. A movie shown in widescreen, also referred to as "letterbox," is presented in its original aspect ratio so that none of the movie is cut from the theatrical release. When a widescreen movie is played on a television, viewers see "black bars," but no data is actually transmitted to those parts of the screen, so referring to them as such is inaccurate. Some people continue to believe that they are missing part of the movie because of the black zone above and below the picture, although they are actually seeing the entire movie, unchanged visually from its original print.

Nearly every Digital Video Disc (DVD) contains the unaltered, widescreen version of the movie, although many also include a pan and scan version, while yet a few others only have the pan and scan edition. Lucasfilm made no plans for the DVD release of *The Phantom Menace* by the time the video was announced, which is rare in the movie industry because almost every new movie is released on both the VHS and DVD formats. Lucasfilm and Fox announced that they had no plans to release a DVD version in the foreseeable future, which did not surprise many industry onlookers, considering that Lucasfilm still had not released the original *Star Wars* movies on the popular format. Nevertheless, the announcement angered many fans of the saga and of the format in general.

Several people claimed George Lucas only delayed the DVD release to 'force' fans to buy the movie on VHS. The viewpoint is somewhat cynical, however, because Lucasfilm constantly attempts to please the fans. Lucas also provided valid reasons for his decision. He emphasized his desire to invest sufficient time on the *Star Wars* DVDs so that he could release a quality product. Lucas said that he did not have time to concentrate on personally overseeing the creation of special features for the DVDs, so he wanted to wait until his schedule cleared, allowing him to focus his efforts on building a quality product.

Many fans wanted Lucasfilm to release a bare-bones DVD of each of the *Star Wars* movies, which would include only the episode, but no extra features. By releasing an inferior product, Lucas would cheapen the *Star Wars* name, which is a symbol of quality and should forever be associated only with superior products. Instead of releasing inferior DVDs, he chose to release the movies on the format only once he knew he had the available time to create a product that satisfied his high standards.

When Lucas released the THX re-mastered version of the *Star Wars Trilogy* on VHS in 1995, he later drew criticism from some fans who felt they wasted their money because the *Star Wars Trilogy: Special Edition* video release occurred just two years later. Lucasfilm wanted to give fans an opportunity to purchase the original version of each movie on VHS before the *Special Editions* came to theaters, but some people did not understand the company's positive intentions. Instead of releasing multiple versions of the movies on DVD and expecting fans to buy each one, Lucas instead hinted at his desire to release all six films on DVD simultaneously after the release of *Episode III*.

Frustrated fans quickly launched petitions and campaigns asking for the immediate release of the movies on DVD. Lucasfilm realized the strong desire for

Star Wars DVDs among the technology-savvy fan base, so rumors began circulating almost immediately that the company had begun preliminary work on a DVD for *The Phantom Menace*. Nevertheless, Lucasfilm made no official announcement indicating the development of any *Star Wars* DVDs at the time, so the wait continued. "Until George has time to concentrate on the DVD, we won't be releasing one," a Lucasfilm spokesman said.

One particularly interesting move by Fox seemed to indicate that *The Phantom Menace* would appear on DVD within a year of its video release, rather than many years later. Several weeks before Fox and Lucasfilm officially announced the details of the VHS release, the studio made a major move that prompted fans and the media to question their motives. Twentieth Century Fox Home Entertainment, which usually uses Deluxe Video Services to duplicate their videos, chose Technicolor Videocassette Services for duplication of *The Phantom Menace*. Paul Scott, senior vice president of worldwide video sales for Technicolor said, "You heard right; we're doing the duplication on *Phantom Menace*."

Most industry analysts believed that Fox switched companies because Technicolor completes replication for DVDs, but Deluxe solely handles VHS. An insider familiar with the deal commented, "It's devastating to Deluxe. This is a big-time kick in the teeth." The loss of the year's biggest title may have cost the company $25 million in revenue and nearly $10 million in lost profits. Despite the switch to Technicolor for replication, Lucasfilm did not elaborate on their motives.

Twentieth Century Fox established a high advertising budget for the release of the video, which they expected would sell extremely well. The company reportedly used $20 million on television spots trumpeting the prequel's release on VHS. In addition, Pepsi, Frito Lay, Hasbro, and Lego all played a role in promoting the movie's video release. Both Hasbro and Lego anticipated a spike in toy sales from the event.

Pre-orders for *The Phantom Menace* videos quickly soared to record highs as the movie became the number one best-seller on e-commerce giant Amazon.com from January through weeks after its release in April. Dean Wilson, executive vice president and chief merchandising officer for Blockbuster, said he believed the video would generate "three million customer visits for us." Likewise, Sean Mahoney, senior director of public affairs and media relations for Hollywood Video said, "We've had a tremendous amount of interest and requests. We expect pre-orders to get into six figures over the course of the next couple of weeks."

In recent years, Easter had become a lucrative holiday for the video sales industry. Craig Thomas, director of video marketing for the Suncoast Motion

Picture Company said, "Parents are looking for an alternative to candy for Easter baskets. Videos have become a gift-giving item." Kevin Brass, executive editor of trade publication *Video Store* said, "There are very few real events in this business, and this is a true event." Despite the optimism of most industry analysts, several people were not as excited about the release.

In March 2000, just weeks before the release of the movie on video, Mark Vrieling, chairman of the Video Software Dealers Association, told the *Los Angeles Times* that he thought the movie would "do well" on video, but not as phenomenally well as many people had predicted. He also stated that the movie lacked the "secondary buzz" that it needed to perform exceptionally well, citing that Jar Jar is an annoying character. Considering that he is supposed to help propel video sales, not hinder them, Vrieling's comments seemed inappropriate. When talking to *Video Business Magazine*, he said, "I don't regret what I said. I'm still pissed off at [Fox] for not doing [a simultaneous] DVD release. I'm more worried about the success of DVD than the success of *Star Wars*." Only weeks later, when *The Phantom Menace* set new VHS sales speed records, Vrieling's comments seemed like bitter criticism of Lucasfilm without objective realization of the popularity of the saga.

The video release became an even more significant event for fans with the announcement that Blockbuster stores around the United States would open at 12:01 a.m. to begin selling *The Phantom Menace*. In addition, fans could enter a drawing to win a life-size Yoda, which stands 36 inches tall and is valued at more than $600. "We're celebrating the release of 1999's biggest film and we decided to add some fun by offering the Yoda contest to our customers," said Curt Andrews, senior vice president of product merchandising and promotions for Blockbuster. At the time, Blockbuster operated 7,100 stores in the United States, its territories, and 26 other countries around the world. The video release for *The Phantom Menace* became a major event at many Blockbuster stores, where eager fans once again formed lines in anticipation of the movie's release.

On April 3, Twentieth Century Fox treated customers at the HMV Trocadero in the United Kingdom to a laser show and also gave the first customer a platinum plaque that commended his dedication. Retailers in the United Kingdom followed suit with those in North America and opened their doors at one minute past midnight to begin selling the most popular video of the year. A spokesman for HMV said, "It was spectacular and the show was a big surprise for customers." Several stores in the United States also celebrated the release in interesting ways.

The Blockbuster flagship store in Kansas City organized a special event for the movie's video premiere. The staff constructed sets from the movie, including one resembling Theed Palace, and they also built a replica podracer. Staff members dressed as various characters from the film, ranging from Darth Maul to Obi-Wan Kenobi, Anakin Skywalker to Queen Amidala. The event started at 5:00 p.m. on April 3 and lasted until 1:00 a.m. the following day. The staff also donned their costumes on Tuesday, April 4 for customers who could not enjoy the midnight festivities.

In Marlton, New Jersey, the Blockbuster store hosted a trivia contest, a costume contest, and a pizza party for fans waiting in line for the video. At the flagship store in Milwaukee, the first 100 people in costume received a free lightsaber. The store even hired stunt artists to perform a lightsaber duel at 9:00 p.m. The event started with the lightsaber duel and concluded at 1:00 a.m. after eager fans had a chance to purchase their videos. In Atlanta, one store gave prizes to the first 25 people in costume. Many other stores also hosted special events, which helped make the video release another major event for the *Star Wars* franchise and its fans.

Upon its release to video stores worldwide, *The Phantom Menace* again became the target of inaccurate media reports. An April 5 headline in *The Boston Globe* read, "'Menace' not a threat." The brief article stated that video sales were progressing slowly, but the journalist based the article on extremely limited information from only several video stores and subsequently made a judgment about the video sales in the city and around the country. Anyone with a limited knowledge of statistics realizes the problems that result from miniscule samples used to make predictions about the entire population. Store manager Meredith O'Donnell said of the prequel, "It's not like *The Sixth Sense*." Although he meant that the prequel was not selling as well as the Bruce Willis thriller, his statement was still unintentionally accurate; *The Phantom Menace* far outsold *The Sixth Sense*.

Another report that followed the movie's release similarly attempted to undermine the prequel's video sales. *The Chicago Sun-Times* published an article titled, "Phantom sales for 'Star Wars'." The article boldly stated that the first day of sales for *The Phantom Menace* contrasted with that of *Titanic*, which is an inaccurate statement because the *Star Wars* prequel sold at least as well on its first day of release as the James Cameron epic. Reporting slow sales at local stores is valid, but both articles attempted to draw conclusions about nationwide sales from just a few selected stores, which is impossible because tens of thousands of retail outlets sell videos.

The continued absurd, inaccurate reporting of *The Phantom Menace's* success mattered little when Fox released the official sales information. In advance of the official statements, industry trade-paper *Variety* reported on April 6 that stores had indicated very strong video sales on the movie's first day. The sales figures for the movie, which Fox released the following day, were astonishing.

Fox reported that *The Phantom Menace* sold five million videos in its first two days alone, which accounted for a whopping $100 million in consumer spending. The movie required five days at the box office to gross the same amount, but in only its first two days selling in video stores, it annihilated the prequel's box office gross over the comparable two-day opening period, which came in at slightly more than $40 million. The sales figures completely shattered previous records and again silenced any doubters.

In the first two days of release, the movie sold 500,000 of the 1.5 million available widescreen collector's editions. The remaining 4.5 million copies sold were pan and scan versions of the film. Mike Dunn, executive vice president of marketing and sales for Fox, said that about 4% of all sales originated from online stores such as Amazon.com. Roughly 200,000 copies sold online, setting a new record. Doug Thomas, New Releases Editor at Amazon.com, said at the time of release, "[Both editions] are still number one and two on our charts. And because of our clientele, the deluxe set is outselling the pan and scan version." Online stores eventually slashed prices on *Titanic* and sold it as a loss-leader, but nothing similar occurred with *The Phantom Menace.*

Before the release of the prequel, Fox had sold a total of more than 70 million copies of various versions of the three previous *Star Wars* movies, 46 million of which came from the United States. *Titanic* sold around 28 million copies in the United States, but *The Lion King* rests atop the charts with 30 million copies sold. After the first two days of sales, *The Phantom Menace* was assured a spot in the all-time top ten best-selling live-action videos. Analysts expected it to reach sales of roughly eighteen million copies, just ahead of the 17.5 million that *Independence Day* sold. Referring to the amazing sales, Lucasfilm spokeswoman Lynne Hale said, "We're absolutely thrilled."

According to the VideoScan data tracking service, and published in the *Hollywood Reporter* on April 20, *The Phantom Menace* had sold about twelve million copies. The prequel crushed the previous top video, *Pokémon the First Movie*, by a margin of 10-to-1. Reports indicated that Fox shipped all of their collector's editions to retailers by the first weekend of release and a majority of stores sold most of their copies shortly thereafter. *The Phantom Menace* did not just succeed in the sales market; it also became a popular rental.

In *The Phantom Menace's* first five days of release, it made $8.5 million in rental revenue, according to *Video Store Magazine* research. The figure set a new record for a movie released for sale and rent simultaneously. The previous record holder, *Mulan* (1998), made $6.8 million, or about 25% less than the *Star Wars* prequel. The rental gross was especially impressive considering that millions of people skipped renting the movie and chose to buy it instead. After one week of rentals, *The Phantom Menace* reached $11.95 million and landed in second place behind *The Sixth Sense*, which could not be purchased at a sell-through price at the time, meaning consumers had to rent it if they wanted to see the popular movie.

During the following week, *The Phantom Menace* added $7.24 million in rentals, falling to third place behind *Three Kings*, which just debuted. Nevertheless, its rental total rose to $19.26 million while the video sales kept skyrocketing as it retained its number one ranking. After its third week, the prequel fell to sixth place, but added $4.82 million, bringing its rental gross to $24.08 million. Through November 26, 2000, *The Phantom Menace* grossed $43.76 million from rentals.

The Phantom Menace continued to sell well throughout its first weeks, remaining the top selling video for more than a month. It also remained in the top ten best selling videos throughout most of the summer of 2000, which is a notable accomplishment considering the sizeable competition in the video sales market. When the year ended, the prequel was crowned the best-selling live-action video of 2000. *The Phantom Menace* VHS also boosted revenue for several video chains because the winter months are often slow for sales and the prequel arrived just after the beginning of spring.

In a company press release on May 4, the Musicland Stores Corporation announced that comparable-store sales increased 17% for the four weeks ended April 29. Keith A. Benson, vice chairman and chief financial officer said, "April sales were terrific. The late Easter combined with vigorous sales of *Star Wars: Episode One*, and strong gains in electronics, DVD and CD sales contributed to the solid results." The Mall Stores Division of Musicland Stores Corporation operates the Suncoast Motion Picture Company, which sold hundreds of thousands of *Phantom Menace* videos nationwide. Year-to-year sales increased 18.6% in April for the Mall Stores Division, which includes Sam Goody.

The difficulty of tracking exact video sales numbers stems from the multitude of stores that sell videos nationwide. VideoScan is the only company that attempts to track actual sales to customers, but even they have difficulty reporting accurate information. According to Scott Hettrick of *Video Business Magazine*, actual sales of *The Phantom Menace* on VHS approached twelve million copies by the end of 2000, although the discrepancy between VideoScan's numbers and Fox's reported sales comes from the copies still on store shelves.

As the video began to fall from the top ten weekly bestsellers, Lucasfilm made no further announcements about a DVD release of the *Star Wars* movies. Nevertheless, fans on the Internet continued to speculate that an announcement was imminent, at least for the DVD of *The Phantom Menace*. On June 19, 2001, Lucasfilm broke their silence with a news story on the Official *Star Wars* Website titled, "DVD: The Wait is Over." The DVD announcement told fans everywhere that *The Phantom Menace* would become available on DVD worldwide by October 16 or shortly thereafter, depending on the country.

Lucasfilm announced the two-disc DVD set by including details about the special features planned for inclusion. In addition to a THX mastered, anamorphic widescreen version of the film for fans to see in all of its digital glory, a team of more than 100 people at Lucasfilm worked for more than eighteen months to build the special features for the DVD. The highlight of the two-disc set is a collection of seven previously unseen, deleted sequences that effects artists at Industrial Light & Magic (ILM) completed specifically for the DVD release.

Never before had a team of visual effects artists finished sequences solely for a DVD release without the intention of having the scenes placed into the finished film. Special effects supervisor Pablo Helman was in charge of all of the work on the deleted scenes, which required 300 special effects shots. Only a few movies in history prior to the DVD release of *The Phantom Menace* had 300 special effects shots total, let alone in just deleted scenes.

Although the deleted scenes remained separate from the film, Lucas liked a few of the changes enough to ask that ILM integrate them into the film for its DVD release. The first such change occurs during the podrace, where numerous small additions add to the second lap of the race, expanding the action and making it feel even more realistic and exhilarating. The second change occurs on Coruscant roughly 82 minutes into the film, where a newly added sequence shows Anakin and Jar Jar joining Padmé on an air taxi that weaves through the planet-wide city until reaching the Queen's quarters. The sequence is brief, but really shows the vastness of the city and its great architecture in even more depth.

Aside from additional scenes both in the movie and as part of the special features section, Lucasfilm packed the DVD for *The Phantom Menace* with plenty of other features. An audio commentary track includes comments from George Lucas, Rick McCallum, co-editor and sound designer Ben Burtt, visual effects supervisors Scott Squires, John Knoll, and Dennis Muren, along with animation supervisor Rob Coleman. Another feature allows viewers to flip from storyboards to animatics to the finished film so fans can see the various stages of production.

Five featurettes give viewers an insight into various aspects of the production process, including the design, fights, story, costumes, and visual effects. Lucasfilm included the twelve-part series of Lynne Hale's diaries on the DVD, all of which originally appeared online. Several galleries full of pictures also appear on the DVD ranging from advertising and print related photos to behind-the-scenes photos. Additionally, theatrical trailers and television spots advertising the movie appear alongside the other extra features.

Besides the numerous extra features already mentioned, the DVD includes a documentary titled "The Beginning," which Stanford film school graduate Jon Shenk put together from more than 600 hours of footage that he filmed over the course of two and a half years. Shenk had just graduated from Stanford a year earlier when Lucasfilm hired him to follow Lucas throughout the filmmaking process and film nearly every detail. Originally, Shenk's footage was just for the purposes of the 20th Century Fox publicity department, although some footage came to the Official *Star Wars* Website.

Shenk always wanted to use his footage as part of an actual documentary on the film, but Lucas was unsure about the idea. Shenk told *The Washington Post*, "The idea was to shoot first and ask questions later. My sense was, 'This is an amazing opportunity to make a great film.'" After his job with Lucasfilm ended, eighteen months elapsed before the company called him again, in February 2001, about turning his footage into a documentary film for the DVD release. Shenk edited together the one-hour documentary in just two months, an impressive accomplishment given the huge wealth of material he had filmed. When speaking of the filming on the movie, he said, "There was a quasi-religious-like feeling of working on *Episode I*. It was like working on a new chapter of the Bible."

Overall, Lucasfilm spent $4 million on the extra features for *The Phantom Menace* DVD, which set a new record for spending on a DVD release. No company had ever created such a high budget DVD production. At a presentation to the media held at Skywalker Ranch, Lucas told reporters of his decision to release *The Phantom Menace* on DVD, despite earlier saying he would only release the *Star Wars* films after Episode III, "There were pressures to release [*The Phantom Menace*]." Lucas said previously, however, that he only wanted to create high quality productions of the films on DVD, so he held to his word with the release of *The Phantom Menace*.

Van Ling, who previously worked on the DVD editions for *The Abyss* (1989) and *Terminator 2: Judgment Day* (1991), produced the DVD for *The Phantom*

Menace, which includes three totally different sets of homepage and chapter menus. McCallum said during a press conference in early September at Sky-walker Ranch, "We knew we didn't want to do the typical thing that happens. There's a video master out there for the videocassette, and then somebody takes that, throws it down, and lays it out on the DVD. You then have 15 minutes of 'How great it is working with George' and 'Isn't Rick nice' and 'His hair is weird' and all the other strange stuff that you get." Unfortunately McCallum's observations are correct; many DVDs, especially ones released earlier in the format's history, just have lame filler for extra features, but no substantial, viewable extras.

During the press conference, Lucas also further explained his motivations for completing the DVD before his original plans. "I really needed to have the people who were involved in [the original production] do it. If I'd waited for another four years, it wouldn't be as easy to accomplish all that." Lucas and McCallum actually had to review work from the DVD for *The Phantom Menace* while film-ing *Episode II* in Australia. McCallum said, "It made our stay in Australia differ-ent because there was virtually no free time whatsoever. We were either shooting or we were working on the DVD." Even with the additions to the DVD, scenes amounting to "another half hour of bits and pieces," according to Lucas, are still unavailable for fans to see.

Lucas and McCallum both emphasized how educational the DVD format can be for young people wanting to enter filmmaking. The behind-the-scenes looks at various movies through their DVD releases really helps potential filmmakers gain a familiarity of the process. Aside from the extra features filmmakers can include on DVDs, Lucas and McCallum both were perhaps happiest just having the film available in such a high quality format for viewers. Lucas said of the DVD for *The Phantom Menace*, "I look at the DVD as the highest quality version of the film that's going to be continuously in the marketplace so I want it to be the best pos-sible way to see the film."

All of the hundreds of hours of work that many people put into creating the two-disc *Phantom Menace* DVD set proved a very rewarding experience when the movie began to set sales records and win awards. Because of the popularity of the film along with an outpouring from fans, including 30,000 signatures in one month from DigitalBits.com, a DVD fan site, asking Lucas to release the film on DVD, analysts expected impressive sales. "It's got every chance of being the fast-est-selling DVD of all time," said Tom Adams of Adams Media Research. Pre-orders from Amazon.com also indicated strong demand.

At the time of release for *The Phantom Menace* on DVD, *Gladiator* (2000) was the best selling disc ever, but *The Mummy Returns* (2001) had just set a sales record the week prior by selling two million copies within one week. When *The Phantom Menace* finally became available on DVD on October 16, consumers spent $17 million on the disc at traditional retail outlets, a new record, according to Fox. "*The Phantom Menace* DVD set a record when it sold more on its release day than any other title in Musicland's DVD history," said Peter Busch, vice president of video operations for Musicland, which operates more than 1,300 Sam Goody, Suncoast, On Cue, and Media Play stores in the United States.

Fox shipped 2.4 million DVD sets on orders of 3.3 million products total, but the first day sales had many stores worried about running out of discs. Fox reported that total consumer spending on the VHS and DVD copies of *The Phantom Menace* had risen to $260 million after the first day of DVD sales, so one could accurately estimate that the VHS version sold at least twelve million copies to consumers at Hettrick had confirmed.

After one week in stores, *The Phantom Menace* set another sales record with 2.2 million copies sold, slightly eclipsing the previous record. Consumers had spent a total of $45 million on the DVD for *The Phantom Menace* after one week. Understandably, Lucasfilm and Fox officials were delighted with the news. "Our tracking shows that the sales velocity for *Episode I* is greater than *Gladiator*, the No. 1-selling DVD of all time, and *The Mummy Returns*, the previous No. 1-selling DVD of the year," said Mike Dunn, executive vice president of sales and marketing at Twentieth Century Fox Home Entertainment. Jim Ward, vice president of marketing for Lucasfilm noted, "This stellar sales performance is even more impressive given that it is nearly three years after its theatrical release and eighteen months after its VHS release."

In September, before the release of the DVD, the Video Premieres Academy, made up of more than 60 voting members from the movie and television communities ranging in profession from directors to critics, nominated *The Phantom Menace* DVD for five awards. It received nominations for Best Overall New Extra Features, Best Original Retrospective Documentary ("The Beginning"), Best New, Enhanced or Reconstructed Movie Scenes, Best Audio Commentary, and Best DVD Menu Design. In October, the Video Premieres Academy announced the winners, which included one win for *The Phantom Menace* for Best DVD Menu Design.

In August 2002, well after the DVD release, *The Phantom Menace* practically swept the 5th Annual DVD Awards, winning in four categories: "Viewer's Choice," "Best Authoring," "Best Menu Design," and "Best Audio Presentation." No other competing DVD at the show, held at the DVD Entertainment Conference & Showcase, won as many awards. Ward said after learning of the awards,

"The *Episode I* disc was really a labor of love, since we knew that fans had been waiting a long time to be able to watch *Star Wars* in the best video format available. We wanted not only to make a disc worthy of that anticipation, but also raise the bar and set a benchmark for what a *Star Wars* DVD should be."

Aside from the VHS and DVD releases of *The Phantom Menace*, the film also enjoyed an impressive network television debut on November 25, 2001, helping Fox during the key sweeps period. The film played from 7:00 p.m. to 10:00 p.m., becoming somewhat of an oddity in the process because it had not played on cable or pay-per-view before its network premiere.

In the key 18-49 age demographic, the film enjoyed a 7.9 rating and an 18 share, meaning 7.9% of all television households in the age range watched the movie while 18% of all televisions on at the time, among the age group, were tuned to *The Phantom Menace*. The stats were the best in eighteen months for any film on network television, helping Fox win the night in all key measurements and also thrusting the network slightly ahead of NBC for the month. No movie in the 18-49 bracket had enjoyed such a high rating since the airing of the first part of CBS's *Jesus* mini-series and no film in the 18-34 age range had such high ratings since *Men in Black* in November 1999. The debut also annihilated *Titanic's* network premiere, which managed a rather unimpressive 6.9 rating and a 15 share on NBC during the previous season.

The success of *The Phantom Menace* on VHS and DVD serves as an upbeat ending to the story of the most anticipated movie of all-time. The strong video and DVD sales supported the impressive box office figures and the widely positive exit polls, which all indicate that audiences overwhelmingly approved of the first prequel and were eager for the next two installments of the saga. The network premiere also exposed a number of other people to the saga, inevitably raising the percentage of audiences familiar with the prequel.

Epilogue

In the history of cinema, few movies have suffered from the same weight of expectation as *The Phantom Menace*. In addition to the preconceived notions of moviegoers and fans, entire industries and corporations relied on the prequel's success to deliver them from difficult times. Despite the incredible expectations, *The Phantom Menace* succeeded at becoming one of the most successful movies of all-time.

The unprecedented media coverage helped introduce the movie, and the saga, to people all over the world, but it also created the expectations that often hindered the accurate reporting of the movie's success. *The Phantom Menace* broke records across many industries, but uninformed members of the media called its performance a disappointment. Most journalists are not qualified to discuss the box office because usually only writers working for industry trade papers such as *Variety* and *The Hollywood Reporter* are knowledgeable about the financial intricacies of the film industry. Nevertheless, the frenzy to find stories about the most anticipated movie of all-time led to many sloppy and inaccurate articles, specifically about the movie's merchandise and ticket sales, as even the media sought to profit from the phenomenon.

After the movie exited theaters, the toy craze died down, fans purchased their videos and DVDs, and the media moved on to the next major story, *The Phantom Menace* had already made its impact on popular culture. The movie became the first to showcase the digital projection technology that is likely to dominate the top quality theaters in the new millennium. It also introduced the superior 6.1 channel sound system that is already used in thousands of auditoriums nationwide, but it accomplished far more than just the introduction of new theater equipment.

The Phantom Menace benefited from an innovative marketing campaign that helped present the film to moviegoers worldwide. The Internet is becoming increasingly important in the promotion of new releases, but studios typically offer a simple Website for their movies that fails to capture the interest of moviegoers and Web surfers. *The Phantom Menace* demonstrated how studios can use the Internet to increase interest in their movies, which travels beyond just cyberspace. Tens of millions of movie fans downloaded each prequel trailer, which helped add to the excitement that continued to build until the movie's release. Daily updates to the Official *Star Wars* Website encouraged visitors to return frequently, unlike many movie Websites that are updated sporadically, if at all.

In addition to the fantastic promotion of *The Phantom Menace* on the Internet, the free advertising that the movie received from newspapers, magazines, and television programs pioneered a new form of advertising. Although the media publishes articles relating to every movie before its release, *The Phantom Menace* enjoyed saturation coverage from hundreds of media outlets nationwide. The media's fascination with *Star Wars* virtually eliminated the need for paid advertising, which is a unique occurrence in the history of movie marketing. The demand and anticipation for the movie forced Twentieth Century Fox and Lucasfilm to exercise caution regarding paid advertising in an attempt to avoid a hype backlash.

The most remarkable feat that *The Phantom Menace* accomplished was giving back to the community and helping less fortunate people in society. Lincoln Gasking and fellow fans who lined up for the movie in front of Mann's Chinese Theatre raised thousands of dollars for the Starlight Children's Foundation while TheForce.net donated almost ten thousand dollars collected from advertising revenue on their Website to the staff members' favorite charities. Most significantly, *The Phantom Menace* premiered first to benefit charities, raising millions of dollars for children's funds across North America. In December 1999, following its successful theatrical run, it became the first movie ever to play in North American theaters for the sole benefit of charity, raising millions of additional dollars for hundreds of nonprofit organizations. The joint effort between major companies and major fans helped make *The Phantom Menace* one of the most charitable movies ever produced.

The Phantom Menace did not please every fan, but it succeeded at introducing the characters and setting up the saga, which the vast majority of moviegoers appreciated. The movie introduced *Star Wars* to many people, young and old. A poll on the Official *Star Wars* Website indicated that 5% of the fans polled between 2/17/00 and 2/24/00 became enthusiasts because of the first prequel. The percentage is likely to grow in the future as more fans see and enjoy the movie on video, DVD, and TV.

George Lucas increased his net worth significantly because of *The Phantom Menace*, which analysts had anticipated well in advance of the movie's release. According to *Forbes* magazine, Lucas earned $400 million in 1999, which easily ranked him first on the celebrity moneymakers list. The second place contender,

Oprah Winfrey, made $150 million, which is a massive total, but far from Lucas's impressive haul.

The magazine ranked Julia Roberts ahead of Lucas on their power list, which seems rather absurd and unjustified. Roberts is a bankable star, but Lucas controls the most powerful movie franchise in existence. *Forbes'* choice is questionable because one can hardly consider a movie star more powerful than the owner of a major studio that provides post-production services for a large percentage of the major movies in Hollywood and the most impressive commercials on TV. The magazine claims that the power list is based on income and on magazine cover appearances, television appearances, and several other factors. Nevertheless, Roberts did not have nearly as many cover appearances as Lucas and his creation, *The Phantom Menace*. In the following year's issue, Lucas once again was the top money earner with $250 million.

The Phantom Menace continued *Star Wars'* reign as the most popular movie saga and placed the prequel trilogy on course to become the highest grossing trilogy of all-time. The original *Star Wars Trilogy* has grossed $1.04 billion at the North American box office, barely ranking it first, above *The Lord of the Rings Trilogy* at $1.03 billion, the first three *Harry Potter* films at $829.1 million, and the *Jurassic Park* movies at $767.3 million. Lucas's own adventure trilogy, the *Indiana Jones Trilogy*, has collected $619.4 million in North America and still ranks among the top film trilogies of all time at the box office. Inevitably, the release of *Spider-Man 3* will put the *Spider-Man Trilogy* ahead of the original *Star Wars Trilogy*, but not before *Star Wars: Episode III—Revenge of the Sith* likely places the prequel trilogy in first place.

Ticket price inflation between 1999 and 2002 gave *Star Wars: Episode II—Attack of the Clones* a slight edge at the box office compared to *The Phantom Menace*, although the prequel sequel had difficulty selling more tickets than the hugely anticipated *Episode I*. Each *Star Wars* movie has performed phenomenally well financially, which continued with *Attack of the Clones*, though not to the same degree as *The Phantom Menace*. Nonetheless, *Attack of the Clones* continued the most epic saga in movie history and also helped illuminate a lot of plot elements in *The Phantom Menace*, making the first prequel an even more enjoyable film.

Lucas's decision to film *Attack of the Clones* entirely with digital equipment assured that the *Star Wars Saga* continued to influence the movie industry and its technology, the effects of which will continue into the future. *Star Wars* has forced Lucasfilm to innovate and use new filmmaking methods to translate Lucas's vision to film. The second prequel offered even more detailed and complicated special effects, which once again raised the bar for other post-production companies.

The release of *The Phantom Menace* began a new era for the *Star Wars Saga*, ending the period of revival that started in 1991 and beginning a new Golden Age that continues through the final prequel, a 2005 event. The prequel era has been an exciting one for *Star Wars* fans, but one with several dangers. Society has become more cynical since the release of the first *Star Wars Trilogy*, making the media eager to build each movie to gargantuan proportions, only to tear it down when they decide it is no longer fashionable.

After hyping *The Phantom Menace* for more than a year, the media began its attempt to tarnish the *Star Wars* name in early May, when the first reviews began to surface. Although the reviewers generally expressed their enjoyment of the movie, they criticized it for the same elements the original trilogy supposedly lacked. The mixed reviews should not have surprised long-time fans because even the first *Star Wars* film in 1977 suffered from a scattering of negative reviews from cynical and narrow-minded critics. Nevertheless, the media began to ridicule *The Phantom Menace* and downplay its success, which continued throughout the summer.

Surprisingly, the combined might of nearly every media empire could not sink *The Phantom Menace* or tarnish the *Star Wars* name. Typically, when the media turns against a film, or a person, recovering from the negative press is almost impossible. *The Phantom Menace* continued to prove its critics wrong and embarrass the media for downplaying the facts. Towards the middle of the summer, another shift in momentum began. After many media organizations realized that perhaps they could not prevent the success of *The Phantom Menace*, they began to abandon their previous negative dispositions.

As *The Phantom Menace* shattered box office records, many magazines and newspapers reluctantly conceded that the movie was a success. The organizations also realized that with two more *Star Wars* movies on the horizon, they had to prepare to use the popularity of the next two prequels for their own profit. Fans anxious to hear any new detail about *The Phantom Menace* snatched up magazines and newspapers containing supposedly exclusive *Star Wars* stories, which boosted sales for the publications significantly. The media did not miss its chance to profit from *Attack of the Clones* and will not miss its chance to benefit from *Episode III* either.

The most surprising media victory for *The Phantom Menace* came months after its release. In issue #540 of *Entertainment Weekly*, printed in the spring of 2000, Jim Mullen declared *The Phantom Menace* the number one most important entertainment event of the entire decade, defeating *Titanic* at number thirteen, the Internet at number ten, and Michael Jordan at number seven, among others. *Entertainment Weekly*, or at least Mullen, finally recognized the importance of *The Phantom Menace* as one of the most influential entertainment events in history.

The Phantom Menace continued the tradition of excellence associated with the *Star Wars Saga* and it serves as a suitable introduction to the characters, the prequel trilogy, and the saga as a whole. *Star Wars: Episode II—Attack of the Clones* is set ten years after the events in the first prequel and stars a more mature Anakin Skywalker. The effects dazzled moviegoers once again, but most importantly, the story for which fans have waited years continued to unravel. *Attack of the Clones* arrived in theaters in May 2002, but until its release, *Star Wars* fans had to wait in anxious anticipation.

Bibliography

"5th person sentenced in 'Star Wars' movie theft." <u>Milwaukee Journal Sentinel</u> 6 Dec. 1999.

"20 Reasons Why Star Wars: The Phantom Menace is Going to be Incredible!" <u>X Posé</u> May 1999.

"60 Minutes on George Lucas." <u>The Official Star Wars Website</u> 16 Mar. 1999. Internet. Available: http://www.starwars.com.

"A Digital Episode I." <u>The Official Star Wars Website</u> 18 Jun. 1999. Internet. Available: http://www.starwars.com.

"A Look at Leavesden." <u>The Official Star Wars Website</u> 9 Mar. 1998. Internet. Available: http://www.starwars.com.

Adams, Doug. "Sounds of the Empire." <u>Film Score Monthly</u> Jun. 1999.

"Additional Guests to Join the Star Wars Celebration." <u>The Official Star Wars Website</u> 29 Mar. 1999. Internet. Available: http://www.starwars.com.

"Advance Phantom Tix Approved." <u>Mr. Show Biz</u> 26 Apr. 1999. Internet. Available: http://www.mrshowbiz.com.

"Amazon.com Announces Hottest Books, Music, Videos and DVDs of the Year as Determined by Editors' Picks and Customer Sales." <u>Amazon</u> 22 Nov. 1999. Internet. Available: http://www.amazon.com.

"At No. 4, It's Still A Menace." <u>Show Biz Data</u> 22 Jun. 1999. Internet. Available: http://www.showbizdata.com.

Albom, Mitch. "'Star Wars' geeks need to get a life." <u>Detroit Free Press</u> 11 Apr. 1999. Internet. Available: http://www.freep.com.

Angelo, Jesse. "Galactic Battle Shaping Up For Gala Premiere Tix." <u>New York Post</u> 18 Apr. 1999. Internet. Available: http://www.nypost.com.

Barry, Dave. "Watch where you stick that light saber, pal." 28 Apr. 1999.

Beck, Rachel. "Stores Prepare for Wars." Associated Press 13 Apr. 1999.

Beggy, Carol, and Beth Carney. "Lucas's sweet charity." Boston Globe 14 Apr. 1999. Internet. Available: http://www.boston.com.

Birchenough, Tom. "Auds say 'da' to 21st Moscow Fest." Variety 2 Aug. 1999. Internet. Available: http://www.variety.com.

Birchenough, Tom. "'Phantom' toppling Russian B.O. records." Variety 20 Aug. 1999. Internet. Available: http://www.variety.com.

Boehm, Erich. "U.K. eyes release dates." Variety 1 Jul. 1999. Internet. Available: http://www.variety.com.

Bond, Jeff. "The Second Coming." Film Score Monthly Jun. 1999.

Bormann, Dawn. "Video store will resemble a galaxy far, far away." The Kansas City Star 31 Mar. 2000. Internet. Available: http://www.kcstar.com.

"Boss Nass to Celebrate with Star Wars Fans." The Official Star Wars Website 17 Feb. 1999. Internet. Available: http://www.starwars.com.

Bowles, Hamish. "Star Wars Couture." Vogue Apr. 1999.

Broersma, Matthew. "'Menace' trailer premieres on the net." ZDNN 11 Mar. 1999. Internet. Available: http://www.zdnet.com.

Broersma, Matthew. "The Force is definitely with them." ZDNN 9 Apr. 1999. Internet. Available: http://www.zdnet.com.

Brown, Janelle. "Official Star Wars Site Launches—But Who Knew?" Wired 3 Dec. 1996. Internet. Available: http://www.wired.com.

"Buzz Wars, Episode One: The Backlash Menace." Newsweek 18 Jan. 1999.

Byrne, Bridget. "Fox Jumps over Cable to Air 'Phantom Menace'." E! Online 25 May 1999. Internet. Available: http://www.eonline.com.

Byrne, Bridget. "'Phantom Menace' Menaced by Expectations." E! Online 23 May 1999. Internet. Available: http://www.eonline.com.

Byrne, Bridget. "'Phantom Menace' Unstoppable." E! Online 6 Jun. 1999. Internet. Available: http://www.eonline.com.

Cahill, Phillippe. "B.O. 'Crown' prince." Variety 8 Sep. 1999. Internet. Available: http://www.variety.com.

Cahill, Phillippe. "Buena Vista Intl. Dominates o'seas b.o." Variety 26 Oct. 1999. Internet. Available: http://www.variety.com.

Cahill, Phillippe. "Fun, fear fly high." Variety 25 Oct. 1999. Internet. Available: http://www.variety.com.

Cahill, Phillippe. "Julia wins o'seas." Variety 4 Oct. 1999. Internet. Available: http://www.variety.com.

Cahill, Phillippe. "'Menace' ascendant." Variety 19 Oct. 1999. Internet. Available: http://www.variety.com.

Cahill, Phillippe. "'Phantom' fantastic." Variety 13 Sep. 1999. Internet. Available: http://www.variety.com.

Carvell, Tim. "Hello, Mr. Chips (Goodbye, Mr. Film) Hollywood gets ready to go digital. All it will take is $1.6 billion, more or less, and cooperation In other words, a miracle.." Fortune 16 Aug. 1999. Internet. Available: http://www.elibrary.com.

"Charity Screenings." The Official Star Wars Website 22 Nov. 1999. Internet. Available: http://www.starwars.com.

Chernoff, Scott. "Child of the Force: Is This 9-Year Old Kid Really Darth Vader?" Star Wars Insider, Issue 39, Aug./Sep. 1998.

Chernoff, Scott. "Evil Has A New Name." Star Wars Insider, Issue 42, Feb./Mar. 1999.

Chernoff, Scott. "Portrait of the Jedi as a young man." Star Wars Insider, Issue 41, Dec./Jan. 1998/1999.

Chernoff, Scott. "Something Wicked This Way Comes." Star Wars Insider, Issue 37, Apr./May 1998.

Chernoff, Scott. "Stamp of Approval." Star Wars Insider, Issue 41, Dec./Jan. 1998/1999.

Chernoff, Scott. "The Quarshie Quotient: An Exclusive, Outspoken Interview with Hugh Quarshie, Episode I's Powerful Captain Panaka." Star Wars Insider, Issue 40, Oct./Nov. 1998.

"Classical." Billboard 2000. Internet. Available: http://www.billboard.com.

Coker, Cheo Hodari. "Shot by Shot." Premiere Jul. 1999.

"COMMTech Gives Kids Innovative Ways to Enjoy Star Wars Episode I." Hasbro 8 Feb. 1999. Internet. Available: http://www.hasbro.com.

Corbin, Jim. Personal interview. 27 Feb. 2001.

Corliss, Richard. "Ready, Set, Glow!" Time 26 Apr. 1999.

Cote, Steve. Personal interview. 7 Mar. 2001.

Cox, Dan. "Portman mulls 'Wars' prequel." Variety 9 Apr. 1997. Internet. Available: http://www.variety.com.

Crabb, Michael. "Phantom Menace fever sweeps Russia." The Arts Report 20 Aug. 1999.

Craughwell, Kathleen. "It's a Long Time to Go for a Movie Far, Far Away." Los Angeles Times 10 Apr. 1999. Internet. Available: http://www.latimes.com.

Cronn, Tad. "'Phantom' shows us our dark side." Seattle Post-Intelligencer 18 Jun. 1999.

Dawtrey, Adam. "April auds dry up in England." Variety 9 Jun. 1999. Internet. Available: http://www.variety.com.

Dawtrey, Adam. "Fox blocks brit exhibs' 'Wars' plan." Variety 1 Jul. 1999. Internet. Available: http://www.variety.com.

Dawtrey, Adam. "O'seas B.O. slump casts pall on Expo." Variety 22 Jun. 1999. Internet. Available: http://www.variety.com.

Dawtrey, Adam. "Profits drop for U.K.'s Odeon chain." <u>Variety</u> 6 Aug. 1999. Internet. Available: <u>http://www.variety.com</u>.

Dawtrey, Adam. "U.K. tix sales dip a bit." <u>Variety</u> 29 Jan. 1999. Internet. Available: <u>http://www.variety.com</u>.

Dempsey, John. "ABC, Disney pinch 'Grinch'." <u>Variety</u> 3 Jan. 2001. Internet. Available: <u>http://www.variety.com</u>.

"Denver goes wacky over 'Star Wars'." <u>Microsoft News</u> 26 Mar. 1999. Internet. Available: <u>http://www.msnbc.com</u>.

Diamond, Jamie. "Portman's Prime." <u>Mademoiselle</u> Nov. 1999.

"Digital 'Menace' Opens." <u>Reuters</u> 18 Jun. 1999. Internet. Available: <u>http://www.wired.com</u>.

"Digital Sound and Advance Ticket Sales." <u>The Official Star Wars Website</u> 24 Mar. 1999. Internet. Available: <u>http://www.starwars.com</u>.

Docherty, Alan. "Star Wars: The British Invasion." <u>Wired</u> 9 Apr. 1999. Internet. Available: <u>http://www.wired.com</u>.

"Domestic Box Office." <u>Variety</u> 27 Dec. 1999. Internet. Available: <u>http://www.variety.com</u>.

"Domestic Box Office." <u>Variety</u> 4 Jan. 2000. Internet. Available: <u>http://www.variety.com</u>.

Donahue, Ann and Tim Swanson. "H'wood hits paydirt in playtime." <u>Variety</u> 20 Dec. 2000. Internet. Available: <u>http://www.variety.com</u>.

Dumas, Alan. "City will host 'Star Wars' convention." <u>Denver Rocky Mountain News</u> 13 Feb. 1999. Internet. Available: <u>http://www.elibrary.com</u>.

Dyer, Richard. "Making Star Wars Sing Again." <u>Film Score Monthly</u> Jun. 1999.

Elliott, Stuart. "The Hype Is With Us: The Lucas Empire Is Invading." <u>New York Times</u> 14 May 1999. Internet. Available: <u>http://www.nytimes.com</u>.

"Episode I News And The Advent Of The Digital Cinema Era: George Lucas Speaks At ShoWest." The Official Star Wars Website 10 Mar. 1999. Internet. Available: http://www.starwars.com.

"Episode I Opening." The Official Star Wars Website 5 Nov. 1999. Internet. Available: http://www.starwars.com.

"Episode I Ticket Update." The Official Star Wars Website 23 Apr. 1999. Internet. Available: http://www.starwars.com.

"Episode I Title." The Official Star Wars Website 25 Sep. 1998. Internet. Available: http://www.starwars.com.

"Episode I To Be Screened Digitally In Four Theaters Starting June 18, 1999." The Official Star Wars Website 3 Jun. 1999. Internet. Available: http://www.starwars.com.

"Episode I Trailer Announcement." The Official Star Wars Website 28 Jan. 1999. Internet. Available: http://www.starwars.com.

"Episode I VHS Releases." The Official Star Wars Website 6 Jan. 2000. Internet. Available: http://www.starwars.com.

Errico, Marcus. "Neeson Could Lead Next 'Star Wars'." E! Online 3 Apr. 1997. Internet. Available: http://www.eonline.com.

Errico, Marcus. "The Force Is with MovieFone." E! Online 23 Apr. 1999. Internet. Available: http://www.eonline.com.

Fader, Shanti. "In Sheep's Clothing: The Face of Evil in The Phantom Menace." Parabola Winter 1999.

Farache, Emily. "America's Wealthiest? Spielberg, Oprah Make Cut." E! Online 24 Sep. 1999. Internet. Available: http://www.eonline.com.

Farache, Emily. "Studios Blocking Box-Office Estimates." E! Online 30 Oct. 1999. Internet. Available: http://www.eonline.com.

Fierman, Daniel and Gilian Flynn. "Jedi Mind Tricks." Entertainment Weekly 21 May 1999.

"First Phase of Episode 1 Production Wraps at Leavesden Studios." The Official Star Wars Website 29 Sep. 1997. Internet. Available: http://www.starwars.com.

"First Strike." The Official Star Wars Website 30 Apr. 1999. Internet. Available: http://www.starwars.com.

Fitzpatrick, Kevin. "The Sound and the Fury." Star Wars Insider, Issue 42, Feb./Mar. 1999.

Fleeman, Michael. "Strict Terms for Star Wars." Associated Press 6 Apr. 1999.

Fleming, Michael. "Dish." Variety 15 Apr. 1997. Internet. Available: http://www.variety.com.

"Fox To Distribute Next Three Star Wars Movies." The Official Star Wars Website 2 Apr. 1998. Internet. Available: http://www.starwars.com.

Frankel, Daniel. "Movies Next Net Piracy Threat, Officials Say." E! Online 17 May 1999. Internet. Available: http://www.eonline.com.

Frankel, Daniel. "'Phantom Menace' Breaking Box-Office Speed Records." E! Online 16 Jun. 1999. Internet. Available: http://www.eonline.com.

Frankel, Daniel. "'Phantom Menace' Copy Stolen in Wisconsin." E! Online 24 May 1999. Internet. Available: http://www.eonline.com.

Frankel, Daniel. "'Star Wars' Deal May End Toy Maker's Story." E! Online 27 Feb. 1998. Internet. Available: http://www.eonline.com.

Frankel, Daniel. "'Star Wars' Junkies: Your Junk Arrives May 3." E! Online 15 Apr. 1999. Internet. Available: http://www.eonline.com.

Frankel, Daniel. "'Star Wars' Takes a Dive." E! Online 21 May 1999. Internet. Available: http://www.eonline.com.

Frankel, Daniel. "'Star Wars' Toy Trouble." E! Online 12 Jul. 1999. Internet. Available: http://www.eonline.com.

Frankel, Daniel. "'Star Wars' Trailer All Over the Web." E! Online 18 Nov. 1998. Internet. Available: http://www.eonline.com.

Frankel, Daniel. "Wisconsin Thieves' 'Star Wars' Plot Unravels." E! Online 26 May 1999. Internet. Available: http://www.eonline.com.

French, Lawrence. "George Lucas returns to the director's chair for Episode 1." Cinefantastique Apr. 1999.

"Galoob Toys Secures Small-Scale-Toy Rights For The Next Three Star Wars Movies; Lucas Companies Take Major Equity Stake in Galoob." Galoob Web Site 14 Oct. 1997. Internet. Available: http://www.galoob.com.

Genovese, Peter. Personal interview. 28 Feb. 2001.

"Germany starry-eyed for 'Star Wars'." Microsoft National Broadcasting Company 19 Aug. 1999. Internet. Available: http://www.msnbc.com.

Goldsmith, Jill. "Fox feels the pinch." Variety 29 Oct. 1999. Internet. Available: http://www.variety.com.

Goldstein, Seth. "Technicolor Nabs 'Star Wars'." Video Store Magazine 21 Dec. 1999. Internet. Available: http://www.videostoremag.com.

Gomez, Linda. Personal interview. 24 Feb. 2001.

Graser, Marc. "Digital 'Menace' unveiled." Variety 18 Jun. 1999. Internet. Available: http://www.variety.com.

Graser, Marc. "Dolby Labs sounds out record sales to exhibs." Variety 19 Oct. 1999. Internet. Available: http://www.variety.com.

Graser, Marc. "Fox hits home with 'Menace'." Variety 6 Jan. 2000. Internet. Available: http://www.variety.com.

Graser, Marc. "'Menace' toys boost Hasbro." Variety 16 Jul. 1999. Internet. Available: http://www.variety.com.

Graser, Marc. "Trailer 'Wars' on Internet." Variety 14 Dec. 1998. Internet. Available: http://www.variety.com.

Graser, Marc. "Trailing 'Wars' web bids." Variety 18 Mar. 1999. Internet. Available: http://www.variety.com.

Griffin, Joshua. Personal interview. 30 August 2000.

Grossberg, Joshua. "'Phantom' Menaces Vid Competition." E! Online 9 Apr. 2000. Internet. Available: http://www.eonline.com.

Grove, Christopher. "Audiophiles prepare for summer of sound." Variety 20 Jan. 1999. Internet. Available: http://www.variety.com.

Groves, Don. "Big pix plow o'seas." Variety 15 Jun. 1999. Internet. Available: http://www.variety.com.

Groves, Don. "Blockbusters bloom o'seas." Variety 8 Nov. 1999. Internet. Available: http://www.variety.com.

Groves, Don. "Bond, 'Tarzan' storm o'seas." Variety 30 Nov. 1999. Internet. Available: http://www.variety.com.

Groves, Don. "B.O. bakes, shakes." Variety 26 Jul. 1999. Internet. Available: http://www.variety.com.

Groves, Don. "B.O. boffo overseas." Variety 29 Jun. 1999. Internet. Available: http://www.variety.com.

Groves, Don. "Counting on 'Sense'." Variety 9 Nov. 1999. Internet. Available: http://www.variety.com.

Groves, Don. "Dollars & 'Sense'." Variety 2 Nov. 1999. Internet. Available: http://www.variety.com.

Groves, Don. "Fall color is green." Variety 20 Sep. 1999. Internet. Available: http://www.variety.com.

Groves, Don. "Fall turning green." Variety 18 Oct. 1999. Internet. Available: http://www.variety.com.

Groves, Don. "Flying and spying." Variety 21 Jun. 1999. Internet. Available: http://www.variety.com.

Groves, Don. "Japan 'Menace'd." Variety 13 Jul. 1999. Internet. Available: http://www.variety.com.

Groves, Don. "'Menace' blasts Oz B.O. records in o'seas debut." Variety 4 Jun. 1999. Internet. Available: http://www.variety.com.

Groves, Don. "'Menace' grows o'seas." Variety 24 Aug. 1999. Internet. Available: http://www.variety.com.

Groves, Don. "'Menace' mauls B.O." Variety 30 Aug. 1999. Internet. Available: http://www.variety.com.

Groves, Don. "'Menace' milestone." Variety 11 Oct. 1999. Internet. Available: http://www.variety.com.

Groves, Don. "'Menace' rolls on." Variety 20 Jul. 1999. Internet. Available: http://www.variety.com.

Groves, Don. "Movie milestones." Variety 23 Aug. 1999. Internet. Available: http://www.variety.com.

Groves, Don. "'Mummy' marches." Variety 6 Jul. 1999. Internet. Available: http://www.variety.com.

Groves, Don. "O'seas auds go ape." Variety 22 Nov. 1999. Internet. Available: http://www.variety.com.

Groves, Don. "O'seas B.O. upswing." Variety 14 Sep. 1999. Internet. Available: http://www.variety.com.

Groves, Don. "O'seas bows wow." Variety 10 Aug. 1999. Internet. Available: http://www.variety.com.

Groves, Don. "O'seas 'Menace' passes $300 mil." Variety 31 Aug. 1999. Internet. Available: http://www.variety.com.

Groves, Don. "O'seas spirits rise." Variety 14 Jun. 1999. Internet. Available: http://www.variety.com.

Groves, Don. "O'seas 'Wide' & 'Wild'." Variety 3 Aug. 1999. Internet. Available: http://www.variety.com.

Groves, Don. "'Pie's' big B.O. slice." Variety 12 Oct. 1999. Internet. Available: http://www.variety.com.

Groves, Don. "'Phantom' fab o'seas." Variety 7 Jun. 1999. Internet. Available: http://www.variety.com.

Groves, Don. "'Phantom' sets marks in six European bows." Variety 23 Aug. 1999. Internet. Available: http://www.variety.com.

Groves, Don. "'Runaway' success." Variety 5 Oct. 1999. Internet. Available: http://www.variety.com.

Groves, Don. "'Stars' over rookies." Variety 2 Aug. 1999. Internet. Available: http://www.variety.com.

Groves, Don. "'Star' rises o'seas." Variety 21 Sep. 1999. Internet. Available: http://www.variety.com.

Groves, Don. "Summer super 'star'." Variety 7 Sep. 1999. Internet. Available: http://www.variety.com.

Groves, Don. "Superhero summit." Variety 6 Dec. 1999. Internet. Available: http://www.variety.com.

Groves, Don. "Trio sizzles o'seas." Variety 12 Jul. 1999. Internet. Available: http://www.variety.com.

Groves, Don. "U.K., France chew oats." Variety 17 Aug. 1999. Internet. Available: http://www.variety.com.

Groves, Don. "Vine guy and ghosts get B.O. o'seas." Variety 16 Nov. 1999. Internet. Available: http://www.variety.com.

Groves, Don. "'Wars' jolts Japan." Variety 19 Jul. 1999. Internet. Available: http://www.variety.com.

Groves, Don. "'Wars' soars ahead." Variety 27 Jul. 1999. Internet. Available: http://www.variety.com.

Groves, Don. "'Wars' still rages." Variety 27 Sep. 1999. Internet. Available: http://www.variety.com.

Groves, Don. "'West' zesty o'seas." Variety 9 Aug. 1999. Internet. Available: http://www.variety.com.

Gurland, Robin. "Casting Director Robin Gurland." By The Official Star Wars Website 7 Jun. 1999. Internet. Available: http://www.starwars.com.

Hachman, Mark. "Lucasfilm to screen all-digital version of new Star Wars movie." Electronic Buyers News 15 Mar. 1999.

Hamilton, Kendall, and Devin Gordon. "Waiting for Star Wars." Newsweek 1 Feb. 1999.

Hamlin, Jesse. "Scary, Baby!" San Francisco Chronicle 13 Oct. 1999.

"Hasbro Offers Fans A Sneak Preview With First Toys From Star Wars Episode I." Official Hasbro Website Oct. 1998. Internet. Available: http://www.hasbro.com.

"Hasbro Reports 33% Increase in Full-Year 1999 Earnings Per Share and Record Results Before Consolidation Program Charges." Hasbro 8 Feb. 2000. Internet. Available: http://www.hasbro.com.

"Hasbro Reports Record Third Quarter Results On Track to Deliver EPS Growth of Approximately 30% This Year." Hasbro 14 Oct. 1999. Internet. Available: http://www.hasbro.com.

"Hasbro sets 3-for-2 stock split, raises div." Reuters 19 Feb. 1999.

Hayes, Dade. "First and goal for 'Sunday'." Variety 27 Dec. 1999. Internet. Available: http://www.variety.com.

Hayes, Dade. "Hasbro, Fox tie-in 'Titan'." Variety 2 Nov. 1999. Internet. Available: http://www.variety.com.

Hayes, Dade. "'Little' win caps big year." Variety 3 Jan. 2000. Internet. Available: http://www.variety.com.

Hayes, Dade. "'Phantom' spirit." Variety 23 Nov. 1999. Internet. Available: http://www.variety.com.

Healy, Michelle. "Action toys will battle for supremacy." USA Today 8 Feb. 1999.

Herskovitz, Jon. "Fox moves to distrib its own films in Japan." Variety 7 Dec. 1998. Internet. Available: http://www.variety.com.

Herskovitz, Jon. "'Menace' hits mark." <u>Variety</u> 22 Jul. 1999. Internet. Available: http://www.variety.com.

Herskovitz, Jon. "'Menace'-ing Japan." <u>Variety</u> 11 Jun. 1999. Internet. Available: http://www.variety.com.

Herskovitz, Jon. "'Menace' keeps record pace in Japan." <u>Variety</u> 27 Jul. 1999. Internet. Available: http://www.variety.com.

Herskovitz, Jon. "'Menace' passes $100 mil in Japan." <u>Variety</u> 13 Sep. 1999. Internet. Available: http://www.variety.com.

Hesseldahl, Arik. "The Power of TheForce.net." <u>Wired</u> 12 Apr. 1999. Internet. Available: http://www.wired.com.

Hettrick, Scott. "A case of misplaced candor." <u>Video Business Online</u> 20 Mar. 2000. Internet. Available: http://www.videobusiness.com.

Hettrick, Scott. Letter to the author. 18 Jan. 2001.

Hettrick, Scott. "'Phantom' on video: $100 mil in 2 days." <u>Variety</u> 7 Apr. 2000. Internet. Available: http://www.variety.com.

Hettrick, Scott. "'Sense'-sational." <u>Variety</u> 6 Apr. 2000. Internet. Available: http://www.variety.com.

Hicks, L. Wayne. "'Phantom' makes first landing at Lowry." <u>Denver Business Journal</u> 15 Feb. 1999. Internet. Available: http://www.amcity.com/denver/

Higgins, Bill. "Episode I: the preems." <u>Variety</u> 17 May 1999. Internet. Available: http://www.variety.com.

Higgins, Bill. "Inside Move." <u>Variety</u> 9 Nov 1998. Internet. Available: http://www.variety.com.

Higgins, Bill. "'Menace' benefit sold out." <u>Variety</u> 4 May 1999. Internet. Available: http://www.variety.com.

Higgins, Bill. "'Star' tourists trek to 'Menace'." <u>Variety</u> 7 Apr. 1999. Internet. Available: http://www.variety.com.

Higgins, Bill. "'Star Wars' L.A. benefit preem set." <u>Variety</u> 13 Apr. 1999. Internet. Available: http://www.variety.com.

Higgins, Bill. "'Star Wars' preems to benefit kids." <u>Variety</u> 24 Mar. 1999. Internet. Available: http://www.variety.com.

Hindes, Andrew and Chris Petrikin. "New 'Star' born with firm terms." <u>Variety</u> 6 Apr. 1999. Internet. Available: http://www.variety.com.

Hindes, Andrew. "'Big Daddy' drives June boom." <u>Variety</u> 28 Jun. 1999. Internet. Available: http://www.variety.com.

Hindes, Andrew. "B.O. high five for 'Phantom'." <u>Variety</u> 24 May 1999. Internet. Available: http://www.variety.com.

Hindes, Andrew. "B.O. turns 'Menace'-ing." <u>Variety</u> 27 May 1999. Internet. Available: http://www.variety.com.

Hindes, Andrew. "Darth mauls theaters." <u>Variety</u> 19 May 1999. Internet. Available: http://www.variety.com.

Hindes, Andrew. "Fandom 'Menace' hits $7.5 mil in first 6 hrs." <u>Variety</u> 20 May 1999. Internet. Available: http://www.variety.com.

Hindes, Andrew. "Inside Move." <u>Variety</u> 18 Nov. 1998. Internet. Available: http://www.variety.com.

Hindes, Andrew. "Jedi's dead-eye at weekend B.O." <u>Variety</u> 7 Jun. 1999. Internet. Available: http://www.variety.com.

Hindes, Andrew. "Jedi masters $200 mil mark." <u>Variety</u> 1 Jun. 1999. Internet. Available: http://www.variety.com.

Hindes, Andrew. "'Jedi' zaps 'privates:' 'Return' tops, 'Jungle' in 2nd, 'Parts' 3rd." <u>Variety</u> 17 Mar. 1997. Internet. Available: http://www.variety.com.

Hindes, Andrew. "July jam Menacing." <u>Variety</u> 27 Apr. 1999. Internet. Available: http://www.variety.com.

Hindes, Andrew. "Lucas Lightning 'Strikes' Twice: $22.3 mil bow may lead to delayed 'Return'." Variety 24 Feb. 1997. Internet. Available: http://www.variety.com.

Hindes, Andrew. "Mega-'Menace'." Variety 21 May 1999. Internet. Available: http://www.variety.com.

Hindes, Andrew. "'Menace' cume boffo." Variety 26 Jul. 1999. Internet. Available: http://www.variety.com.

Hindes, Andrew. "'Menace' digital in L.A., N.J." Variety 4 Jun. 1999. Internet. Available: http://www.variety.com.

Hindes, Andrew. "'Menace' maneuvers." Variety 14 May 1999. Internet. Available: http://www.variety.com.

Hindes, Andrew. "'Menace' to preem new Dolby system." Variety 8 Dec. 1998. Internet. Available: http://www.variety.com.

Hindes, Andrew. "'Mum's' the word." Variety 17 May 1999. Internet. Available: http://www.variety.com.

Hindes, Andrew. "Pix musical chairs." Variety 5 May 1999. Internet. Available: http://www.variety.com.

Hindes, Andrew. "Sound investment." Variety 18 May 1999. Internet. Available: http://www.variety.com.

Hindes, Andrew. "'Star' booking miffs exhibs." Variety 16 Apr. 1999. Internet. Available: http://www.variety.com.

Hindes, Andrew. "'Star' crossed?" Variety 6 May 1999. Internet. Available: http://www.variety.com.

Hindes, Andrew. "'Star' has trailer hitch." Variety 8 Apr. 1999. Internet. Available: http://www.variety.com.

Hindes, Andrew. "Sunday B.O. a 'Star' sign." Variety 25 May 1999. Internet. Available: http://www.variety.com.

Hindes, Andrew. "'Tarzan' well-swung at B.O." Variety 21 Jun. 1999. Internet. Available: http://www.variety.com.

Hindes, Andrew. "Theaters surround Dolby EX." Variety 8 Mar. 1999. Internet. Available: http://www.variety.com.

Hindes, Andrew. "Warp Speed Ahead: $35.9 mil 'Star Wars' B.O. makes pic No. 2 of all-time." Variety 4 Feb. 1997. Internet. Available: http://www.variety.com.

Hindes, Andrew and Eric J. Olson. "Fresh 'Star' sounds." Variety 15 Oct. 1998. Internet. Available: http://www.variety.com.

"Hints pay off for Samuel L. Jackson." Reuters 29 Apr. 1999.

Hirschler, Ben and Merissa Mar. "Pearson to buy Dorling Kindersley." Reuters 31 Mar. 2000.

Hobson, Katherine. "Black Market Readies for The Phantom Menace." The Street 6 May 1999. Internet. Available: http://www.thestreet.com.

Hoffmann, Bill. "$99,000 For Tix? You Bidder Believe It!" New York Post 14 May 1999. Internet. Available: http://www.nypost.com.

Hoffmann, Bill. "No-Shows At Work May See Dark Side Of Boss." New York Post 15 May 1999. Internet. Available: http://www.nypost.com.

Hoffmann, Bill. "Reel Crime Has Cops On 'Wars' Path." New York Post 25 May 1999. Internet. Available: http://www.nypost.com.

Hoffmann, Bill. "Selling 'Star Wars' Will Be Child's Play." New York Post 5 Apr. 1999. Internet. Available: http://www.nypost.com.

Horn, John. "'Phantom' Legacy." Premiere Jul. 1999.

Horowitz, Sarah. "Visions of Tatooine." Metropolis May 1999.

Howard, Ron. "Pick on Someone Your Own Size." Newsweek 1 Feb. 1999.

"Howard Defends Star Wars Kid." Mr. Show Biz 28 Jan. 1999. Internet. Available: http://www.mrshowbiz.com.

Ingram, Holly. Letter to the author. 8 Mar. 2000.

"Intertops.com Posts Odds On Opening Weekend Success Of New Star Wars Movie." <u>Intertops Official Website</u> 17 Apr. 1999. Internet. Available: <u>http://www.intertops.com</u>.

"Int'l auds stagnant despite multiplexes." <u>Variety</u> 3 Jan. 2000. Internet. Available: <u>http://www.variety.com</u>.

"It's a Blue World." <u>The Official Star Wars Website</u> 20 Mar. 1998. Internet. Available: <u>http://www.starwars.com</u>.

"It's Here!" <u>The Official Star Wars Website</u> 17 Nov. 1998. Internet. Available: <u>http://www.starwars.com</u>.

"It's Official! 'Digimon' One of Top Ten Best-Selling Action Toys of 2000." <u>Business Wire</u> 11 Dec. 2000.

Intertops.com. Letter to the author. 6 Mar. 2000.

Intertops.com. Letter to the author. 7 Mar. 2000.

Jenkins, Garry. <u>Empire Building</u>. New Jersey: Carol Publishing Group, 1997.

Jensen, Jeff. "A Sho of Force." <u>Entertainment Weekly</u> 26 Mar. 1999.

Jensen, Jorn Rossing. "Impressive Finnish." <u>Variety</u> 17 Jan. 2000. Internet. Available: <u>http://www.variety.com</u>.

Jensen, Kris. "Kosmos gets 'Star Wars' check for $1,894." <u>Grand Forks Herald</u> 4 Feb. 2000.

Kane, Margaret. "High-tech toy fair: plug and play." <u>ZDNN</u> 8 Feb. 1999. Internet. Available: <u>http://www.zdnet.com</u>.

Kaplan, David A. "The Selling of Star Wars." <u>Newsweek</u> 17 May 1999.

"Katzmark pleads innocent to misdemeanor theft." <u>Associated Press</u> 18 Aug. 1999.

Keller, Julie. "'Phantom Menace' Returns!" <u>E! Online</u> 23 Nov. 1999. Internet. Available: <u>http://www.eonline.com</u>.

"Kids Fuel 'Phantom Menace' Success." <u>Associated Press</u> 22 May 1999.

Kirk, Kolby. Personal interview. 25, 26, and 27 Feb. 2001 and 3 Mar. 2001.

Kivlehan, Chris. "Kliffs Notes on Lucas' Star Wars." <u>Sci-Fi World</u> Summer 1999.

Klady, Leonard. "B.O. goes Judd, thud." <u>Variety</u> 27 Sep. 1999. Internet. Available: <u>http://www.variety.com</u>.

Klady, Leonard. "B.O. record broken." <u>Variety</u> 23 Jun. 1999. Internet. Available: <u>http://www.variety.com</u>.

Klady, Leonard. "Heat wave at summer box office." <u>Variety</u> 7 Sep. 1999. Internet. Available: <u>http://www.variety.com</u>.

Klady, Leonard. "July pix melt B.O. records with $917 mil." <u>Variety</u> 3 Aug. 1999. Internet. Available: <u>http://www.variety.com</u>.

Klady, Leonard. "June busts all over." <u>Variety</u> 2 Jul. 1999. Internet. Available: <u>http://www.variety.com</u>.

Klady, Leonard. "'Phantom' pushes Fox to market share lead." <u>Variety</u> 9 Jun. 1999. Internet. Available: <u>http://www.variety.com</u>.

Klosterman, Chuck. "Hype makes the world go 'round." <u>The Dallas Morning News</u> 11 Mar. 1999. Internet. Available: <u>http://www.elibrary.com</u>.

Krakow, Gary. "VCDs: What's the big deal?" <u>MSNBC</u> 14 Apr. 2000. Internet. Available: <u>http://www.msnbc.com</u>.

Lamb, Gregory M. "A Day at the Cinema." <u>The Christian Science Monitor</u> 9 Apr. 1999. Internet. Available: <u>http://www.elibrary.com</u>.

Lamorte, Chris. "Star Hustlers." <u>Westword</u> 5 Mar. 1999. Internet. Available: <u>http://www.westword.com</u>.

Lavoie, Denise. "Lego looks to soar with Luke Skywalker, Darth Vader." <u>Associated Press</u> 30 Apr. 1998.

"Leavesden: Back in Action." <u>The Official Star Wars Website</u> 18 Mar. 1998. Internet. Available: <u>http://www.starwars.com</u>.

"Leavesden Studios will be bulldozed." <u>BBC</u> 29 Oct. 1999. Internet. Available: http://www.bbc.co.uk.

Levin, Gary. "Toy Story: Rights 'Wars'." <u>Variety</u> 10 Feb. 1997. Internet. Available: http://www.variety.com.

"Liam Neeson Tapped for Star Wars Prequel." <u>Mr. Show Biz</u> 3 Apr. 1997. Internet. Available: http://www.mrshowbiz.com.

"Licensee & Exhibitor Listings." <u>Star Wars Celebration Official Program Guide</u> 30 Apr. 1999.

Liebenson, Donald. "'Phantom' Shows Its Power in Video Arena." <u>Los Angeles Times</u> 14 Mar. 2000. Internet. Available: http://www.latimes.com.

"Lift Off For Star Wars Video." <u>Empire Online</u> 3 Apr. 2000. Internet. Available: http://www.empireonline.co.uk.

Lippman, John. "'Star Wars' Distribution Deal Leaves 20th Century Fox With Power of Force." <u>Wall Street Journal</u> 3 Apr. 1998.

Lloren, Jason. "'Phantom' Love Fest." <u>San Francisco Examiner</u> 17 May 1999.

Longino, Bob. "May The Hype Be With You: 'Star Wars: Phantom Menace' mania likely to produce staggering May box office debut." <u>Atlanta Journal and Constitution</u> 25 Feb. 1999. Internet. Available: http://www.elibrary.com.

Lucas, George. "George Lucas, on *Star Wars:* Episode I." By Lynne Hale. *Star Wars: Episode I The Phantom Menace* Unabridged Production. 1 Nov. 1994.

Lucas, George. "Grand Illusion." By Paula Parisi. <u>Wired</u> May 1999.

Lucas, George. "Of Myth and Men." By Bill Moyers. <u>Time</u> 26 Apr. 1999.

Lucas, George. "The Future Starts Here." <u>Premiere</u> Feb. 1999.

"Lucas Says Media Spread Inaccuracies Like a Virus." <u>San Francisco Chronicle</u> 17 Feb. 2000. Internet. Available: http://www.sfgate.com.

"Lucasfilm THX and Dolby Unveil Dolby Digital—Surround EX, The Latest Advance in Digital Surround Sound Technology." Official THX Web Site 20 Oct. 1998. Internet. Available: http://www.thx.com.

Luff, David, and Bill Hoffmann. "Computer Tix Mixup Sparks Ziegfeld Follies." New York Post 20 May 1999. Internet. Available: http://www.nypost.com.

Macintosh News Network 12 Mar. 1999.

Madsen, Dan. "Prequel Update: New Star Wars Stars!" Star Wars Insider 34 (Spring 1997).

Mann's Chinese Theatre Hollywood Souvenir Brochure. 1992.

"Mark your calendars: Star Wars: Episode I has a release date." Mr. Show Biz 11 Aug. 1998. Internet. Available: http://www.mrshowbiz.com.

Marx, Andy and Max Alexander. "The Force is with him: 'Star Wars' savant Lucas plans celluloid comeback." Variety 4 Oct. 1993.

Mathews, Jack. "George Lucas IS the Force/Preparing 'The Phantom Menace,' the first of his 'Star Wars' prequels, the director defends his legacy—the blockbuster movie." Newsday 17 Jan. 1999.

"May the Bandwidth Be with You." Wired 20 Nov. 1998. Internet. Available: http://www.wired.com.

"May the profit be with you." BBC 17 Jul. 1999. Internet. Available: http://www.bbc.co.uk.

McCallum, Rick. "A Yahoo! Chat with Rick McCallum." The Official Star Wars Website 4 Mar. 1999. Internet. Available: http://www.starwars.com.

McCauley, Mary Carole. "'Phantom Menace' already casting a long shadow." Milwaukee Journal Sentinel 18 Mar. 1999. Internet. Available: http://www.elibrary.com.

McCarthy, Todd. "Deep Focus." Variety 25 Jun. 1999. Internet. Available: http://www.variety.com.

McElwee, Kathleen R. "Hasbro Announces Definitive Agreement To Acquire Galoob Toys, Inc." <u>Galoob Official Web Site</u> 28 Sep. 1998. Internet. Available: <u>http://www.galoob.com</u>.

McKenzie, Aline. "Starstruck. 'Star Wars' screening wows benefactors of children's hospital." <u>The Dallas Morning News</u> 17 May 1999.

McNary, Dave. "Rival Studios Find It Useless To Resist, Surrender May To Darth Side." <u>Los Angeles Daily News</u> 14 Mar. 1999.

"'Menace' not a threat." <u>The Boston Globe</u> 5 Apr. 2000. Internet. Available: <u>http://www.boston.com</u>.

"Menace Raking In the Green…Sort Of." <u>Mr. Show Biz</u> 21 May 1999. Internet. Available: <u>http://www.mrshowbiz.com</u>.

"Millions to Choose Menace Over Work." <u>Mr. Show Biz</u> 5 May 1999. Internet. Available: <u>http://www.mrshowbiz.com</u>.

"MLG April Comp-Store Sales Up 17.0 Percent." <u>Business Wire</u> 4 May 2000.

Morgan, Richard. "Hasbro goes solo." <u>Variety</u> 29 Sep. 1998. Internet. Available: <u>http://www.variety.com</u>.

Morgan, Richard. "Lucasfilm defends Lego 'Star Wars' deal: Other licensees Hasbro and Galoob dissatisfied." <u>Variety</u> 1 May 1998. Internet. Available: <u>http://www.variety.com</u>.

Morgan, Richard. "'Menace' masters market." <u>Variety</u> 26 May 1999. Internet. Available: <u>http://www.variety.com</u>.

Morgan, Richard. "Star Wars toy fans get peek." <u>Variety</u> 8 Oct. 1998. Internet. Available: <u>http://www.variety.com</u>.

Morgan, Richard. "Toy 'Wars' invasion." <u>Variety</u> 4 May 1999. Internet. Available: <u>http://www.variety.com</u>.

Morgan, Richard. "Wal-Mart loading up for 'Star Wars'." <u>Variety</u> 19 Apr. 1999. Internet. Available: <u>http://www.variety.com</u>.

"MovieFone Will Make Star Wars Tickets Available On Wednesday, May 12th At 3pm." Business Wire 23 Apr. 1999.

"Movies at the Cutting Edge." New York Daily News 11 Apr. 1999.

Mullen, Jim. "Jim Mullen's Hot Sheet: What the country was talking about this decade." Entertainment Weekly Spring 2000.

"Neeson In Force Field." Variety 3 Apr. 1997. Internet. Available: http:// www.variety.com.

Nesheim, Jay Jay. Letter to the author. 13 Mar. 2001.

Newport, Frank. "Seven out of Ten American Families Will Be Giving Out Treats This Halloween." Gallup News Service 29 Oct. 1999. Internet. Available: http://www.gallup.com.

"New Star Wars: Episode I Website Merges Incredible Technology With Electronic Toys." Hasbro 20 May 1999. Internet. Available: http://www. hasbro.com.

"New Star Wars Trailer Released Online By Lucasfilm And Apple." The Official Star Wars Website 10 Mar. 1999. Internet. Available: http://www. starwars.com.

"New York Toy Fair: Pokémon latest hot property in toy industry." Atlanta Journal and Constitution 11 Feb. 1999. Internet. Available: http://www. elibrary.com.

"No. 1 Pirate Video: Phantom Menace." Show Biz Data 24 Dec. 1999. Internet. Available: http://www.showbizdata.com.

"North American Top Box Office Actuals." Yahoo! 10 Jan. 2000. Internet. Available: http://www.yahoo.com.

"North American Top Box Office Actuals." Yahoo! 17 Jan. 2000. Internet. Available: http://www.yahoo.com.

"North American Top Box Office Actuals." Yahoo! 24 Jan. 2000. Internet. Available: http://www.yahoo.com.

"North American Top Box Office Actuals." Yahoo! 31 Jan. 2000. Internet. Available: http://www.yahoo.com.

Oakes, Chris. "Phantom MPEG Hits Net." Wired 27 May 1999. Internet. Available: http://www.wired.com.

Oaks, Travess. Personal interview. 6 Apr. 2000.

Osaki, Tad. "'Menace' minces Japan B.O." Variety 12 Jul. 1999. Internet. Available: http://www.variety.com.

Oz, Frank. "Blizzard of Oz." By Scott Chernoff. Star Wars Insider, Issue 42, Feb./Mar. 1999.

Pappas, Ben. "Star bucks." Forbes 17 May 1999. Internet. Available: http://www.elibrary.com.

Pearlman, Cindy. "Big Screen Chameleon Samuel L. Jackson Feels the Force in Star Wars: Episode One." Cinescape Magazine Jul./Aug. 1998.

Peers, Martin, and Andrew Hindes. "Loews defends 'Menace' hardball." Variety 21 May 1999. Internet. Available: http://www.variety.com.

Peers, Martin. "AMC in post-boat dip as net loss rises." Variety 19 May 1999. Internet. Available: http://www.variety.com.

Peers, Martin. "Carmike quarter sours." Variety 10 Feb. 1999. Internet. Available: http://www.variety.com.

Peers, Martin. "Exhib Carmike reports loss despite cost cuts." Variety 30 Apr. 1999. Internet. Available: http://www.variety.com.

Peers, Martin. "Exhib UA losses triple." Variety 17 May 1999. Internet. Available: http://www.variety.com.

Pegoraro, Rob. "Logging On: DVD Fans Refuse the Force." Washington Post 11 Feb. 2000. Internet. Available: http://www.washingtonpost.com.

Pereira, Joseph. "Did Impossibly High 'Star Wars' Hopes Unfairly Zap Hasbro Stock to Dark Side?" The Wall Street Journal 13 Aug. 1999.

Pereira, Joseph. "'Star Wars' Film May Drive Staff Far, Far Away." The Wall Street Journal 6 May 1999.

Petrikin, Chris. "Force returns to Fox field." Variety 3 Apr. 1998. Internet. Available: http://www.variety.com.

Petrikin, Chris. "Lucasfilm force goes with Hasbro, Galoob." Variety 15 Oct. 1997. Internet. Available: http://www.variety.com.

Petrikin, Chris. "Star of trailer wars." Variety 12 Mar. 1999. Internet. Available: http://www.variety.com.

"Phantom Breaks Down Under." Mr. Show Biz 3 Jun. 1999. Internet. Available: http://www.mrshowbiz.com.

"Phantom Crooks Surrender." Mr. Show Biz 26 May 1999. Internet. Available: http://www.mrshowbiz.com.

"Phantom Fans Form Lines; Fox May OK Advance Tix." Mr. Show Biz 12 Apr. 1999. Internet. Available: http://www.mrshowbiz.com.

"Phantom Huge, But Not Biggest Ever." Mr. Show Biz 23 May 1999. Internet. Available: http://www.mrshowbiz.com.

"Phantom Leads, Austin Follows." Mr. Show Biz 13 May 1999. Internet. Available: http://www.mrshowbiz.com.

"Phantom Makes Money, Gets Pirated, Draws Protests." Mr. Show Biz 27 May 1999. Internet. Available: http://www.mrshowbiz.com.

"Phantom Outcries Continue." Mr. Show Biz 28 May 1999. Internet. Available: http://www.mrshowbiz.com.

"Phantom Ticket Frenzy Begins." Mr. Show Biz 12 May 1999. Internet. Available: http://www.mrshowbiz.com.

"Phantom Trailer II on Web." Wired 12 Mar. 1999. Internet. Available: http://www.wired.com.

"'Phantom' video fades Pokémon'." Hollywood Reporter 20 Apr. 2000. Internet. Available: http://www.hollywoodreporter.com.

Phillips, Ty, and Susan Nickell. "'Star Wars' fans a 'Menace' at toy stores." The Modesto Bee 4 May 1999. Internet. Available: http://www.modbee.com.

Portman, Natalie. "Natalie au naturel." By Susan Sarandon. Jane Sep. 1999.

"Press Conference in Italy." The Official Star Wars Website 25 Jul. 1997. Internet. Available: http://www.starwars.com.

"Profile: Robin Gurland, Casting Director." The Official Star Wars Website 12 Feb. 1998. Internet. Available: http://www.starwars.com.

Puig, Claudia. "Women's films face 'Menace'." USA Today 1 Apr. 1999.

Punter, Jennie. "Sound revolution." Toronto Star 29 Jan. 1999. Internet. Available: http://www.thestar.com.

Rausa, Janet. "Phantom sales for 'Star Wars'." Chicago Sun-Times 5 Apr. 2000. Internet. Available: http://www.suntimes.com.

"Ray Park to Attend Star Wars Celebration." The Official Star Wars Website 12 Feb. 1999. Internet. Available: http://www.starwars.com.

Rea, Steven. "Lucas strikes again: Trying for the magic of 1977." Philadelphia Inquirer 25 Apr. 1999. Internet. Available: http://www.phillynews.com.

Reynolds, David West. "From Concept To Screen: A Conversation With Episode I Concept Designer Doug Chiang." Star Wars Insider, Issue 39, Aug./ Sep. 1998.

"Rick McCallum Interview." The Official Star Wars Website 2 Jun. 1997. Internet. Available: http://www.starwars.com.

Rivero, Enrique. "Biggest piracy bust in two years nets 35,000 tapes." Video Business Online 30 Aug. 1999. Internet. Available: http://www. videobusiness.com.

Ryan, Joal. "A MovieFone Spelling Bee." E! Online 13 Feb. 1999. Internet. Available: http://www.eonline.com.

Ryan, Joal. "Jail Time for 'Phantom Menace' Thieves." E! Online 29 Jun. 1999. Internet. Available: http://www.eonline.com.

Ryan, Joal. "New Chapter in 'Star Wars' Toy Story." E! Online 29 Sep. 1998. Internet. Available: http://www.eonline.com.

Ryan, Joal. "New 'Star Wars' Flick a 'Phantom Menace'." E! Online 28 Sep. 1998. Internet. Available: http://eonline.com.

Ryan, Joal. "Opie Backs Darth Vader." E! Online 29 Jan. 1999. Internet. Available: http://www.eonline.com.

Ryan, Joal. "'Phantom Menace' Breaks $400 million." E! Online 26 Jul. 1999. Internet. Available: http://www.eonline.com.

Ryan, Joal. "'Phantom Menace' Works Work Week." E! Online 27 May 1999. Internet. Available: http://www.eonline.com.

Ryan, Joal. "Sly Fox Snares 'Star Wars'." E! Online 3 Apr. 1998. Internet. Available: http://www.eonline.com.

Ryan, Joal. "'Star Wars' Ticket Rush!" E! Online 12 May 1999. Internet. Available: http://www.eonline.com.

Ryan, Joal. "'Star Wars' Toys Talk the Talk." E! Online 8 Feb. 1999. Internet. Available: http://www.eonline.com.

Ryfle, Steve. "'Phantom Menace' Takes Over the World." Hollywood 5 Jan. 2000. Internet. Available: http://www.hollywood.com.

Saunders, Doug. "A picture worth thousands of words?" The Globe and Mail 4 May 1999.

Sauriol, Patrick. "'Star Wars' Prequels Being Filmed." Sci-Fi Invasion! Fall 1997.

Shachtman, Noah. "'Phantom Menace' Stalks the Net." Wired 13 Nov. 1998. Internet. Available: http://www.wired.com.

Selkokari, Antti. "Finnish start big for 'star'." Variety 11 Aug. 1999. Internet. Available: http://www.variety.com.

Serwer, Andrew E. "Who gets what in the 'Star Wars' toy deal." Fortune 18 Aug. 1997. Internet. Available: http://www.elibrary.com.

Silberman, Steve. "G Force." Wired May 1999.

"Simultaneous Worldwide VHS Video Debut of Episode I." <u>The Official Star Wars Website</u> 5 Jan. 2000. Internet. Available: <u>http://www.starwars.com</u>.

Shirkani, K.D., and Jill Goldsmith. "Pix, TV buoy toys." <u>Variety</u> 11 Feb. 2000. Internet. Available: <u>http://www.variety.com</u>.

Slotek, Jim. "'Phantom' Profits Out Of This World \ Box Office Records Fall Weekly." <u>The Arizona Republic</u> 29 Jun. 1999. Internet. Available: <u>http://www.elibrary.com</u>.

Snider, Mike. "Early start for toy sales." <u>USA Today</u> 15 Apr. 1999.

Snider, Mike. "Studio Web Sites Offer Even Earlier Peeks at Films." <u>USA Today</u> 8 Oct. 1997.

Snider, Mike. "The 'Star Wars' force is with Apple." <u>USA Today</u> 12 Mar. 1999. Internet. Available: <u>http://www.USAToday.com</u>.

Snyder, John Bradley. "Prequel Profile: Casting Director Robin Gurland's World of Possibilities." <u>Star Wars Insider</u>, Issue 36, Feb./Mar. 1998.

Snyder, Jon Bradley. "Star Wars Celebration." <u>Star Wars Insider</u>, Issue 42, Feb./Mar. 1999.

Snyder, John Bradley. "The Fan Event is Coming." <u>Star Wars Insider</u>, Issue 40, Oct./Nov. 1998.

Soriano, César G. "Looks like lines: No pre-sale for 'Menace' tickets." <u>USA Today</u> 29 Mar. 1999.

"So you think you're a Star Wars fan." <u>BBC</u> 13 May 1999. Internet. Available: <u>http://www.bbc.co.uk</u>.

"Special Announcement: Trailer Release Date." <u>The Official Star Wars Website</u> 6 Nov. 1998. Internet. Available: <u>http://www.starwars.com</u>.

Stack, Peter. "Fans Hail 'Phantom's' Force." <u>San Francisco Chronicle</u> 17 May 1999.

Stack, Peter. "'Phantom' Opening-Day Tickets Are Selling at Full Force." <u>San Francisco Chronicle</u> 14 May 1999.

"Star Wars A Hot News Topic In May." Show Biz Data 4 Jun. 1999. Internet. Available: http://www.showbizdata.com.

"'Star Wars' beats rivals at European box office." Agence France-Presse 13 May 2000. Internet. Available: http://www.nandotimes.com.

"Star Wars Book Busts British Publisher." Show Biz Data 7 Mar. 2000. Internet. Available: http://www.showbizdata.com.

"Star Wars book flop hits DK." BBC 24 Jan. 2000. Internet. Available: http://www.bbc.co.uk.

"Star Wars Celebration Activities." Star Wars Celebration Official Program Guide 30 Apr. 1999.

Star Wars: Episode I—The Phantom Menace. Dir. George Lucas. With Liam Neeson, Natalie Portman, Ewan McGregor, and Jake Lloyd. Twentieth Century Fox and Lucasfilm, 1999.

"Star Wars: Episode I—The Phantom Menace." Cinefex Jul. 1999.

"'Star Wars: Episode I—the Phantom Menace' Releases On Video Tuesday, April 4." Blockbuster 28 Mar. 2000.

"Star Wars: Episode I The Phantom Menace To Be First Motion Picture Released in Digital Projection." The Official Star Wars Website 12 Mar. 1999. Internet. Available: http://www.starwars.com.

"Star Wars: Episode I To Premiere in 11 Cities On May 16th To Benefit Children's Charities." The Official Star Wars Website 12 Apr. 1999. Internet. Available: http://www.starwars.com.

"Star Wars: Lucas strikes back." BBC 14 Jul 1999. Internet. Available: http://www.bbc.co.uk.

"'Star Wars' mania strikes at midnight." Associated Press 3 May 1999.

"Star Wars prequel drawing movie lines just for 2-minute preview." Associated Press 18 Nov. 1998.

"Star Wars Products Land At Toys 'R' US At 12:01 AM On May 3." <u>Toys "R" Us</u> 14 Apr. 1999.

"Star Wars stops Dublin traffic." <u>BBC</u> 16 Jul. 1999. Internet. Available: <u>http://www.bbc.co.uk</u>.

"Star Wars: The Phantom Memo." <u>E! Online</u> 1 May 1999. Internet. Available: <u>http://www.eonline.com</u>.

"Star Wars: The Phantom Memo." <u>E! Online</u> 15 May 1999. Internet. Available: <u>http://www.eonline.com</u>.

"Star Wars toys cloaked in secrecy." <u>The Providence Journal</u> 9 Feb. 1999.

"Star Wars Toys Help Hasbro Beat Target." <u>Reuters</u> 15 Jul. 1999.

"Star Wars Trailer and Timelines." <u>The Official Star Wars Website</u> 25 Nov. 1998. Internet. Available: <u>http://www.starwars.com</u>.

"Star Wars Trailer Attracts Over 3.5 Million Downloads." <u>The Official Star Wars Website</u> 16 Mar. 1999. Internet. Available: <u>http://www.starwars.com</u>.

"Star Wars Trailer Previewed." <u>Mr. Show Biz</u> 17 Nov. 1998. Internet. Available: <u>http://www.mrshowbiz.com</u>.

"Star Wars TV Special." <u>The Detroit News</u> 26 May 1999.

"Storm Hits Star Wars Production in Tunisia." <u>The Official Star Wars Website</u> 29 Jul. 1997. Internet. Available: <u>http://www.starwars.com</u>.

Stroud, Michael. "Star Wars' Digital Experiment." <u>Wired</u> 16 Mar. 1999. Internet. Available: <u>http://www.wired.com</u>.

Stroud, Michael. "The Force for Good Isn't Cheap." <u>Wired</u> 22 Mar. 1999. Internet. Available: <u>http://www.wired.com</u>.

Sullivan, Maureen. "MPAA pledges to keep heat on piracy in Asia." <u>Variety</u> 3 Dec. 1999. Internet. Available: <u>http://www.variety.com</u>.

"Surprise Hits Like Blair Witch Set B.O Record." <u>Mr. Show Biz</u> 15 Dec. 1999. Internet. Available: <u>http://www.mrshowbiz.com</u>.

Talmadge, Candace. "Media Hype Replaces Advertising for 'Star Wars' film." Reuters 11 May 1999.

Tanner, Mike. "Web-Site Force Is With Hasbro, Not Lucas." Wired 25 Jan. 1997. Internet. Available: http://www.wired.com.

"Terry Brooks to Attend Star Wars Celebration." The Official Star Wars Website 22 Feb. 1999. Internet. Available: http://www.starwars.com.

Theobald, Steven. "Star Wars flick lovers flocking to the stores." Toronto Star 4 May 1999. Internet. Available: http://www.thestar.com.

"The Big Tease Is Here Now; Movies: First peek at prequel to 'Star Wars' film series gets a six-month jump on premiere, eliciting TV coverage and even paying customers—for a trailer." Los Angeles Times 21 Nov. 1998. Internet. Available: http://www.latimes.com.

"The Forbes Celebrity 100." Forbes 2 Mar. 2000. Internet. Available: http://www.forbes.com.

"The Force Is Back." Vanity Fair Feb. 1999.

"The Force is with Hasbro as it Enters Into Agreement for Expanded Worldwide Rights to Star Wars Toys and Games Through the Next Three Star Wars Movies." Hasbro 14 Oct. 1997. Internet. Available: http://www. hasbro.com.

The Guinness Book of Records 1999. New York: Bantam Books, 1999.

"The LEGO Group Acquires Global Star Wars License." Lego Official Web Site 30 Apr. 1998. Internet. Available: http://www.lego.com.

"The New Episode I Trailer!" The Official Star Wars Website 8 Mar. 1999. Internet. Available: http://www.starwars.com.

"The Price Of The Phantom Menace." Official Empire Magazine Web Site 23 Mar. 1999. Internet. Available: http://www.empireonline.co.uk.

Thompson, Gary. "'Star Wars' tickets, the sequel." Philadelphia Daily News 21 Apr. 1999.

"Three Ziff-Davis Magazines Feature First Coverage of Star Wars: Episode I—The Phantom Menace Games." PR Newswire 7 Apr. 1999.

"Top-20 toy licenses." Microsoft National Broadcast Network 7 Dec. 1999. Internet. Available: http.//www.msnbc.com.

"'Toy' keeps B.O. in toon." Variety 6 Dec. 1999. Internet. Available: http:// www.variety.com.

"Trailer Running Time Confirmed." The Official Star Wars Website 16 Feb. 1999. Internet. Available: http://www.starwars.com.

"Trinity." Play Incorporated 27 Feb. 2001. Internet. Available: http:// www.play.com.

"Two Minutes And Ten Seconds of History in the Making." The Hollywood Stock Exchange 17 Nov. 1998. Internet. Available: http://www.hsx.com.

"U.K. Moviegoers Return En Masse To Theaters." Show Biz Data 25 Aug. 1999. Internet. Available: http://www.showbizdata.com.

Variety Staff, and Leonard Klady. "Early 'Star Wars' reviews irk Fox." Variety 10 May 1999. Internet. Available: http://www.variety.com.

Verdon, Joan. "'Menace,' anyone? Yes, say 'Star Wars' shoppers." Bergen Record Corporation 4 May 1999. Internet. Available: http://www.elibrary.com.

Villalva, Maribel. "'Menace' video moves mountains of money." USA Today 11 Apr. 2000.

Waxman, Sharon. "Irresistible Force Meets Unmoving Match." Washington Post 17 Apr. 1999. Internet. Available: http://www.washingtonpost.com.

Weiner, Rex. "Lucas the Loner Returns to 'Wars'." Variety 5-11 Jun. 1995.

Wells, Jeffrey. "Trail of the *Phantom*." Mr. Show Biz 17 Nov. 1998. Internet. Available: http://www.mrshowbiz.com.

Whipp, Glenn. "Tour de Force for 'Star Wars' \ 'Episode 1' Months Off, But Fans Already in Tizzy and Soon To Be In Line." The Arizona Republic 22 Jan. 1999. Internet. Available: http://www.elibrary.com.

Whipps, Clare. Personal interview. 10 Mar. 2000.

White, Michael. "Star Wars Tickets Available Wed." <u>Associated Press</u> 11 May 1999.

Willman, Chris. "Hear and Now: This week on the music beat." <u>Entertainment Weekly</u> 9 Apr. 1999.

"Will The Next *Star Wars* Sink *Titanic*?" <u>Entertainment Weekly</u> 1 May 1998.

Wilner, Richard. "License Wars For 'Star Wars' Toys." <u>New York Post</u> 25 Nov. 1997. Internet. Available: <u>http://www.nypost.com</u>.

Wilson, Jim. "The Machines of Star Wars: Episode I—The Phantom Menace." <u>Popular Mechanics</u> Jun. 1999.

"Wings Over The Rockies Air And Space Museum: Hangar Map." <u>Star Wars Celebration Official Program Guide</u> 30 Apr. 1999.

Winterbottom, Helen. Personal interview. 13 Mar. 2000.

Wolk, Josh. "Dwindling Force?" <u>Entertainment Weekly</u> 7 Jun. 1999. Internet. Available: <u>http://www.ew.com</u>.

Wolk, Josh. "Flip the Record." <u>Entertainment Weekly</u> 24 May 1999. Internet. Available: <u>http://www.ew.com</u>.

Woods, Mark. "'Matrix' maps B.O." <u>Variety</u> 28 Jun. 1999. Internet. Available: <u>http://www.variety.com</u>.

Woods, Mark. "Oz-based exhib Hoyts posts flat half-year." <u>Variety</u> 26 Feb. 1999. Internet. Available: <u>http://www.variety.com</u>.

Woods, Mark. "'Phantom' phenom." <u>Variety</u> 16 Aug. 1999. Internet. Available: <u>http://www.variety.com</u>.

Wuensch, Yuri. "Stores brace for Star Wars onslaught." <u>Edmonton Sun</u> 4 Apr. 2000. Internet. Available: <u>http://www.canoe.com</u>.

Wuntch, Philip. "'Star Wars' screening to help out charities." <u>The Dallas Morning News</u> 14 Apr. 1999. Internet. Available: <u>http://www.elibrary.com</u>.

Index

978-0-595-67148-9
0-595-67148-9

Printed in the United States
29872LVS00002B/3

9 780595 671489